FIFTH WEDNESDAY

JOURNAL

Defining literature. In real context.

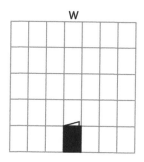

POSTMASTER:
Send address changes to: Fifth Wednesday Books, Inc., P.O. Box 4033, Lisle, IL 60532-9033

FIFTH WEDNESDAY
JOURNAL

Defining literature. In real context.
www.fifthwednesdayjournal.org

FALL 2011 • ISSUE 9

GUEST POETRY EDITOR
Christina Pugh

GUEST FICTION EDITORS
Jonis Agee
Brent Spencer

PUBLISHER AND EDITOR	Vern Miller
MANAGING EDITOR	Rachel Hamsmith
ART EDITOR	Jenn Hollmeyer
NONFICTION EDITOR	Monica Berlin
BOOK REVIEWS EDITOR	Daniel Libman
LAYOUT & DESIGN EDITOR	Kat Sanchez
COPY EDITOR	Sherry Stratton
ADVISORY EDITORS	James Ballowe, Nina Corwin
ASSISTANT EDITORS	Kelly Davio, Denise Dirks, Gro Flatebo, Maddie Freeman, Nathan Fulkerson, Yliana Gonzalez, Susen James, Angela Just, Sarah Kelley, Christopher Lowe, Terry Lucas, Sandra Marchetti, Danielle Newton, Meredith Noseworthy, Sherry O'Keefe, Susan Azar Porterfield, Donna Pucciani, Laura Salamy
CONTRIBUTING EDITORS	Carolyn Alessio, Michael Anania, John Bradley, Susan Hahn, Anna Leahy, Laurence Lieberman, Molly McNett, Edie Meidav, Amy Newman, Lon Otto
WEBMASTER	Barbara Barasa
INTERNS	Madeline Marucha, Rebecca Sage, Frank Schweihs

FWJ IN THE CLASSROOM

Our mission is to the larger community of writers, artists, our readers, and our supporters. FWJ has undertaken an active program of outreach with FWJ in the Classroom, a program offering subscriptions at deeply discounted rates to students of creative writing at colleges and universities in the continental United States. Professors receive free desk copies under certain conditions. We also offer a visit in person or via electronic media (Skype, etc.) by one of our editors when possible. We expect to extend this offer to more than 350 academic programs and an additional 350 academic libraries by the end of this year.

Familiarity with literary magazines and their role in nurturing literature in this country is important to early success for writers of creative work. A writer's first taste of success is usually in a literary magazine such as FWJ. In the past four years we have published more than 340 writers and photographers, 31 of whom saw their first publications in our pages.

Our editors volunteer their services, but printing and distributing flyers, shipping the books, and related expenses will add up to more than $400 this year. We hope to expand the program during 2012 with total expenditures expected to reach $600 to $800. Support for the program is needed and very much appreciated.

Fifth Wednesday Journal is a nonprofit 501(c)(3) organization, and donations are tax deductible to the full extent of the law. Donations may be made by check to

Fifth Wednesday Books, Inc.
P. O. Box 4033
Lisle, IL 60532-9033

or online with PayPal or a charge card.

For a complete program description, please visit www.fifthwednesdayjournal.org.

SPRING 2012 GUEST EDITORS

GUEST FICTION EDITOR

Donna Seaman is a senior editor for *Booklist*, a book critic for *Chicago Public Radio*, and a reviewer for the *Los Angeles Times*, *Chicago Tribune*, *Kansas City Star*, *Bookforum*, and other venues. A recipient of *Writer Magazine*'s Writers Who Make a Difference Award, the James Friend Memorial Award for Literary Criticism, the Studs Terkel Humanities Service Award, and several Pushcart Prize Special Mentions, Seaman was a finalist for the National Book Critics Circle Nona Balakian Citation for Excellence in Reviewing. Seaman's essays and interviews have appeared in *Creative Nonfiction, F Magazine*, and *TriQuarterly*. A contributor to *Home Ground: Language for an American Landscape*, edited by Barry Lopez and Debra Gwartney, Seaman created the fiction anthology *In Our Nature: Stories of Wildness*, and her author interviews are collected in *Writers on the Air: Conversations about Books*, and at www.openbooksradio.org.

GUEST POETRY EDITOR

Kevin Stein has published ten books of poetry and criticism, including the essay book *Poetry's Afterlife: Verse in the Digital Age* (University of Michigan Press, 2010). Among his recent poetry collections are *Sufficiency of the Actual* (University of Illinois Press, 2009) and *American Ghost Roses* (University of Illinois Press, 2005), winner of the Society of Midland Authors Poetry Award. Stein edited two anthologies of Illinois poetry: the audio CD *Bread & Steel* and *Illinois Voices*, the latter with the late G. E. Murray. His poems and essays have appeared in numerous journals, including *American Poetry Review, Boulevard, Colorado Review, The Gettysburg Review, The Kenyon Review, Poetry*, and *TriQuarterly*. His poems have also earned the Frederick Bock Prize from *Poetry*, the *Indiana Review* Poetry Prize, the Devins Award, an NEA fellowship, and other distinctions. Since 2003 he's served as Illinois Poet Laureate. For more information go to www.bradley.edu/poet/stein.

COMING IN 2012

TAKING THE FIFTH

FWJ is pleased to announce novelist, poet, and essayist Ana Castillo will be Taking the Fifth with Daniel Libman in 2012. She is the author of numerous books, including *Psst . . .: I Have Something To Tell You, Mi Amour* (two plays, 2005), *Watercolor Women/Opaque Men: A Novel in Verse* (2005), *Peel My Love Like an Onion* (2000), *Loverboys: Stories* (1996), *My Father Was a Toltec: And Selected Poems* (1995), and *The Mixquiahuala Letters*, which won the American Book Award in 1987. Her recent novel *The Guardians* (Random House, 2007) is a compelling story of a family caught up in the human smuggling along the Mexico-United States border. Learn more about Ana Castillo at her website, www.anacastillo.com.

TENTH ISSUE CELEBRATION

FWJ will celebrate release of the tenth issue in the first week of May 2012. The issue will feature new poetry by some of America's best-known poets, including Kim Addonizio, Bob Hicok, Donald Revell, and Dean Young. It will contain outstanding new fiction by some of Chicago's best young fiction writers, including Joe Meno, Christine Sneed, and Pulitzer Prize winner Achy Obejas. A special photography feature with Petra Ford will mark this issue. We are planning a new feature in which members of our editorial team tell you about some of their favorite books. A new subscription by November 1, 2011, will include this extraordinary issue at no extra cost. Look for more information on our website and sign up for our e-Newsletters as we approach our tenth issue celebration in Chicago during the first week of May.

ILLINOIS POETS PAST AND PRESENT

FWJ will host a special reading by Illinois poets on the evening of Friday, March 2, 2012. This event will be held in the new Poetry Foundation Building located at 61 W. Superior Street, only a short distance from the Chicago Loop and the shores of Lake Michigan. Poets reading from both their own work and the work of past Illinois poets will include Susan Hahn, Larry Lieberman, Christina Pugh, Ed Roberson, and Kevin Stein. In addition to their own poetry, they will read poems by Archibald MacLeish, G. E. Murray, Gwendolyn Brooks, and Carl Sandburg. This event is free and open to the public. Look for more information on our website and elsewhere.

TABLE OF CONTENTS

EDITOR'S NOTES

When the clutter on the editor's desk recedes like an outgoing tide, when the e-mail inbox contains less noise than news and fewer items than the outbox, when the telephone's ring changes from stridency to appeal, when the strings of sticky notes dangling from one another down the sides and across the bottom of the computer screen grow shorter each hour, when the urgent notes from the copy editor and the proofreaders have dwindled to one a day, another cycle has reached its close; only the Editor's Note remains and the issue will be complete. At last, it's the editor's opportunity to have a say about the matters at hand; and with the final period to a brief essay, the three-day vacation begins.

With this issue, number nine, *Fifth Wednesday Journal* begins the fifth year of publication. So let's be on with it. To begin, interviews with two of America's best practitioners of the literary arts. Elizabeth Strout shares with Daniel Libman the reasons behind her flirtation with stand-up comedy, as well as her appreciation for literary magazines. Ed Roberson discusses with Jim Ballowe his remarkable beginning as a poet when he won a competition sponsored by *The Atlantic Monthly*. He also talks about his love of the natural world as a scientist (limnologist) and a hobbyist (birder). In addition, our editors have selected more than 200 pages of challenging and entertaining literature by both established and newer writers.

In this issue we announce the winners of the 2011 Editor's Prizes. Every editor is convinced that all the work in the magazine is worthy of prizes and awards. The editor does not envy the task set to the judges to put down a finger and say, "This is the one." Still, the editor may have a private favorite among the candidates. So it is that the judges' choices may both please and disappoint the editor. This year the judges' fingers landed on work by Jonis Agee, Norman Lock, and Jessica Hubbard Marr. Congratulations to each of them. No disappointment here.

Readers will notice an addition to our masthead. *Fifth Wednesday Journal* now enjoys the support and good wishes of a favorite group, our Contributing Editors, all of whom were Guest Editors for an earlier issue. Welcome and thanks.

Finally, I want to extend an invitation to everyone to a special event on March 2, 2012, in Chicago. *Fifth Wednesday Journal* will host a program featuring Illinois poets of the past and the present. Read the announcement elsewhere in these pages and watch for more details on our website. Now, for that three-day vacation.

EDITOR'S PRIZES

POETRY

The 2011 Editor's Prize winner is "Alphabet of the Eels" by **Norman Lock** (FWJ fall 2010). Our judge, Natania Rosenfeld, read the sixty-seven poems published in the fall 2010 and spring 2011 issues before making her selection. She wrote that she chose Lock:

for his magical "Alphabet of the Eels," in which the sinuous syntax mimics the subject with great wit and with a notable consciousness of the diction of Dr. Johnson's own era. Rarely is a prose poem as rhythmic as this one, and the alliteration is fine, clever, never cloying: "the sprat prized by penurious Londoners" spits itself out subtly (quite a feat); "words both rare and radiant, which to pronounce was to explicate" is at once stately and concise. Lock puns like Shakespeare or Joyce — "the grave mystery of death" — and if at times he sounds a bit imitative, such imitation of masters is eminently forgivable. Like J. M. Coetzee in his novel *Foe* or W. G. Sebald in *Rings of Saturn*, Lock fully conveys the sensuality as well as the cataloguing mania of an earlier era, that "Enlightenment" which is actually full of dark and slippery corners. His poem throbs with life.

Norman Lock's many published works include the novels *Shadowplay* (Ellipsis Press), *A History of the Imagination* (FC2), *The King of Sweden*, and *The Long Rowing Unto Morning* (Ravenna Press); the novella *Land of the Snow Men* (Calamari Press); the prose sequences "Joseph Cornell's Operas," "Émigrés," and "Grim Tales" in *Trio* (Triple Press); and *The House of Correction* (Broadway Play Publishing Co.).

Rosenfeld named two honorable mentions: **John Matthias** for "A Slashed Painting by John Singer Sargent" and **Joe Francis Doerr** for "Drapetomania" (both in FWJ spring 2011). She writes that both poems are tight and entertaining in rhythm and stanzaic form, historically aware, and engaging. Both poets, without sacrificing subtlety, lyricism, or craft, comment on a compelling, uniquely American history of sexism, racism, and masculine self-aggrandizement — one we would do well to consider in our era of arrogance and fear.

Natania Rosenfeld is professor of English at Knox College and author of *Outsiders Together: Virginia and Leonard Woolf* (Princeton, 2000). Her poetry, essays, and fiction have appeared in journals including *The American Poetry Review*, *Raritan*, *Fairy Tale Review*, */nor*, and *Prairie Schooner*. She has no hobbies but reads voraciously and spends time, whenever possible, in New York, Berlin, London, and Tel Aviv.

PHOTOGRAPHY

Our choice for the 2011 Editor's Prize for photography is **Jessica Hubbard Marr**'s photograph "The Gaze (London, 2010)," which was published in the spring 2011 issue. Marr is currently pursuing her master's degree in the history and theory of photography at Sotheby's Institute of Art in London. She received her BA in English literature from Kenyon College in 2005. She spent two years living and working in Oaxaca de Juarez, Mexico. To view more of her work, visit jessicahubbardmarr.com.

Our judge, Jeff Curto, reviewed the twenty-six photographs published in the fall 2010 and spring 2011 issues of FWJ. He wrote of his choice:

It was a great honor to judge the *Fifth Wednesday Journal*'s photo contest. All of the images were wonderful and interesting, but one photograph really stood out for me. "The Gaze (London, 2010)" cuts to the essence of what photography is all about. For me, photography is about the act of looking on an intense level. It's a very specific sort of pointing at something and imploring, "Look; this is interesting."

When I saw that the camera had been pointed at a little boy who was then fixing his gaze on another picture, it magnified that experience of looking and pointing. The fact that he's "focusing" his gaze with glasses adds another dimension. The symbolic connection is enhanced with the humor of the boy's gaze being directed towards a pinup drawing, which is in turn juxtaposed with caricatures of boxers. It's a photograph that provides many levels of things to view, consider, and digest.

I have to give an honorable mention to "Adiós" by **Peter D. Schaller** (fall 2010). The closing of a casket is a heavily symbolic event, whether or not a camera is there to record it. In this image, hands bathed in glowing light add a greater depth. The living hands are so elegant and evocative of both grief and acceptance. The hands of the deceased are seen in that ultimate pose of resignation.

Peter is a community development specialist who lives and works in Nicaragua. His free time is dedicated to writing and taking photographs.

Jeff Curto is professor of photography at College of DuPage in Glen Ellyn, Illinois. He was awarded a master of fine arts degree from Bennington College. He attended Ansel Adams' last workshop in Carmel, California, in 1983. Jeff hosts two popular podcasts: his History of Photography class sessions from College of DuPage (photohistory.jeffcurto.com) and Camera Position that discusses photography's creative aspects (www.cameraposition.com). He also leads photography workshops in Italy — www.photographitaly.com.

FICTION

Our choice for fiction is **Jonis Agee**'s story "The Plane of Primary Focus," which appeared in the fall 2010 issue. Agee is the author of thirteen books, three of them — *Strange Angels*, *Bend This Heart*, and *Sweet Eyes* — named Notable Books of the Year by the *New York Times*. Her most recent novel is *The River Wife* (Random House, 2007). Other honors include the Mark Twain Award and the John Gardner Fiction Award. She is the Adele Hall Professor of English at the University of Nebraska-Lincoln, where she teaches creative writing and contemporary fiction.

Here is what our judge, Edie Meidav, told us about her decision:

True to its title, Jonis Agee's story "The Plane of Primary Focus" works like a Möbius strip of suffering. Right when you think you know where this chatty aggrieved narrator, who holds you tight by the lapels, has her sights fixed, you find she and Agee have placed you in a completely different room. If fiction is a house, as Henry James suggests, Agee's story would be like that of the famously nutty widow, somewhere near San Jose, California, who kept crafting additions to her house which were, essentially, architectural red herrings: closet doors opening to nothing, stairways doubling upon themselves. By Agee's story's end, we swallow, along with our surprising narrator, a lump in the throat. The repressed will return. Yet in Agee's masterful hands, this eventuality has less to do with time and more with that excruciating pain: focus.

Meidav noted these commendable stories: "There is Nothing Left to Lose" by **Dave Onofrychuk** (fall 2010), "The Weight of Snow" by **Julian Hoffman** (spring 2011), "If I Set Up the Chairs" by **Susan Hahn** (fall 2010), and "Postmortem Literature" by **Charles Lamar Phillips** (spring 2011), along with too many others to cite here.

Edie Meidav's novel, *Lola, California*, was released by Farrar, Straus & Giroux in July 2011. She is the author of *The Far Field: A Novel of Ceylon* and *Crawl Space*. Winner of a Lannan Fellowship, a Howard Fellowship, the Kafka Prize for Fiction by an American Woman, and the Bard Fiction Prize, she teaches at Bard College. She was guest fiction editor at FWJ in spring 2010. Visit her website at www.ediemeidav.com.

JAMES BALLOWE

Mechanisms of Emotion:
An Interview with Ed Roberson

Sometime last spring I mentioned to my friend Lisel Mueller that FWJ would be doing an interview with Ed Roberson, this issue's featured poet. She immediately accepted my casual invitation to come along, saying she would like to know Ed better, having met him only twice before, once in the eighties at Goddard where she was teaching and more recently at an event in Chicago. Ed, too, was delighted to spend some time with Lisel, whose *Alive Together* was recognized in 1997 with a Pulitzer Prize.

So in June the three of us sat down for a weekday lunch at Francesca's Bryn Mawr on Chicago's Far North Side. As if we had known each other forever, the conversation immediately began to flow around what we were doing, family, acquaintances, travel, and life in general. Soon I found myself thinking, here I am admiring the talk of two of the most interesting folks I have ever met while drifting from my purpose as designated interviewer. Then Lisel quietly focused the moment for us with a question that was far from being preemptive, merely a continuance of the conversation. She and I then soon found ourselves under the spell of Ed's calm, certain, and illuminating narrative responses.

Lisel Mueller: *Did you always want to be a writer?*

Ed Roberson: No. I started out in the sciences, wanting to be a scientist. That's what I was studying in college.

LM: *Well, how old were you when you began to think about writing?*

ER: It wasn't until I was a couple of years into college. I would have been about twenty. I had one teacher, Mrs. Graham. I had to take her writing course. When I turned in my papers, she was always encouraging. At the end of the semester, she said, "You keep this up, you're going to be a writer." I don't mean I decided right then. I took it as a compliment, but she certainly sparked my curiosity. Me, a writer? So what I did the rest of my college career, I got involved with some friends who were working at the lab, and who were also working with the literary magazine. So there was this connection of people between the two, and gradually I just gravitated toward writing.

I had no idea whether it was going to be poetry or prose, because I hadn't even made up my mind what I was doing. It was more general, "Art." Then I took a couple of courses from Professors Tim Philbrick, Charles Crow, and Richard Tobias. Those were the folks who pulled me aside and sort of led me to really get serious. I took Dr. Tobias's Renaissance course, and I was a terrible student. Sometimes I'd go to class and discover something that I would want to go to the library and look up. In his class he taught the sonnets of Wyatt and Sidney, and I started looking at these things to see how they were pieced together, to see how they affected me the way they did. And this sort of introduced me to the composition of poetry through the mechanism of the sonnet. And it was almost like, for me, the kind of cumulative, rational discovery that comes in the science lab, not just a fit of emotion. I could see how all the pieces fit together, and I could see how it was meant to work . . . composed to work.

LM: *Did you figure that out by yourself?*

ER: Well, I was intrigued enough to go to the library and look at some of the facsimiles of the sonnets, and I began to actually write sonnets just to see how you do the structures and counts, how you make it work. I was looking at these things as little mechanisms of emotion, rather than literature, you know. And I was writing sonnets and really writing a lot.

In one of Dr. Tobias's classes he made the remark that it was sad that people weren't writing sonnets anymore, and this was one of the things he thought was going to disappear. And here I am sitting in a class with a stack of these. So when I left the class I dropped a bunch of these things on his desk. So the next time I came to class, he said in a low voice, "Mr. Roberson." And I had to go up and see him after class. And he told me that he felt I knew what I was doing and that I should get serious. And then he failed me because I didn't attend enough of his classes. But what he really did was show me where I was going right. Years later, when I was actually an adjunct professor at Pittsburgh I met him in an elevator, and he laughed and said, "See, it's good I failed you." He was laughing the whole time. But he was like a kick in the butt, you know, for the writing.

And then Dr. Crow was, like, one of those people who knew everything, and he was always willing to have some conversation about ideas. A student would casually make a remark about something, and he would say, "Yes, that's true, but . . . " And then we'd get this broad-ranging little lecture. And you always learned something from that "but." Those guys got me to thinking seriously about the techniques of writing. At the same time, there were a bunch of artists in the city [Pittsburgh]. Thad Mosley had a gallery on the North Side where a lot of young black writers, poets, dancers, and artists hung out. Everyone would also go to this gallery in the Hill District, Harambe House with the New Horizons Theater. There was a strong community arts movement of black consciousness there. I was getting everything. I was getting the school thing, I was getting the community arts thing, black arts, some of the folks who had done trips to the south — the Freedom Riders. It was a tremendously rich time for me, but I didn't know then that it was a rich time. I was sort of just there looking at everything, taking it in.

FWJ: *Was this in the sixties?*

ER: Yes, the early sixties. I was just there sucking it all up. I didn't know that this was an unusual time. This was what art was supposed to be. So, you know, I just kept working and writing and not really thinking anything was going to happen with it. I was just wanting to know how to do it right or how to do it well. Thoreau was always about doing it right and doing it well. So I wanted to do that kind of thing. So, there was no real training in college. I was just more living and enjoying it all rather than having someone sitting me down and saying, "Do this right."

LM: *When did you start becoming a published writer? Was that your intention?*

ER: No. That was an accident. I was working on the literary magazine, reading other people's writing. Of course, I was trying my own writing, and we had an advisor for the magazine, Irving Rothman, a Milton or Defoe scholar now at the University of Houston, I believe. He took us all to lunch once and said there was this contest *The Atlantic Monthly* had for college students' writing. He thought it would be a good idea for one of us to enter. And it was actually like the situation in the old cereal commercial, where the little kid's brothers gang up on him to try the new stuff and they say, "Let's get Mikey!" There was actually a moment when we were all walking back from lunch, and everyone said, "Let's get Ed!" So they entered me in the contest, and I won. So my first published piece outside of school was in *The Atlantic Monthly*. The grand prize. It was an opportunity to attend Breadloaf. But I didn't go to Breadloaf. At the time, I was with the Pittsburgh Explorers Club, doing rock climbing. The Explorers Club was going to climb in South

America. So instead of going to Breadloaf, I went to South America, and we climbed mountains in Peru and Ecuador.

I want to say that writing was serious, but it wasn't a directed goal. Even after I started getting published, it was mostly enjoying it with friends and picking up books and passing them around. One of the guys I hung out with, Gerry Rhodes, would bring stuff back from New York, and he'd just say, "Here read this." So I got to read things like Frank O'Hara's "Personism," his manifesto on poetry that appeared in *Yugen* before it was ever anthologized in the *New American Poetry: 1945–1960* book. So, like I said, we didn't know where we were going, and I definitely didn't know where I was going.

We were listening to music, too, at that time. I discovered Thelonious Monk. One of my fraternity brothers had this album — I can't remember which one. It was the album that had "Tea For Two" on it. I went out and bought my own copy. I just loved it. The wrong notes would be all the right notes. It was the most exciting thing. You could see that little shift. And Miles Davis was doing things. At the same time I was appreciating Monk's twists, I was getting these real pure, minimal sounds from Miles. It just seemed so rich, so much going on. I didn't play an instrument or anything. At that point I wished I did. I just followed folks around.

FWJ: *What about Coltrane?*

ER: I came to Coltrane much later.

LM: *Coltrane was wonderful. I still listen to a lot of his music.*

ER: Yeah. I came to him much later. For me it was Monk, then Miles, then Coltrane. I guess the transition into Coltrane actually came through Alice Coltrane, his wife. Someone took me to hear her doing a concert. She was not only playing the piano, but also there was a full, auditorium organ there. So she got up from the piano, walked across the stage, and sat down at this organ. To me, it was totally unexpected. I mean she just hit these notes, and the whole place just lifted off the ground. I thought that I had better look this stuff up. So I started listening to her, then discovered John.

You know, one of the things that gets me when I look back and sort of assess whether I did things right, is . . . well, don't you wish you had paid better attention to stuff? I was just going along as if looking at the birdies, just collecting what I wanted. Not a directed research. I was just sort of enjoying whatever.

LM: *Are you talking about birds? Real birds?*

ER: Well, I had a housemate, Darrell Gray, who knew birds. It was the first time I had ever seen, you know, the identifying book the birders use.

FWJ: *A field guide to birds, like Peterson's?*

ER: Yes. Darrell had two of those things. One Saturday we jumped up and ran up to Lake Pymatuning, which is a wildlife preserve near Lake Erie, north of Pittsburgh. And it was just beautiful. And all of a sudden, Darrell whispers, "Look!" And a heron came by out of the fog, and I had never seen a heron. You know, with the neck furled back and this beautiful soar? Your breath just stops.

FWJ: *So you remember when you were introduced to things like that.*

ER: I'm a birder. In that way, I study the lake birds.

FWJ: *As in "Air Mail"?*

ER: "Air Mail"?

FWJ: *You know, your poem in this issue of FWJ. [Reads a bit of it.] I love this poem.*

ER: Of course. I'd forgotten about that. But I don't remember the poem. I write them and forget them. [*Laughter*] I guess I don't pay attention to what I've written.

FWJ: *Well, you make other people pay attention.*

ER: I'm paying attention to trying to get it into words and get it out, and sometimes that's not really the same place as the public's poem. Where I am when I'm writing, it's like an interrogation; sometimes it uses torture to get the truth.

FWJ: *You haven't seen these poems yet, Lisel. They are so distinctive and have such a wonderful line. There's "Air Mail," and the fine, metaphoric "Slow Moon." "Under the Influence" is such a graphic poem with etched references, quite different from the other poems.*

LM: *"Under the Influence"? What are the references, the influences to that poem? Would you read it to us, Ed?*

ER: [*Reads.*]

LM: *And this is based on reality, I assume.*

ER: Yes.

FWJ: *Lisel is persuasive. Could you read "Air Mail" for us?*

ER: [*Reads.*]

FWJ: *Where did you see those snakes?*

ER: Those are the Asian flying snakes. There's a filmed study of how those snakes glide that way. It's similar to how the cobras' necks flatten out. And they manipulate their body like the wing of a plane. They just sort of glide through the air.

What I saw in South America were the coral snakes and a kind of puff adder. I nearly stepped on one of those things in Ecuador in the Amazon. They make a sound with their tail in the leaves. Our guide called out, "Danger! Danger!" When I looked down, I saw this blast of yellow, and then it was gone.

FWJ: *There's a whole community of writers whose principal subject is natural history. I would say that some of my favorite poems in* To See the Earth Before the End of the World, *a book just brimming with compelling poems, remind me of the best work of Gary Snyder.*

ER: Well, yes. I really admire Snyder, too.

FWJ: *I don't mean to suggest that I see echoes of him in your work, though.*

ER: Well, when I said that my friends were passing things around for me to read, Snyder is one of the ones I was handed. And I'm sure I picked up a sense of certain things from Snyder. I take the comparison as a compliment.

FWJ: *So many of your poems are about humans as a part of nature. Is this a conclusion you drew from your science training and your interest in limnology?*

ER: People would say we don't need nature poems. And my reaction is that humans are nature. Nature is us. Nature is not a separate thing.

FWJ: *You started off as a scientist and with teachers who brought you deeply into their work and field experiences.*

ER: When I was an undergraduate, Drs. Richard Dugdale and Vera Dugdale-Alexander packed up the lab into two outfitted VW buses and drove from Pittsburgh up the Alaska Highway to Anchorage, then flew us from there out onto the islands. But Anchorage was our base and we were always passing Portage Glacier up top of Cook Inlet. Then a year ago I read a *New York Times* article about global warming that said glaciers were melting so fast you now had to drive back up into the valley to get to Portage Glacier. I remember it right there off the side of the main road, and now you have to take a drive up the valley. That really shook me, and I wrote the title poem. Other poems that I had lying around then fell into place, and the manuscript started to take shape.

FWJ: *So a lot of what's happening to the natural world influences your work.*

ER: I didn't want to write something that was just pretty. I wanted to write something not just because of the sound or the beauty thing, but because of something that was reaching much farther. The world setting is much bigger than one person. I was raised in a church, a Southern African Methodist Church with all the emotional trimmings. I was never a real believer. But what I did believe in was what music of the stories allowed people to feel. What the musical structures of the religious allowed you to think or feel. How it could give you the experience of things so deep that you would break into tears. Whereas, sitting in a bar, the stories don't move me that way. Communal as they are, those experiences don't go beyond the bar. So, what I always wanted to do was not write the stuff that's pretty but write the stuff that cut way deeper, that was almost terror to deal with. Was hard to look at. The things that scare you, that were hard to look at or listen to, that described those parts of the day when you just sort of sit down and have to shut up. It's best for me when I am humbled into writing. Or look at it, be silenced but enabled to stand up to it and write a poem that says here's a response to the call of that moment, that music. It will make you think. I remember those sung sermons, the sermons of the black southern preachers.

FWJ: *That language is in your poems. You also have street language. And then there's this interesting syntax. Here and there, you drop a verb; you drop a preposition. They are just not there, and as a reader I'm looking at these words juxtaposed and I'm thinking, yes!*

ER: You know, a sculptor once told me it had to do with the speed, that my words go so fast you have to read slowly, then again out loud.

I sometimes don't take time to put in the prepositions, the connectives, and just let things hang together in time, in the music. As he says it, "Ed just doesn't have any patience." It's not that I don't have any patience, but it's that I want people to hear the alternate sentences, both languages. Sometimes the connection that's supposed to be in there is so tight that it doesn't allow you to hear other layers or voicings. I want people to hear of them separately as lines in a chorus. Does that make sense? And I want you to be able to hear this sentence complete and that sentence complete. And I want you to hear them at the same time. Two voices. And to put that preposition in there actually takes away from that. So yes, I'm not patient, because I want you to make that leap, and I'm not going to make that leap for you. You can hear both of these ideas going at the same time. It's the way they are working against each other, fighting against each other, and creating an impossibility that actually resolves itself.

LM: *When I read your poems I'll have to think of that.*

FWJ: *Sounds as if we're back to Thelonious Monk.*

ER: Well, that all comes into it.

James Ballowe, FWJ advisory editor, is Distinguished Professor of English Emeritus at Bradley University. His biography of Joy Morton, *A Man of Salt and Trees: The Life of Joy Morton*, was published by Northern Illinois University Press in 2009. In 2010 the University of Illinois Press published his anthology, *Christmas in Illinois*.

ED ROBERSON

Air Mail

Planes have no way
no reason to undress
from their wings,
birds fold theirs away
in a chest or hang them up
behind a feather door on angel's racks
no one can see.

No one can see why
birds should take more space
than walking
on the ground, rich as they are in air,
the luxury class more
dimensions they can afford,
they drop to land

trees and not
climbed cliff sides. Almost
contemptuous. Against which take
the satisfaction in being here of snakes
rubbing bellies with an earth
they don't mind
is contagious, rubs off on

all the measured feet
they don't have
going   for distance   the length
where others have step
and takeoff.
They keep contact.
And never undress from the ground.

Except for the few
airmailed calligraphic glides
branch to branch
then the down to earth
coming in
clear   nothing to wipe
no fumes

ED ROBERSON

Snow Moon

In that moment   I thought it might be
ceramic   the ground snow   moon-glazed that blue,

blue so pale it's felt as much as seen almost
not there   a shade of longing to   be its bowl,

as I thought it might be   a thought made solid
a skip of state   as to sublime   be you.

ED ROBERSON

Under the Influence

Empty, boarded up stores push on the street
that emptiness; street addicts have to have it
to take what they see   in the windows,
strung out across the sidewalk, holding up
walls   with that lean.

                              The sight sells it,
the look of it pushes into a street
its block going nowhere I have to take
to get through   to the train   to work.

This how I get to the job, strung out through
this   how I arrive, a high like the bottom
and have to team with the high on white trip
in from the suburbs.

                           Always ready to arrest,
the law and their order bunch pull my work
over per their addiction,

                       but my papers are clean.

ED ROBERSON

Winter Solstice

The noon daylight already   almost flat,
my head bumps on the daze under it.

Torn off the back-less tablet pool of dark
by the dawn   is this clean sheet of light that we,

by simply standing,   write in overhead
the common halo of the human on its feet,

a cloud of bruises   whose rain falls so short
of tallying the blows   as to be cartoon:

a jagged scribble blackens the balloon
above my head with cursing,   we darken

the ceilinged sky, close as if cave already
of its year;   our light remaining upright though,

we weld it up and open   'til earth engraves
its day   light flattens completely out.

ED ROBERSON

Poem Beginning with Transparent Line

..in its hand painted camouflage of mid-air
the swan dive is flying, the sky dive floats
its calligraphy of gravities down the scroll
      the ancient poem in this
      :……..

..lived fabric well rendered as so   can be elaborate
quotations of how practiced we can be
in our falling
      tries   by melted wing, blinded eye
      or straight down collapse

through dust   cloud   practiced
lift to fall step   into step as walking some of us
clumsy waters of life fall
      step as stairs   laughter
      rather than any Niagara's awe

..ink all over
the expensive papers of breath
camouflage of mid-air
      the ancient poem in this
      smudged fingerprint

..transparent
for being so
now permanently
      unobstructed

ED ROBERSON

Who You Callin'

Mosquito-ish angel, ladle of rescue,
helicopter skidding through a flight turn
sideways   moving forward out of the curve
before straightening out   it tilts ahead;

the center of all these forces slops around
without a spill, the mixture somehow smoothed,
dips them out   Angel, ladle of rescue,
swatting the loss away, stings death.
                                    The cursing!
Both arrogant sons of bitches at
their game   each in the image of the other,
death and rescue skid ass-wise around
the corner neither knows: death   being

inevitable the essence is when,
that point   on which the odds get even   sucker!

ED ROBERSON

Ulysses For Sale

a lot of things but for example he
had reading the bible on his
life's to do list all his life   or many
of the great philosophies   the novels
building the boat or plane unfinished
in the garage   some achievement or what
some experience held for him   would do
to him would make him   then
he gave the books away and sold the kit
to the plane   yes
                lines as things never finish
there is the infinite   but to admit
he will never finish things is a different
book never thought to have been read writing it
all along   piecing itself together   the end of it

RICHARD HACKLER

Eating Little Fish

Nonfiction

I can't help it: it is March in Michigan's Upper Peninsula, and I haven't been able to linger in my shirtsleeves and stare at the harbor in months. I can't help pausing before I walk into Thill's Fish House, wavering on my feet, slumping against the door frame and taking in this early, unseasonable spring.

I look out at Lake Superior: at the ore dock jutting into the harbor, flaking off rust, so enormous and out of place in Marquette's gentrified downtown that it might have fallen here from space; at the seagulls, scattered against the pale sky as though they were tossed there, like dice. I look at the water itself until I can't anymore, until my eyes dry up, until I need to shut them against the wind and sun. And when I shut my eyes, I listen — to the sharp cries of the circling gulls, to the steady whoosh of the downtown traffic, to a flag somewhere snapping taut in the wind.

Earlier today, I invited my friend Aubrey over for lunch. "Come to my house later," I said. "We'll eat fish!" Now, outside of Thill's, out in the bright afternoon, I'm rocking on my feet in anticipation: we'll crank open my windows, Aubrey and I, and let our hair blow around in the breeze. We'll talk about gardens and baseball, our words mushed between mouthfuls of herring, and pretend that spring has won, that winter is dead, that we'll never have to shut our windows again.

"Excuse me," says a voice behind me. I turn around and see, staring hard at me, an old man, stout and flannelled, with gleaming, deeply set eyes the color of faded denim. He looks, as so many of Marquette's men look, exactly like Ernest Hemingway.

"I'm sorry," I say, and he flashes a quick, tight smile. I understand, his smile says. The afternoon is warm, and it is natural to linger outside, to stare at the harbor. I pull open the door and follow him inside.

And there, inside the shop, is the smell. Most of the fish at Thill's are gutted and filleted in the backroom, and the steam rises from the sinks in back, gathers the smell, and pours out to the front of the shop. If you could wring out this air, the stench would puddle on the linoleum floor and soak through your shoes.

But it doesn't matter. This is my favorite place in Marquette. I walk here at least twice a week, and leave with my arms full of fish: jars of pickled herring, slabs of whitefish wrapped in newspaper, fillets of smoked trout so salty they leave your tongue feeling wrung out, dead.

It thrills me to live here, in a town whose residents still look to their surroundings for sustenance, rather than driving their minivans to the nearest Walmart when they need groceries. And where people like this old man still walk to the fish shop, still furrow their brows and crouch to the floor to warily consider today's catch.

Though I'm not from here — have only lived here, in fact, for seven months — I feel at home in Marquette. And never more than when I'm standing in Thill's, breathing through my mouth, my head buzzing from this steamy rush of fish reek.

The old man stares and frowns for a minute more before looking up, hacking clear his throat, and saying, in a voice that sounds as though it should be coming from behind a podium, "How fresh are those walleye fillets, son?"

"Got 'em this morning," says the clerk, a thin, thirtyish man in brown overalls. He crosses his wrists behind his back and stares at the old man through heavy-lidded eyes. If this clerk's hair weren't thinning, and if he weren't standing behind the counter at the fish house, I might mistake him for a bored seventh-grader.

"Very good," says the old man, nodding. He pauses, staring into the display case, before nodding again. "I'll take a pound."

While the clerk wraps up Hemingway's walleye, I crouch in front of the display case to consider my options. The salmon fillets, their rubied flesh bright as Easter eggs, are twelve dollars a pound, and shipped here from Washington, anyway; and it would be very sad, I think, to leave Thill's with a package of fish that arrived in Michigan on an airplane. Which leaves the whitefish fillets — their skins gray, and shining so brilliantly in the florescent light that they look blue, almost holographic; the herring — smoked whole, ghastly, their eyes as bright and empty as marbles; and the smelt.

Smelt are tiny fish, no longer than my pinky, and there are hundreds of them piled in this display case. Next to the others, they look hapless: their scales intact, their heads lopped off, their tails drooping as if in surrender. If this were a zoo, I might feed them to a seal.

"Tell me about the smelt," I say to the clerk. The old man has gone home with his walleye, and I have the shop to myself.

"Well," he says, and looks up at the ceiling. We've talked before, this clerk and I, and he hovers over each word, chooses them as carefully as if he were carving them into a rock. "These ones are from Lake Michigan, actually. They catch them this time of year by deep-water trolling."

"But what do they taste like?" I ask. "Are they really fishy?" I'm thinking now of a story a friend told me once, about a party she attended at which everyone around her swallowed live goldfish and washed them down with pulls of tequila.

"Oh, I don't think so," says the clerk. "They're good! Just fry them up in some oil." He stops, looks at the floor, looks up again. "The old-timers go crazy for them. Eat them like French fries." He raises his right hand to his mouth and pretends to bite a French fry, or a headless fish, in half.

I laugh, a little uncertainly, and stare at the smelt. I think about goldfish, their wriggling bodies sliding down the throats of whooping teenagers. I think about smelt, and think that I've never spent money on such a sad-looking food.

My family has been eating little fish for generations. My mom's side arrived here from Sweden a hundred twenty years ago and brought with them Lutheranism, stoicism, and a love of oily fish. After settling in central Minnesota, my great-great-grandparents survived the winter on buckets of pickled herring. Herring fillets were cheap at the local market, and soaking them in vinegar preserved them for months. My great-grandmother grew sick of it — the piercing smell, the sour, overflowing taste — but it was better than going hungry, so she managed.

My grandfather's childhood is also full of herring, but his memories are fonder. "It was a treat," he told me, "when my dad would bring home a jar of herring." Of course, this was during the Depression, so his memory might be skewed. "We were probably excited to be eating at all."

When my dad was seventeen, he worked for a year at Viking Herring and Lutefisk in Minneapolis. "Making the lutefisk was the worst," he said. "They didn't give us masks back then, and the lye would spray in our eyes. I had to go to the doctor three, four times that year." This brush with blindness somehow didn't rob him of his passion for little fish: he still flushes my mom from the kitchen with his pickled herring, its juices soaking through Saltines, through paper towels, riddling the counter with sour little puddles that he'll need to wipe up later.

I acquired my family's taste for oily fish very suddenly — lying in bed two months ago, staring at my ceiling and wanting, more than I'd wanted anything in a long time, a piece of herring on a Triscuit. It was a phantom pain, this feeling, a wanting like an absence, as though something vital had been scooped whole from my chest. I thought about Christmas Eve, about my dad perched over his jar, a fork in his hand, raising a chunk, dripping, up to his mouth, laughing as my nieces wrinkled their noses and skittered downstairs with their cell phones.

What's happening to me? I thought, trying to fall asleep. Something in my blood, something dormant in me has woken and rushed me back to my roots. I wished it weren't so late. I wished I could call my dad.

I went to Thill's the next morning. I've been a regular ever since.

But still: *smelt*. Herring, at least, is recognizable as food. Cut into pieces, surrounded by onions and bay leaves and peppercorns, it looks like something a person could conceivably eat. A smelt, though, looks like bait that someone might use to catch other, better fish.

"I'll take a pound," I say to the clerk. "And," because I do not trust the smelt, and because I'm buying lunch for two, "a couple of smoked herring."

The clerk wraps the herring in parchment paper and dumps my smelt into a plastic grocery bag. "Enjoy!" he says, handing them to me across the counter.

"I'll do my best," I say, and walk out into the bright afternoon, the hollowed corpses of two herring tucked under my arm, a bag of headless fish swinging from my right hand. I am a Norse warrior, I think. I am a pillager of the sea.

In Marquette, I'm told, we do not believe in spring. We hear things, of course — we have friends downstate, relatives in Minneapolis and Madison, people who call us late in March and tell us, their voices as full as rain barrels, that they've seen tulips, brag about their brightening lawns and promising gardens. They ask us who we like in the Central Division this year, ask us if we want to come camping with them — if the weather keeps up, who knows? They might make it out in a couple of weeks! We listen politely, we nod, we smile at their trilling voices, as clear as birdsong, but we don't believe a word.

In Marquette, spring is a trick: the sunny week in mid-March before the bracing, soppy snowstorms of early April. It deceives us, cajoles us into putting away our boots and dragging our lawn chairs out from the shed, before it cripples us again.

Or this is what my friends have told me. I'm new to Marquette, and haven't absorbed the native skepticism. Right now, out on the sidewalk, on this unseasonable day in early March, blinking and dazed with the other sunstruck locals running their afternoon errands, the idea of snow seems to me as remote as polar bears or volcanoes.

I grew up in central Minnesota, in the sprawling stripmallscape that creeps northward from Minneapolis, up toward Saint Cloud. My parents tried to flee the encroaching ugliness, moving farther and farther north — from Minneapolis to Crystal, from Crystal to Maple Grove, and from Maple Grove to Big Lake, forty miles north of the city, where I grew up — but it caught up with them. Now even the woods behind their house — the dense, unbroken woods I used to wade through with my dad, entire afternoons spent tripping over roots, bloodying our arms against thorn bushes, hopping over patches of itch weed and poison sumac — are scarred with housing developments.

Central Minnesota is a place with a beauty of its own, of course, but a beauty entombed beneath layers and layers of concrete. When you need a loaf of bread, you drive to the nearest Cub Foods; when you need a bottle of shampoo, you drive to the nearest Target. Nobody walks, because there aren't sidewalks. And you cannot throw a rock without shattering the window of a Chipotle Burrito Shop.

So what a thrill to live in Marquette. What a thrill to walk past the Safety Store, to imagine myself someday needing an orange vest and a roll of caution tape, and then walking downtown, brimming with the knowledge that there is a place for me. What a thrill to walk past the vintage photography store and to consider that, in this outpost of twenty thousand people, there is a market for sepia photographs and antique postcards. And Higgins' Bingo Supplies! When I walk by today, I press my face against the glass and stare at the stacks of bingo cards, the rows of daubers, the old woman paging through a magazine behind the counter, because I find it a source of wonder and gratitude to live near a store that deals solely in bingo supplies.

We are so much ourselves in Marquette. While other towns raze their Main Streets and build Super Walmarts out by the highway, our downtown remains unique and vital. It must be the isolation. We're an eight-hour drive from any major metropolitan area, and a town set so deeply in the woods, so far away from the rest of the world, must attract a particular sort of person: someone who wants only to be left alone, to let his beard grow long and crazy, to earn his living selling hardhats and yellow caution tape.

In the Upper Peninsula, we drift just outside the steadying orbit of society. We will buy our fish from the fish market and our bread from the bakery. We will help our neighbor shovel his driveway and jump-start his car when mornings are cold. We are alone out here, together in the woods, and we will make the best of it.

Aubrey and I have been blessed, and we know it. So we walk lazily down the sidewalk, stepping deftly over potholes and hardened clumps of black snow, wringing all that we can from this afternoon. We ease past the hospital, past the university buzzing with students, talking slowly about the smelt we'll eat, the beer we'll drink, pausing to notice the shadows of bare trees waving on the sidewalk, the pools of reflected light in the potholes full of melted snow.

We're a few blocks from my house when we look up and see, suddenly in front of us, walking in the opposite direction, Ted and Veronica.

"Come eat smelt with us," I say. "Come drink beer!" Veronica is on her way to work, but Ted's afternoon is free. He says goodbye to Veronica, turns around, and now there are three of us.

"I've never eaten smelt before," Ted says, matching his stride to ours. We feel brave and expectant, like pioneers.

An hour earlier, after walking home and dropping the smelt in the kitchen sink, I turned on my computer to learn what I could about our lunch before leaving to fetch Aubrey. Smelt, I discovered, were a staple for early New England settlers. Like herring, smelt is a small, oily fish that has never commanded a high price on the market. It is a food for lean winters, an abundant fish that's easy to catch — smelt swim in large schools and are caught by wading into creeks at night, shining a headlamp into the water, and scooping them out with a net. If my ancestors had grown up in New England, they would have survived the winters on smelt and pickled beets, not herring soaking in buckets of vinegar.

"I don't know if this'll be any good," I say now to Aubrey and Ted, unlocking my front door, walking into my house. I'd left the windows open, and my kitchen is as fragrant and bright as a city park. "It really is just a bag of headless fish." I hold it up, the soggy bag of corpses, for illustration.

Nobody seems to mind, though. I overturn the smelt into a pan with a lump of butter and grab each of us a beer.

"This is a good day," says Ted, and we all sit down, stunned by our good fortune, as the room fills up with the odors of spring, butter, and frying smelt.

We are so far away from our families, my friends and I. We are so far away from our hometowns. But right now, gathered around my kitchen table, leaning on our elbows, drinking our beer and talking through mouthfuls of fish, it doesn't matter.

"I just want a job," Aubrey is saying, chewing on a piece of smoked herring, "that doesn't drain me. That lets me go home at night with the energy to write."

We've built this moment ourselves: carved it from our lives the way, a hundred fifty years ago, loggers and miners and fishermen carved Marquette from the boundless, rocky woods. Or the way, thirty years later, my ancestors built a livelihood on the central Minnesota prairie.

"Or one that doesn't leave you feeling like an asshole when you get home at night," says Ted.

"And one," I say, holding a smelt, pointing it to emphasize my words, "that gives you enough money to pay your rent." I bite into it, drop its tail on my plate. "That's all I want! Enough money to pay my rent."

"It isn't too much to ask," says Aubrey.

"We want so little."

The smelt is better than I imagined, but it isn't good. In texture and taste, it reminds me of a school cafeteria fish stick.

Ted picks one up, stares avidly into it. "Check it out," he says, and pulls from his smelt, stunningly whole, an entire little spine.

Aubrey shudders. "I've been eating my spines," she says. "Is that OK?"

"Oh, no," he says, grabbing another smelt, talking as he chews. "That spine is going to cut up all of your organs. It's going to be really painful for you." He shakes his head, rips out another spine.

"I've been eating my spines, too," I say to Aubrey, and I have: I've eaten seven of them. I learned earlier that it's customary to eat the spines.

I want you to see us here. I want you to picture us from above, from space, a dot on a map, and then zoom in, into the Upper Peninsula, this lonely jut of land arching out into the Great Lakes, and come farther in, into the forest, unbroken for hundreds of miles, and then into Marquette, and consider how strange it is that we live here, that anyone lives here, in this tiny, wooded middle of nowhere, and come in closer, until you're in my kitchen, closer, until you're hovering over my table, until you see us, all of us — Aubrey leaning back in her chair, closing her eyes against the sun, folding her hands on her floral-print dress as though she might start praying; Ted leaning forward, his elbows propped on the table, turning a smelt in his hands, one eye closed, as though he were approximating its value; me, looking out at the street, my hair waving around in the breeze, my eyes drooping shut — and think of how strange and miraculous it is — Aubrey from Iowa, Ted from Chicago, me from Minnesota — that we've found each other here, that we're gathered together on this bright, breezy, impossibly warm afternoon, sitting around my table, united by this greasy, this ugly, this unremarkable fish.

The Magician's Assistant

Fiction

Morty hesitated on the fourth floor landing, listening to his mother. It wasn't his fault he could hear every word. Sounds carried in the narrow hallways. His mother was washing dishes, and her voice rose over the clatter and splash.

"With brains like his, he will be a rabbi."

There was a rustling of a newspaper, and Morty held his breath, waiting for his father's reply.

"Better he should be a doctor. People are always falling apart."

"*Oy!* All that sickness and dying. Not Morty."

"First he should get through school."

"A rabbi! You wait and see."

"First he should come home for dinner. Where is he?"

He didn't move. That his mother thought he would be a rabbi didn't surprise him. He knew his mother thought he could do anything. But that his father thought he should be a doctor — this was something to think about. He hoped his father would say more. His father had never talked much, but lately he talked even less. Just the night before, he had said something to his mother about it when his father was taking an after-dinner *shpatsir*.

"He hardly talks at all now."

"What do you mean?"

"Haven't you noticed? He says as few words as possible."

"He should be singing and dancing? The man works sunup to sundown, chained to a sewing machine! They have to shout to be heard. It's a miracle he has a voice left. A man comes home, he should have some quiet."

His mother had collected the dishes, angrily plunking them down in the sink.

"Mama, I'm sorry, I was only saying —"

"I know what you were saying. Now do your homework."

They had finished the night in silence, even his mother, who usually talked enough for all three of them. The next morning she had given him an especially big bowl of oatmeal. As he was buttoning his coat, she had flung her arms around him.

"You know I love you."

He had leaned against her, giving himself up to her embrace. He knew his mother loved him, all right. It was his father he wondered about.

His father hadn't always been like this. Only last summer, the two of them had sat together after dinner by the fire escape, their faces turned towards the evening breeze. And then there was the time last year when he had had a fever, and his father had checked on him in the middle of the night. Morty had opened his eyes, and his father had stroked his cheek. "*Shlof, mayn kind.*" All night he had felt protected by his father's hand.

But ever since his father had gotten the job at the tie shop in September, things had been different. Now when Morty woke up for school, his father was already at work. They saw one another for the first time at dinner. Maybe his mother was satisfied by the handful of words his father uttered over the course of a meal, but he wasn't. And when he had had a cold a few weeks ago, his father had never checked on him at all. Morty knew this, but he had asked his mother the next morning, hoping he had been wrong.

"*Tatele*, you've got to understand. Your father put his head on the pillow and he was out."

He knew it was the end of something. He just didn't know what.

He studied the poorly lit stairs, their treads sagging in the middle as if they might tumble to the floor below. So his father thought he should be a doctor. He hated science class. He hated math class. He hated school, period. His thoughts swung to the colored pencils in the stationer's window that he had seen on the way home from *kheyder*. In the twilight darkened by rain, the pencils with their names printed in miniature gold letters were the only bright thing on the entire street. Cerise, aquamarine, burnt umber — he loved even the words. He had torn his eyes away from them to stare at the price. A dollar! He had walked home in the rain, his hands shoved in his pockets, scanning the gutters for fallen change. He hadn't found a cent.

He could hear his mother setting the table. There was no point thinking about the pencils. He banged on the door.

"*Gotenyu!* Where were you all this time?"

"Just walking."

"In the freezing cold? The pouring rain? Take off those shoes and socks!"

His mother threw herself into action, running for a towel, grabbing clean socks, and heaping three plates with roast chicken, fried onions, and kasha. His father only looked at him, clearing the newspaper from the table. Morty flushed beneath his glance.

"Hi, Papa."

"Sit. Eat."

His father's voice was raspy. Maybe his mother was right. Maybe his father was just hoarse from shouting over the sewing machines all day. Morty looked at him furtively. His skin looked yellow. Maybe his father was sick. He pushed the thought away, avoiding his father's eyes.

Even though his mother had made one of his favorite meals, he could barely eat. He stared at the onions on his plate, thinking of burnt umber. His mother felt his forehead and insisted he go to bed early. She bustled in and out of his bedroom, plumping up his quilt, straightening his room, hovering over him. One more kiss, and he was alone. He was glad to be in bed, even though he wasn't tired. He needed to think.

He drew every moment he could manage it: the tenements on Rivington Street, the guys playing handball, his mother making strudel, his father in his *tefillin*. Sure, his mother and father saw him drawing, but to them it meant nothing. His mother said he would hurt his eyes doing such nonsense in poor light. His father only shook his head. And he should tell them he wanted colored pencils? Even if he could tell them why he wanted them, which he couldn't, and even if they understood him after he told them, which they wouldn't, they could never afford colored pencils. Colored pencils? He could hear his mother's voice rise up in a shriek. The whole thing was impossible. No, he would have to earn the money himself. He only had a few free hours a week, what with school and *kheyder*, but somehow he would manage it. He was eleven years old, almost twelve. He would do it himself. Rolling over, he thought of the pencil called obsidian and fell asleep.

"I might know a fella who needs somebody like you."

Morty waited as Lou Posner stirred the pile of roasting chestnuts. For once, the chestnuts were not demanding his attention. He looked anxiously at Posner's lined face, the stubble of white beard, the broken nose, the bloodshot eyes. The sleeves of Posner's wool coat were rolled up, exposing bony wrists and chapped hands weathered by years of exposure to the wind and cold. For most of the school year the man was outside Seward Park High School, and with each year he seemed to get smaller and smaller, as if one day he would vanish into the pavement.

"My sister's daughter Flossie, her husband Itzie's got this friend who's got some extra thing going on Sundays. Wants somebody to help him out. Wanted Itzie to do it, but Flossie, she put her foot down."

"So do you think he still needs somebody?"

Posner shot him a crooked smile.

"For you, I'll find out. You come back tomorrow, and I'll let you know. As for today, my friend, how 'bout a chestnut? Brain food, you know. Gotta feed the brain, a smart boy like you."

So Morty bought a chestnut from Lou Posner, even though he couldn't help but think that it took him that much farther away from the colored pencils. Still, it paid off, because the next day, Posner handed him a scrap of paper with the address of Itzie's friend scribbled on it.

"He calls himself The Great Zablonsky. Does magic shows. And he needs an assistant."

Morty studied the address, panic stirring in the pit of his stomach. Who was this guy he was about to meet, and what would his parents think of him working for anybody, let alone a magician?

"What does he need an assistant for?"

"What do I know from magic? But he'll tell you all about it. Itzie says he's a nice guy. Works as a presser and does magic on the side. But you better talk to him today, 'cause Itzie says he's in a hurry to find somebody. Just say you're the boy Lou sent."

"Thanks, Mr. Posner. I'll go see him after *kheyder*. I'll let you know what happens."

"You do that. You come see me and fill me in. But no magic tricks, hunh? I'm an old man. Can't take no surprises."

That evening, he hurried out of *kheyder* while his friends loitered behind him. After the stuffy classroom, the chill November wind made his eyes water. By the time he arrived at the tenement on Essex Street, stars shone above the fire escapes. He climbed three sets of stairs, made his way past peeling walls and a burnt-out light bulb, and found Zablonsky's door in the back. He felt far away from everyone he knew, and for a moment he considered bolting down the stairs. Then he thought of the pencils, and their colors seemed to shimmer in the dark hallway. He knocked.

A man opened the door, flooding the hallway with light. He was short and skinny in a way that made him seem young, but the lines in his face told a different story. Then, too, he was almost completely bald, with only a wisp of hair combed over his crown. Dressed in black pants and a white shirt, he looked like a regular enough guy. Still, his naked head cast a strange shadow in the hallway, and Morty felt a shiver of fear. The man looked at him inquiringly.

"You the kid that Itzie told me about? Posner's friend?"

"Yeah. I heard you needed an assistant."

"You heard right. Nice to meet you. Frankie Zablonsky."

"Morty Weissman."

He had never shaken hands with a stranger without his parents around. But the magician didn't know that.

"So, ever see a magic show?"

"No, but I'd like to."

"How old are you?"

"Twelve."

The man raised his eyebrows.

"Almost twelve."

"OK, Mr. Almost, I see you're looking to the future. That makes two of us. You scared of being in front of people?"

"Better in front than in back."

"No kidding. There's a routine you'd have to learn."

"Can't be harder than the Talmud."

"You got a point. You free on Sundays at two? I got a steady thing going at the Royale the third Sunday each month. And when I don't have a show, I wanna use that time to go over the moves. We'd work right here. You free then?"

"Yeah, sure."

"You'd have to tell your parents, you got that? I don't want anybody getting mad at me for working with almost-twelve-year-old kids."

"I'll tell 'em."

"I won't pay you for practicing. Only for the shows."

"How much?"

"How 'bout a quarter?"

"Sounds good." Morty's thoughts raced. Four shows and he could buy the pencils.

"If the practice this Sunday goes all right, you got a deal. And I'll be counting on you for some publicity. You tell your folks The Great Zablonsky has a show at the Royale two Sundays from now. They can come see you and me perform and bring the whole *mishpokhe*."

They grinned at one another, equally pleased.

"So you wanna come in and see the stuff?"

Zablonsky's kitchen was even smaller than the one his mother commanded. A grimy stove, a sink stacked with dishes, a beat-up icebox. A table and chair by a narrow window looked out over the fire escape. Crammed under the table was a pile of bags and satchels. Zablonsky yanked one open and pulled out a frayed crimson handkerchief, a top hat, a pair of white gloves, and a deck of cards, tossing each one onto the table with a flourish. They gave off a stale, chalky odor.

"This is just some of my stuff. I got loads more. I do the moves, and you're there to hand me things. Smile at the audience. Maybe talk a little. Distract 'em, you know. We'll practice all the tricks, so don't worry. Mostly what you gotta do is keep secrets."

"No problem. I keep secrets backwards and forwards."

"Because how I do my tricks — it takes years of work, and besides, it's nobody's business, right?"

"Right."

"Because it's delicate work, and seeing is believing, right?"

"So we gotta help the customers see."

"You got it!" Zablonsky punched him lightly on the shoulder. "Kid, I got a feeling about you. I think you're gonna be good at this."

The magician put an arm around Morty and gestured proudly with the other at his collection of props. They didn't look like much to Morty, but he could see that Zablonsky thought they were out of this world.

His mother closed the door behind him, marched to the stove, and then shook her ladle at him.

"What took so long this time?"

"I'm sorry, Ma. I had to do something."

He had run all the way home, and with each step he had tried to prepare himself for his mother's questions. Now he couldn't remember a single excuse. His father looked up from the newspaper. One of his parents at a time he could deal with. Two, it was impossible.

"What kind of something?"

"I — I wanted to see something before it got dark. I'm drawing it."

"He's drawing it! I should be grateful it isn't midnight!"

"Ma, it's not that late! Besides, what other time do I have? I'm in school from sunup to sundown!"

His mother gave him a look.

"So what is it already? I got ears."

"Lottie. Enough."

His father put down the newspaper, and for a moment, all three of them were motionless. Then his mother turned back to her stove with her head held high, as if she had more important business. A wave of gratitude swept over Morty. His father had come to his rescue! A wild hope flared inside him even as he braced himself for his father to interrogate him. Maybe his father would ask him about his drawing. Maybe this was a way to tell them about the pencils. The truth trembled inside him.

But his father only returned his gaze, his dark eyes intense, brooding. He looked more tired than usual, his face pale, his eyes ringed with shadows, his beard shot with gray. Another instant of his father's gaze and he would have told him everything: the pencils, Lou Posner, Zablonsky, the show two Sundays from now. But the words died inside him as his father looked away. Morty shoved his hands in his pockets and was startled to feel the scrap of paper with Zablonsky's address. He clenched it in his fist as if to hide it from his father's eyes.

"I'm sorry I'm late. I didn't mean to worry you."

"*Mayn kind!*" his mother exclaimed, throwing her arms around him. "What would we do without you?"

Over his mother's shoulder, he could see a wan smile flicker across his father's worn face. Why had his father said "Enough"? Was his father trying to help him, or did he only want his dinner? Even then, if his father had looked at him once more, he would have told them everything. But no. His father folded the newspaper. His mother served the soup.

For the rest of the week, Morty told himself that the next day he would tell his parents everything. But each day came and went, and he told his parents nothing. At dinner he sat with them in their customary triangle, his father uttering a handful of words while he ate slowly, his mother talking nonstop, ferrying food from the stove to the table. Morty wondered how their conversation could be so ordinary when what he wasn't telling them pressed like a stone upon his heart. He had never lied to them before. He had never thought about lying. Why was he doing it now? For a bunch of colored pencils in a cardboard box? Over and over he considered telling Zablonsky that he couldn't do it. He could say he had changed his mind. He could say his parents wouldn't let him. But that would be lying too. He wanted those pencils. He couldn't pretend he didn't.

No, the only thing to do was to tell his parents. But he knew they would never understand. His mother would raise her arms up to heaven. For this your father works himself to death? For this we gave up everything and came to this country? So that you could work for a magician? And grow up to be an actor? She would throw her apron over her face and sob. But his father's silence would be worse, much worse. He would not even look at him. He would pick up his newspaper, fold it in half, and walk out of the room.

No, he could never tell them. If he did, it wouldn't be just the pencils he would lose. He would lose something else — he wasn't sure what — but the thought of his father walking out of the kitchen filled him with fear. No, the only thing to do was to work for the magician without them knowing. The pencils cost a dollar. He would get a quarter each month. Four months. Sixteen Sundays. He could do it. He'd be extra good with his homework. He'd work hard in *kheyder*. He'd help his mother with the dishes. After the show in February, he'd tell Zablonsky that he had to stop.

So each day he woke up and went to school and went to *kheyder* and came home, and each day the secret accompanied him. As soon as he saw his mother in the morning, her face still creased from sleep — as soon as he saw his father in the evening, his hands looking broken, as if the sewing machine had worn them out, the secret came between them. Then, too, when he was alone in his room on the other side of the kitchen, the secret was always there. Night after night the streetlight shone through the curtains and cast a filmy shadow against his bedroom wall, and night after night the secret followed him. Cerise, aquamarine, burnt umber. Blood, sea, earth. It swallowed him.

Sunday morning he could barely think. How would he get to Zablonsky's by two? What would he say to his parents?

But after lunch, his father went to visit a friend who was sick, and his mother was busy with the washing.

"Ma, I'm going out to play handball."

She looked up from the tub, her arms wet up to the elbows.

"Button that coat. And don't be home late."

His heart was beating so hard he was sure she would hear it, but she returned to her scrubbing. The instant he hit the street, he started running. If he wasn't at Zablonsky's for long, he would definitely play handball. He owed his mother that much.

The magician's door was ajar. Morty knocked, and a voice called out from the bedroom.

"Hey, Mr. Almost! Come on in! I'll be right with you."

He looked uneasily at the props piled under the table and peered out over the fire escape. The iron bars were flaking with rust. Beyond them, a clothesline stretched across an inner courtyard littered with broken chairs and weeds. He imagined eating meal after meal by that window, staring out at the view. No wonder Zablonsky had turned to magic. He was just thinking of drawing the magician bent over a bowl of soup, framed by the fire escape, when Zablonsky leapt into the room.

"Ta-da! Lesson number one: start with a bang! Give 'em a show they won't forget! So — how you doing? You tell your ma and pop you're here?"

"Yeah." A pang of misery shot through him. Now he was lying to Zablonsky as well as his parents. It was all he could do to meet the magician's eyes.

"Take off your coat already. You wanna glass of water or something?"

"No, thanks. I'm fine."

"So lemme tell you about the Royale. When I get there, they put me in the main room of the café, right with the customers, so I have no place to get revved up before the show. All I can do is set the props, sit in the back, and wait till I go on. Maybe you're thinking that's not such a big deal, but the thing is — the entrance. You gotta make an entrance. Even if you're right there in front of 'em, you gotta come in — boom!" Morty flinched as the magician stamped his heavy black shoe on the linoleum floor. "So here's the question: how do we come in when we're already there?"

The magician looked at him expectantly, but he had no idea what to say. Some assistant he was. Zablonsky looked right through him and turned his back on him. OK, it was all over. If he was lucky, he'd earn money helping Posner with the chestnuts.

But he had no time to plan things further. Zablonsky spun around, flinging open his arms.

"Ladies and gents! It's time for *The Great Zablonsky*!"

The magician held his pose for a dazzling moment, his eyes sparkling, his chest swelling with pride. Even his white shirt seemed to shine, as if it were lit from within by a spotlight. Then just as abruptly, he dropped his arms. Morty realized that was his cue.

"Wow! That was great."

"Really? You think so?"

"Yeah, that was fabulous. And you scared me, too."

"They should be scared! I want 'em at the edge of their seats!"

"They'll be at the edge, all right."

The magician beamed, and his gaunt face seemed smooth, young again.

"So now you know. It don't matter if you're right in front of 'em! It don't matter if you're in their faces and up their noses! What matters is style. That's the beginning and the end of magic. You remember that."

He patted his wisp of hair into place, smiling at his reflection in the windowpane. Then he fished the white gloves out of a bag.

"You see these? Top of every show, you give 'em to me. But you can't just hand 'em over. These are not any gloves. They're The Great Zablonsky's gloves. We're talking power. Mystery. Magic. So let's see what you can do."

The magician tossed the gloves onto the table, and Morty picked them up gingerly. The fabric was soft and pleasing, but one of the gloves had been mended along the outside seam, and both of them had grimy fingertips. He turned his back on Zablonsky and took a few steps away, trying to think of something. He figured he should whip around, wave his arms, blast out the words. But his heart was beating like a drum and his mouth refused to speak because he was no longer Lottie and Abe's son, no longer even the kid who wanted colored pencils. He was the magician's assistant.

With a sudden movement, he thrust the gloves upward as if they were the Statue of Liberty's torch. Turning around, he locked eyes with the magician. Then slowly, he lowered the gloves, gave them to Zablonsky, and bowed.

When the magician finally spoke, his voice was hoarse with emotion.

"You and me, kid. We're gonna go places."

The hardest part wasn't learning the moves.

It wasn't sitting with his hands ice cold and his stomach in a knot while he and Zablonsky waited to go on. It was coming home to his mother and father after the show and acting like nothing had happened.

He watched himself as he listened to his father pray, as he ate his dinner, as he helped his mother with the dishes. He couldn't believe what had happened to him. He had not only become a magician's assistant. He had become a liar. That night in bed, he turned the quarter over and over, as if something on the surface might help him trace the way back to the boy he used to be.

He thought his mother would corner him one day in the kitchen, shaking her finger at him, her eyes wide with indignation, but she never did. He thought his father would appear at Zablonsky's or show up at the Royale, even though Morty knew this was a crazy idea. His father would never go to a place filled with actors and writers, people who never dreamed of being doctors or rabbis.

But he had to admit it: he liked going to the Royale. He liked listening to the conversations and watching people's faces, wondering how they earned a living and what their apartments were like. He felt a thrill of pride when he and Zablonsky took their bows at the end of their shows and people clapped. He was good at what he did. He knew that. Then, too, he felt a different kind of thrill when he studied the quarters he kept in a sock in the back of one of his dresser drawers. He checked on them every night. He walked by the stationer's shop every afternoon, peering in the window, waiting for the time when the pencils would be his.

But when that time finally came, how would he tell Zablonsky that he had to quit? What would he say? And what would Zablonsky say? Every time he showed up at the magician's door, the man greeted him with a different nickname. First he had been "Mr. Almost," then he had been "Mr. A." Somewhere along the line, Zablonsky had switched to the other end of the alphabet, although how he had come up with "Ziggy," Morty had no idea. Now whenever Morty arrived, the magician would throw open the apartment door and announce, "Ladies and gents! It's Ziggy Weissman!" Then the magician would clap him on the back, offer him a glass of water, and the two of them would go over their routine. There was always some adjustment or new trick that Zablonsky wanted to discuss with him. It had even gotten to the point where Morty had made a few suggestions. They would talk, they would argue, and Zablonsky's lined face would flush with excitement, his wisp of hair falling into his eyes while he paced his cramped kitchen. At the end of a particularly good practice session, the magician would announce, "This is what I get for hiring a *kheyder yingl*!" It was Zablonsky's highest compliment, but it made Morty feel like a traitor. How could he work with the man for four months and then quit? Zablonsky would never understand. It was the one thing the magician had in common with his parents.

It was the third Sunday in January, and he was sitting with Zablonsky in the Royale, waiting to go on. He studied the people around him, wishing he could draw a skinny lady with a pink hat and a man with a potbelly whose hair stuck out in all directions. He was just thinking that the man's head looked like a porcupine when Zablonsky interrupted his thoughts.

"Ziggy! Where are the gloves?"

"Aren't they in the black bag?"

Zablonsky shook his head, his face contorted with panic. Morty searched the other bags, but it was useless. The gloves were nowhere. The magician pawed through everything all over again, his hands shaking. Morty knew he had to say something fast.

"Look, it's OK. I'll do the exact same thing to open the show, just without the gloves. Nobody will know but us. Everything will be fine."

"No it won't! They've got to be here!"

Zablonsky bent over the black bag for the millionth time, his white shirt sticking to his back, drenched with sweat.

"*Oy Gotenyu!* I washed them last night and put them on the clothesline to dry!"

"You want I should run and get them?"

"No! I'll do it myself!"

"But what should I tell Mr. Glickman?"

"Tell him I'll be back in a half-hour!"

Zablonsky darted through the crowded café and out the door.

Morty stuffed everything back in the bags and sat down, hoping the owner wouldn't notice him. But there he was, coming straight at him, a short, stocky man with coarse features and thick hands, whose shirt buttons looked ready to pop any moment. Squeezed into his suit, the man reminded Morty of a sausage.

"So what happened to the magician? I thought he stayed and the coin vanished." Glickman chuckled at his own joke, but Morty could see that he did not look pleased.

"I'm sorry, Mr. Glickman. Zablonsky will be right back."

"Like in two minutes?"

"Like in thirty minutes."

"Oh yeah? Well that's twenty-eight minutes too late."

"But he forgot something he needs."

"Well, I got customers who need entertainment!" Glickman jabbed his stubby finger into Morty's chest. It was the hairiest finger he had ever seen, and he wished he could draw it even as it was being jammed into his breastbone. "The show must go on, kiddo, so get on with it! You're a magician too, right? Give us a little warm-up act while we're waiting for Zablonsky."

Every pore in Morty's body burst into sweat.

"I just help Zablonsky. I can't —"

"Can't, schman't. Do you sing?"

"No."

"Dance?"

"No!"

"Well, what *can* you do, sonny? I got customers here!"

"I — I can draw."

"Can you draw people?"

Morty shrugged. That was all the answer Glickman needed.

"Hey, folks! We got a Rembrandt here! The real McCoy! This kid can draw!"

There was a murmur of interest. People put down their coffee cups and smiled in his direction. Glickman pulled him to the front of the café and sat him down at a table. Feeling more dazed with every second, Morty watched as Glickman grabbed a stack of menus, turned one over, and shoved it in front of him.

"You got a pencil?"

"Yeah, I got a pencil."

Glickman leaned into his ear.

"At least you come prepared. More than I can say for Zablonsky." He straightened up and bellowed in a voice that made Morty wince. "Who wants to be the first person to get his portrait done by Picasso here?"

There were titters of laughter, and several people raised their hands. Glickman slapped him on the back.

"OK, pal. You got a buncha takers. You choose."

So what could he do? He chose the guy with the belly and the porcupine hair. The man sat down across from him and mopped his face with a handkerchief.

"Usually I don't *shvits* like this. But this kind of thing, in front of so many people —"

"It's OK. Don't worry."

He couldn't believe he was comforting this guy. All he had to do was sit in his chair and do nothing. With a shock, Morty realized that the room had fallen silent. All eyes were on him. A bead of sweat slid down his forehead as he stared at the man's hair. It was thick and wiry, and in the late afternoon light, it glinted like metal. Without thinking, he started drawing.

It seemed only a few minutes later that the man was shaking his hand and pushing two dimes across the table at him. Glickman clapped the guy on the back.

"Who knew you looked so good, hunh? Your wife's gonna want that framed. An heirloom for the *kinder*." Glickman nudged Morty. "Hey kid, don't stop now. Who's next?"

Morty couldn't help himself. He chose the lady in the pink hat. Two seconds later, he was wishing he hadn't, because she smiled so sweetly at him when she sat down at his table that he had trouble concentrating. Then a whiff of her perfume hit him, and he thought everything was all over. He would never be able to draw while the lady sat opposite him, a faint blue vein running down her neck and disappearing in the rosy glow of her collarbone. Again the room fell silent. He reached for another menu, turned it over, and thought about one of the pencils he had seen in the shop window, the one labeled "Carnation." It was the exact shade of the lady's hat. What a color. The lady raised a hand to her hat.

"Should I take this off?"

"Oh, no. Please don't."

She smiled and gazed out the café window. Grateful that her eyes were no longer on him, he drew slowly, taking in the texture of the old menu, the thick paper fuzzy in places, smooth in others. With the porcupine guy he had been certain, and the lines had come easily to him. But with the lady it felt as if his hand were moving through water. The heel of his palm made a whispering sound as it moved against the menu. A chair scraped the floor. There was the chink of china and silverware. Outside the café, somebody laughed. His pencil pulled him through the waves of sound.

When he pushed the drawing towards the lady, she looked at it and said nothing. All right, she didn't like it. He was just bracing himself for Glickman to tell him off when the lady rose from her chair and kissed him on the top of his head. Right in front of everybody! He held his breath as the lady fumbled with her purse, found a quarter and a dime, and left them on the table. Nodding to Glickman, she walked to her seat, holding the drawing carefully in front of her. People gathered around her to study it. He stared at the coins in his hand, still feeling the pressure of the woman's lips on his head. He had enough money to buy the pencils — a whole month earlier than he had expected! He was still staring at the money when Glickman's loudspeaker voice split the room.

"OK, folks. Sorry to get your hopes up, but it's my turn next." The man plopped down in the chair in front of Morty. "Hey, Michelangelo, my wife would really like one of these."

Glickman's hands rested on the table like slabs of meat. The clean, well-trimmed nails seemed somehow a front, a disguise. It was the black fuzzy hair sprouting from the backs of the fingers that really was Glickman. Morty had just started drawing those fingers when Zablonsky burst through the door.

"Mr. Glickman, I'm so sorry."

"Too late, pal. We got a real nice thing going with your buddy here. We'll talk later."

Zablonsky stood rooted to the spot. Morty rose from his seat, but Glickman grabbed his elbow and yanked him down.

"Hey, Mikey. You ain't finished. Get on with it."

Morty shot an agonized glance at Zablonsky, whose dark eyes turned on him accusingly. Without a word, he collected his bags. As he headed for the door, he stopped behind Morty and looked at his drawing. Then he walked out of the café.

There was a rushing in Morty's ears, and his hand shook. It was all he could do to look at Glickman, who flashed him a self-satisfied smile and sat formally, his feet planted on the floor, his shoulders back, his chin held high. Morty hated the man's smug face, his beefy fingers, his shiny teeth. How could Glickman smile like that when he had shamed Zablonsky in front of all those people? Morty knew he had to finish the portrait, but all he wanted to do was rip up the menu and run.

Finally it was over. Glickman scooped some coins out of his pocket and dropped them on the table. Ten, twenty, thirty-five, fifty cents! For one drawing! Morty recounted the money from the porcupine guy and the pink lady, his joy mixing with dread.

He had done it. The next day, he could walk into the stationer's shop, count out the money, and the pencils would be his. And then he'd have to tell Zablonsky that he had to stop.

Morty was dimly aware of Glickman smiling at his portrait while people crowded around, peering over his shoulder. Glickman was shaking his hand.

"Hey kid. You got talent. Any time you want to earn some money, you gimme a call."

Mumbling his thanks, he promised he would come again and hurried out of the café. He didn't stop running until he was pounding on the magician's door.

"I'm sorry! Lemme explain what happened!"

Zablonsky let him in without looking at him. Dropping into his chair at the kitchen table, he shuffled the cards he used for his act.

"Well, you made off good. You've probably been waiting for something like this. Bet you were planning everything all out."

"What are you talking about? You left the gloves on the clothesline! I didn't plan anything!"

"Sure, sure. That's right." The magician tapped the cards against the table, straightening their edges as if he were preparing to do a trick. "Tell the old man off. I'm losing my grip. I'm just a presser, right? Who'm I kidding? Stupid idea. Stupid idea from the beginning."

With a bitter smile, he flung the deck against the wall. The cards exploded over the sink and stove, landing in a splash of black and red against the dirty linoleum. Zablonsky stared at the cards, then buried his face in his hands. Morty stumbled forward as a strangled sob came from the magician. He wanted to touch Zablonsky's shoulder, but all he could do was look down at the bald head, the scalp blotchy and shiny in the electric light.

"It was Glickman's idea, not mine! You've got to believe me! He told me I had to do something, and all I could do was draw! He made me do it!"

The sobs subsided, and Zablonsky raised his head. One slow tear made its way down his cheek. The magician surveyed the bags of props scattered around him as if they were so many dead bodies, then looked out the window at the clothesline. He seemed oblivious of the boy beside him, beyond embarrassment, far away. When he spoke, his voice seemed as empty as the sagging line stretching across the barren space.

"Somebody teach you all that drawing stuff?"

"No."

The magician seemed to turn this over in his mind, his eyes fixed on the building across the courtyard, as if his gaze could find a way through the stone and mortar to some place only he could see.

"Bet your parents want you to be a big *makher* when you grow up. A rabbi or a big-shot lawyer, right? Not a presser, hunh? They never come to our shows. They know you're working with me?"

"No."

"You told me different."

"I know. I'm sorry. They wouldn't have let me if I had."

"So why you doing this? You burning to be a magician when you grow up?"

"I want to buy a box of colored pencils."

He had said it. He had wanted to tell his father, but it was the magician he had told. It was a relief to have said the words, and yet something inside him ached.

Zablonsky narrowed his eyes in disbelief.

"You're almost as crazy as me, you know that? So what do they cost, these fancy pencils?"

"A dollar."

"For that, they better have every color in the rainbow. How much you make today?"

"A dollar and five cents."

"For how many pictures?"

"Three."

"I hate to think how many pants I press for that. I should make up a trick and name it after you. Call it 'The One-Two-Three.'"

Their eyes met, and for a moment they seemed to breathe in unison. Then Zablonsky turned back to the window, and Morty knew it was time for him to go.

But first he had to do something. Pulling some change from his pocket, he laid it on the table. A quarter rolled off the edge and landed with a clatter on the floor. Zablonsky made no move to pick up the money, but he looked down at the coins, and his lips trembled.

Never had a Monday felt so endless. It was all he could do to get through the school day. Finally, some time before three o'clock, he stepped inside the stationer's shop. Shelves from floor to ceiling were crammed with paper and card stock. Pens of every kind and rows of gleaming ink bottles stood behind glass. Typewriters in need of repair lined the floor and were stacked in corners. He stood just within the threshold, taking in the smell of ink, grease, and dust, his eyes adjusting to the light cast by a green shade. A wizened shopkeeper sat behind a counter, poring over a typewriter whose parts were laid out before him. The man looked up at him, his gnarled hands resting on the machine. In the glow cast by the emerald shade, the room seemed to be underwater.

"What can I do for you?"

"The colored pencils in the window. I want to buy them."

The shopkeeper removed his glasses and studied him, his wispy eyebrows drawing together. Beneath them, his eyes were a pure blue, a strangely bright color in so lined a face.

"They are a lot of money, *mayn kind*. One dollar."

"I know. I have it."

Shooting him another glance from beneath his eyebrows, the old man got down from his stool, surveyed the shelves behind him, and selected a narrow, flat box.

"These pencils, they are special. You spend a lot of time drawing?"

"As much as I can."

The old man considered this.

"Your parents — they give you this money?"

"No." He looked straight into the shopkeeper's eyes. In the quiet shop, with the old man listening, he could say anything. "I got a job. I've been saving my money."

The shopkeeper nodded.

"Good. Good."

Morty bowed his head. Was it good? He could buy the pencils, and he would never have to lie to his parents again. He could buy the pencils, and he would never work with Zablonsky again. He thought of the magician's last words. *I should make up a trick and name it after you. Call it "The One-Two-Three."*

"Something is wrong, *mayn kind*?"

"No. I'm fine."

The old man's eyes seemed to penetrate him, and Morty put his hand in his pocket, grateful to have the money to think about, anything to make him stop thinking about Zablonsky. The old man climbed onto his stool and moved the typewriter out of the way.

"Come. You want to see these pencils, yes?" The old man opened the box, tipped the pencils into his hand, and spread them out in a fan.

Morty moved into the circle of light, gazing at each brilliant color, the sharpened tips, the gold lettering, the precise, faceted sides. The pencils had a faint metallic smell, and he inhaled deeply, holding on to the counter as if he might fall headlong down some abyss.

"When did you start drawing?"

"A long time ago."

The old man gave him a bittersweet smile.

"You will like these pencils. You will not be disappointed."

One by one, the shopkeeper put the pencils back into the box. Then he wrote out a receipt, placed the pencils in a brown paper bag, and folded the top over securely. When he handed the bag to Morty, their fingers touched.

"Draw well, *mayn kind. Zay gezunt.*"

He looked into the shopkeeper's eyes, clutching the pencils to his chest.

That night he lay in bed, listening to his father in the kitchen. Every night his father made a glass of tea. Every night his father pulled his chair up to the kitchen table, sipping his tea while the sugar cube between his teeth grew smaller and smaller. It used to frighten him that his father drank his tea in the dark, the kitchen lit only by moonlight. He used to be afraid his father cried there, or almost cried, and the thought made him cringe in his bed, terrified of what might be happening on the other side of the wall.

But now as he listened to his father, he was no longer frightened. Now he knew why his father sat alone in the kitchen at night. Now he knew why his father had said to his mother, "Enough."

His father also had secrets. Things he could say to no one because no one would understand. And when you had secrets, it was good to be alone in the dark. You could forget the narrow halls smelling of dinner, forget the people above and below you packed inside small rooms, forget even the city pressing against the window. It was good to drink tea in the dark, and Morty wished he could pull his chair up to the kitchen table and sit beside his father. Instead, he lay in bed, waiting until his father put his glass in the sink, came back from the bathroom down the hall, locked their door, and joined his mother.

It was only when he heard the bedroom door close that he slipped the pencils out of their box and spread them across his pillow. In the moonlight, they were something fallen out of a dream, blazing instruments that he was almost afraid to touch. He thought of his father drinking tea, the shopkeeper bending over his typewriter, the magician sobbing at his table, his cards a stain on the linoleum floor. The pictures crowded in on him like flares in the night. His father locking the door. The shopkeeper handing him the bag. Zablonsky lifting his face.

He lay in the darkness, searching for a pencil the color of tears.

KAREN AN-HWEI LEE

Prayer in the Language of Ash

". . . a crown of beauty instead of ashes . . ." — Isaiah 61:3

dear reader   promise me
in the language of ash

not wealth in currency or lilies
          nor a notary seal   this grass in essence

                    sea of psalms
     rising over aphasia
     sky-torn world   vellum   even skin

     glassine   a thin flame   not yet written
      my mother's goat-hair brushes

     or love's adversary
                    I desire your forgiveness   as a woman's hands

               bless a girl mei mei

                         who awaits
                         womanhood.

On Twelve Minor Seas

The sea becomes the shore, the shore becomes the sea.
— *Indonesian Proverb*

Salt of Sargasso Sea
No sailors
in sargassum,
sea of kelp.

Salt of Cosmonaut Sea
It is polynya,
sparse sea ice
nearly polar.

Salt of East China Sea
Internal waves
salt the tongues
of my ancestors.

Salt of Kara Sea
Is it radiological?
No one sees
the waste.

Salt of White Sea
North inlet
almost locks
winter ice.

Salt of Andaman Sea
Coral languishes
as algae migrate
to cooler waters.

Salt of Chukchi Sea
At a high latitude
the beluga
calve, feed, molt.

Salt of Yellow Sea
Fishing boats
of Huanghai
disperse light.

Salt of North Sea
Shallow or epeiric
sea on a shelf
in my hands.

Salt of Bering Sea
Water basin
of gray whales,
acres of cloud.

Salt of Aral Sea
Saline lake
vanishes
right here.

Salt of Arafura Sea
Wealth lies
in fishing nets,
prayers.

HARRIET J. MELROSE

The Ghost Garden

The landscaper looks at the garden, gives me a quote. It's work
I used to do myself. I always know more than the experts.
We gaze at the garden. I know he has a different vision.

I see the stand of Siberian Iris where the ground's overtaken
by obedience plants, a casualty of *bilateral adhesive capsulitis*.
In front of the yew, the hybrid lilies — now I count only one.

Under the fringe tree, I remember the bride's veil astilbe.
The ligularia, delphiniums, and monk's head, the tallest
at the back, gone during the first hand surgery and ten months

of rehab. The peonies and Asiatic lilies still flourish. Flowering
bushes stand and the huge spread of anemones, now the star
of the garden. The day lilies kill a perennial every year: this time,

a small spirea, an offshoot of the original, which seeded
itself in a perfect spot. The landscaper sees a garden overrun
with periwinkle, obedience, ivy, deadly nightshade, violets,

and weeds I can't name. He sees elm saplings grow in the center
of two flowering bushes: a Miss Kim lilac and a spirea.
He imagines the difficulty of separating the roots. He notices

an oak leaf hydrangea with half its branches dead, covered
by the living foliage and cone-shaped blooms — the miniature
peach tree's in a similar state. The yew encroaches on the windows.

I stopped the equinox rituals: removal of dead maple leaves in fall,
adding mulch and pruning in spring. Gardens have a life of their own,
demanding attention. I can't keep up, but I like to preserve the original

sense of the garden, which still can amaze: even out of zone, the fringe tree
blooms, the intense purple of the Japanese Iris, peonies the neighbors
can't resist picking; and in early spring, rare white, pink, and green tulips.

Studio Royale

Fiction

Tom Mays hid his wife's favorite nightgown and the earrings she claimed she loved. She was packing for Safe Harbor, and he watched her in the bedroom as she ravaged bureau drawers and her jewelry box. "What's wrong, Paula?" he asked.

"I can't find my nightgown and my earrings, the ones you gave me," she said.

"Maybe you should reconsider the trip."

She shook her head. "Because I can't find things?"

She was going tomorrow to a place devoted to addictions. Paula drank occasionally and took pills sometimes to sleep, but the real abuse was food, according to her. She'd gained twelve pounds. She didn't tell him how long she'd be gone, or how she found out about Safe Harbor. She gave him a brochure two weeks ago that showed the usual rosy Colorado views — mountains, a ranch setting, horses in a corral. The couple that ran the place, the Kiels, had been drinkers, but went on the wagon. The Kiels stood near a Conestoga wagon, ringing a dinner bell, a border collie nearby. Tom didn't know what he was feeling exactly, except a fear of letting Paula go, and a desire to be the one the Kiels called to the dinner table.

He knew they couldn't afford the fees. They ran Studio Royale, a name she picked. He specialized in commercial photography, and she handled personal portraits. Maybe one of her clients told her about Safe Harbor.

They'd been married four years. He was fifty-two, and she was thirty-six. They met when she took a photography course he taught at the community college, and married three months later. A colleague had warned him about marrying Paula. He mentioned the age difference and Paula's flightiness. "She's a good soul, but doesn't it strike you that everything seems like a hobby to her?" Tom had defended Paula, angry with his colleague, and feeling forced to describe Paula's positive traits, as if he were composing a letter of recommendation. She wasn't cynical, and she approached every endeavor honestly and enthusiastically.

"I drink, take pills, and I overeat," he pictured her telling the other substance abusers.

"You're not taking cameras?" he asked when Paula finished packing.

"No. I'm not taking cigarettes, either."

"Good," he said, "but what's the deal about the cameras?"

"I'm leaving them behind," she said, an edge to her voice, but she surprised him by suggesting they go out for a fling.

They went to a steak house, drank wine, and smoked flagrantly. He watched her devour the surf and turf special, and then a big chunk of cake. She looked radiant.

They returned home and drank tequila in the kitchen. Paula talked about how she'd miss her garden. He hoped she'd say that she changed her mind about leaving, but she took his hand and led him to the bedroom. He felt a voluptuous thrill when she swept her arms across the bed, knocking the suitcase to the floor.

"You know what I'm going to do tomorrow?" he said, and joined her on the bed.

"I'm going to —"

She pressed her fingers against his lips. "Do me," she whispered.

He thought she had already left the following morning when he awoke with a shocking headache, but he heard noise in the kitchen. He stayed in bed and thought about what he tried to tell Paula right before they made love last night — that he was going to take better care of her.

She wore a blazer and a skirt, and brought coffee and toast to him, her hands shaking.

"See what it does to me. I've got to quit drinking. You don't have to get rid of the booze, though. Maybe I'll be strong enough to give it up, maybe give up other things, too. I might just see things differently."

"We should've talked about this last night, Paula."

"I liked what we did. Besides, if we talked, you would've blamed yourself. It's my problem. All mine."

"What do you think will happen?" he asked.

"At Safe Harbor? Well, I think it'll be like everything else in my life. Not exceptionally bad or good."

He stood by her car in his pajamas, barefoot, and sick to his stomach. He heard the phone in the house. "Maybe it's the Kiels," he said, but Paula drove off.

"Some things you need to know," said a man's voice on the answering machine. "Esther and I met in Lincoln, Nebraska. We were married on May 16, 1950. I ranched and farmed there, Esther worked for Mutual of Omaha, and then we moved to West Pawnee, Colorado. I play golf. I enjoy cattle and —"

The machine had cut the man off. Tom was heading to the bedroom when the phone rang.

"I don't like talking to machines," said the man. "I enjoy cattle and auctions. We have two children. They'll be the hosts of our anniversary party. We have five grandchildren, one great-grandchild."

"What do you want? Why are you telling me this?"

"Do I have to start all over again? Esther and I are celebrating our fiftieth wedding anniversary. Didn't your secretary tell you?"

"My wife," Tom said. "You probably talked to her."

"Esther did the talking, and I composed an article for the newspaper. I'm giving you the same facts because your wife told Esther she wanted information. Esther," the man shouted, "what's the story here?"

The woman got on the phone. "Paula wanted our history. For our portrait. Is she around?"

"She had to leave town unexpectedly."

"Oh, no. Illness?"

"Yes," Tom said. "I was just getting around to looking at her appointment book."

"Bless your heart. You'll find us there for Wednesday at 8:00 a.m., but you probably got your hands full. Where's she at?"

"Oh, she's in good place. They've got a reputation." His heart raced, and he knew he could go on, earning this woman's sympathy. And when he spoke with Paula again, he could say, "Honey, I did something strange while you were away, and I didn't feel exceptionally bad or good about it."

"Well," the woman said, "we'll just find another studio. We want our deposit back ASAP. We're living on a fixed income."

"I'll do it."

"You're in the picture business, too?"

He felt foolish, listing his credentials, and at the end of the call, he glanced at Paula's appointment book, and found notes for the Toomeys.

"Esther enjoys country music and travel. Has lived way out in the Pawnee Grasslands for thirty years. Not much travel for poor Esther."

He rifled through the book, and saw "Canceled" slashed across some appointments scheduled for the following weeks. On today's date, she'd written, "Safe Harbor. Dale and Kathryn Kiel. Married twenty-two years. Trouble at midway point. On the wagon eight years. Dale likes fly-fishing. Kathryn loves to cook. Safe Harbor her idea, but he does all the talking."

He found similar notes for earlier appointments about people's backgrounds, hobbies, and corny ideas for portrait themes. He tried to imagine what Paula was feeling right now. Thrilled to be away from him? A cold sensation rippled across his back.

He would quit smoking today. He searched around, and threw away every pack. Despite his hangover, he'd keep his appointment at a bank that was changing its name, logo, and location, and that had hired him to design brochures assuring customers that the switch wouldn't cause disruption.

He called another of Paula's clients who was scheduled for an appointment tomorrow, but there was no answer.

He photographed the president and staff members outside the new building.

There was no message from her at home, and when he called Safe Harbor, Mrs. Kiel assured him that Paula arrived safely, and was fitting right in. "She took a nap. She's out walking now."

He heard music in the background and people talking. "Alone?" he asked.

"She's fine. Now don't you worry, Mr. Mays."

"Well, I just wanted to make sure she's all right. Will you tell her to call me?"

"Sure. We're having our juice and pre-dinner talk right now."

"Shouldn't Paula be there?"

"It's up to her. She's in for a rigorous schedule tomorrow. Breakfast, group, horseback riding, journaling, lunch, another group session, free time, dinner, and a movie."

She finally called at nine, telling him about the gorgeous scenery at Safe Harbor. "Oh, Tom, you should see the view. I'm looking at the mountains right now. The people are real nice. I haven't had a drink or a cigarette, and God, the meal! Roast lamb, mashed potatoes, homemade bread, and a fresh salad. Kathryn said I could work in the garden if I want."

"I spoke with the Toomeys. Remember them?"

"There are five other guests here. People come from all over. One man from California's been here two months."

He tried to remain calm. "How long do people usually stay?"

"It varies."

"I checked your appointment book. The Toomeys are coming Wednesday. I tried calling tomorrow's customer, but no answer. What's the story?"

"Story? The other client? A birthday picture. I feel so different up here."

"Good thing you left your appointment book behind, or else I wouldn't have a clue about what's going on."

"I canceled what I could. I'm sorry, but I don't want to think about that now."

"Hey, I found your nightgown and the earrings. Want me to bring them?"

"No visitors our first week here. I'll call you every night. I have to go now."

"I miss you." He waited, but no response from her. "I'm surprised they feed you such rich meals."

"They know what they're doing. Besides, my problem is the secret eating."

"I quit smoking today."

"That's wonderful. Well, I don't want to hog the phone. Goodnight, sweetheart."

"Son of a bitch," he muttered. "Son of a bitch." How could he sleep now? Who could after such a call? There was probably a name for his disorder, and a group that specialized in regret and the remorse over things that people wished they'd said to their mates. "Your problem, sweetie, is that you've been eating away at me."

And now, at Safe Harbor, the other residents were probably hearing Paula describe her last fling, and how she ate, danced, drank, smoked, and generally behaved like a soldier about to ship out for battle.

He began to look through her portrait portfolios. She'd arranged old wedding pictures next to current anniversary shots. He felt a stab of sadness, seeing the current shots, the couples sitting side by side. Paula had used a soft focus to try to minimize the way people had aged, and it troubled him to think that they all looked alike, the sort of elderly people you see on the street and soon forget, or maybe you want to forget that it's going to happen to you. On the bureau that Paula had ravaged the night before was their wedding picture, an ordinary Polaroid taken by a girl at a tiny chapel in Las Vegas. He had a sunburn, and his ears looked raw in the picture, his eyes puffy. Paula had worn a fancy blue dress, a corsage pinned to the bodice. His skin bristled when she kissed him, the corsage feeling like a head of lettuce.

He was working the following morning on the bank brochure when the doorbell rang. A woman who looked to be in her thirties smiled at him. A little girl and a homely basset hound were behind her. The girl wore a yellow dress tiered in stiff ruffles, her face as mournful as the dog's. The woman introduced herself as Ellie Holtzinger and the girl as Doris. "I told Paula we'd be here at ten, but we got delayed."

"Paula's out of commission. I'll be taking the pictures." He expected a reaction and questions, but the woman looked unperturbed. "What's the dog's name?"

"Amigo," the girl said. "She picked the name."

"Tell him the story, Doris."

"He was supposed to get killed," the girl said, "but she put a stop to that."

"I found him out in the country, near our place. I brought him to the Humane Society and put an ad in the paper. Not a single call, except from the Humane Society, telling me when the dog would go under."

The girl grinned.

"I got there in the nick of time," Ellie said. "Fate. The hand of fortune. This sweet fellow was scheduled for the procedure on Doris's birthday, so Amigo was her present."

"Fate," the girl said, addressing the dog. "The hand of fortune."

"Paula told Doris to wear her favorite outfit, but her father bought her this dress, so we thought he should at least see her in it."

"We're sending him pictures of someone else's old dog," the girl said. "She shampooed him. That's why we were tardy."

Ellie laughed. "Sounds just like her father. Just like him. Divorced," she whispered to Tom.

He led them to Paula's side of the studio, and told Doris to sit on the chair while he arranged the lights and chose one of Paula's backdrops — a field of yellow flowers and a blue sky. Ellie put Amigo on the girl's lap, its long ears flopping over her dress, like pennants. The dog pointed its solemn face at Tom and struggled to stand, its stubby legs rasping on the girl's dress. Doris smacked the dog on the nose.

Asking this kid to smile would be out of the question. He shot the pictures quickly, and then Doris rushed outside. Amigo collapsed into the chair.

"Would you take some pictures for me?" Ellie asked. She placed the dog on her lap, and smiled in such a way as to suggest that this was not a hard thing to do. "You know what her father sent, along with that dumb dress? A picture of himself with his new boat. Happy as a clam, that one."

He wondered what Paula might've told Ellie about her own troubles. "You have to wonder what gets in people's heads."

"A waste of time, trying to figure that out," she said, and left with Amigo.

He developed the pictures. Doris's shots surprised him. She looked all right, softer than in person. He poured a drink, took the contact sheets into the bedroom, and stared at Ellie's pictures. He could call, deliver the sheets, and let her choose. He lifted the phone, then replaced it, feeling a catch in his heart at the image of Paula devouring the surf and turf special last night, and then he conjured details of last year's anniversary trip to a mountain resort, and how a waitress had hurt Paula by asking her twice if she really wanted such a big breakfast. He'd felt noble by insisting that Paula be given whatever she wanted. After that, she spent the next two mornings in the hotel's workout room, and told him about exercise regimens they could do together. They rented bicycles, and he felt a mixture of pity and fear, seeing her pumping hard in her tight cycling outfit. He gave her the silver earrings that night. She cried, and said she loved them.

The phone rang while he was rifling through the wastebasket for a cigarette. He felt breathless, but it was Ellie Holtzinger calling.

"Amigo," she said. "He's gone. I've lost him."

"Oh, no. I'm sorry. You loved that dog."

"I let him outside to do his business. I had my hands full with the surprise party for Doris and her friends. I lost track of time and poor Amigo." She began to sob.

Tom visualized Amigo, dead, run over. "Poor Amigo. He was a good dog."

"Doris and I have been looking for hours, but no sign of him."

"Jesus," Tom said. He wished he could confide in someone to try to describe his conviction that loss seemed like the one sure thing. "Did you call the Humane Society?"

"Yes, of course." She sounded exasperated. "Maybe they're trying to call me right now, so I'll cut to the chase. I want those pictures of Amigo. I'm going to make some posters. Can you bring the pictures out here?"

"Yes, sure."

He showered and shaved, and was considering what he'd wear, but kept thinking about his first date with Paula. He'd asked her to see a movie, and picked her up at a grim apartment complex, fringed by a stingy lawn. She wore high heels, a silky dress, and pearls, and showed him photographs she'd taken of her family back East, her grandparents' farm, and many shots of a yellow cat. Sentimental pictures, not to his liking, but he'd been moved, and the feeling continued during the movie, when she finished off a tub of popcorn, and cried when the music swelled during a sad scene, and even clapped at the end, when things turned out all right.

He felt a flutter of excitement on the drive to Ellie Holtzinger's, the landscape cooperating with his mood. A clear sky, a fat moon, and an unspoiled countryside.

Ellie, Doris, and Amigo were on a porch glider. Ellie waved and lifted Amigo in front of her face. "He found his way home!" she shouted. "Our little miracle dog."

"I will never forget this birthday," Doris said in a sarcastic way.

Ellie didn't invite him inside. She looked at the pictures on the porch, rejecting some shots and choosing others, bartering with him as if at a swap meet, even telling him that the price was higher than the one Paula quoted.

He sold the pictures at Paula's price, eager to escape, and furious to hear Ellie say that with Amigo back, she didn't need lots of photos of him. "I've got the real thing."

He rushed home, finding a message from Paula on the machine.

"Oh, I wish you could've seen me today. I hiked and worked in the garden. Slept right through dinner. I've been doing a lot of thinking and writing in my journal. All kinds of discoveries. We'll talk, OK?"

She would call it a discovery, but it would really be a list of his faults and probably some new resolution to get at the root of her problems, and he'd be that root.

Someone at Safe Harbor was hogging the phone. He'd wanted to tell her that he'd been thinking of her all day, making some discoveries himself, but the phone hog ruined that.

He took two of Paula's Ambiens and was overcome with a sensation of everything slowing down. He felt he was underwater, and above him was a rapping sound, like the oars of a boat, and then a woman whispering, and he wanted to stay with the dream, but heard loud pounding.

He was at the door, in his pajamas, facing an elderly couple, the man in a brown suit, the woman in an orchid dress. "The Toomeys," she said. The man cast Tom a dismissive look.

"Sorry, but I stayed up late last night working, and I had to look for a dog." He led them into the studio, the floor feeling clammy on his bare feet.

"What kind of dog?" Mrs. Toomey asked.

"Basset hound."

"We have a German Shepherd," she said. "John prefers the larger breeds."

Tom grinned, and Mr. Toomey glared at him. "The newspaper people have strict deadlines," he said. "They want our wedding picture with the new one right next to it. Before and after."

He gave Tom the wedding picture. The photographer had added blush to their cheeks and had retouched their teeth, making them impossibly white.

"We look like clowns in that picture," Mr. Toomey said, "for our solemn occasion. Just make us look dignified."

"I hope your wife's on the mend," said Mrs. Toomey. "What's she got wrong with her?"

"Esther," Mr. Toomey said. "It's none of our business. Can't you see that he's a little out of sorts?"

"I'm doing just fine," Tom insisted. "Paula's not out of the woods yet, but she's improving, making gains every day."

He didn't change the backdrop he used yesterday. He looked at the Toomeys through the viewfinder and began shooting, surprised to be thinking about his own parents. His mother had taken off for a while when Tom was ten, and he'd resented how his father had talked about her in the barber shop, standing in his white smock like a dentist trying to explain necessary procedures. "This is the worst part, but try to picture a good outcome," he'd told Tom, and then his father drove one night to a motel on the outskirts of town, where Tom's mother's car was parked.

"This is what she picked," his father had told him. "Just so you know."

Tom had watched him later, joshing with customers as if nothing had happened, even joking about Tom's mother. "She's like a submarine. She goes under for a while, comes back up, but never lets you know what she saw down there."

When she returned, Tom's father acted like he never knew where she went, and he and Tom listened to her tales about the fabulous sights she'd seen out West.

Tom had told Paula the story, the way people do at the beginning, to offer up keys to themselves, and Paula had said it was the saddest story she'd ever heard.

"Your mother all by herself in a motel room."

"What if she was with someone, though?"

"The outcome's the same."

"Want to know our secret?" Mrs. Toomey asked. "Everyone's been asking us that question. Well, we don't have any secrets. That's exactly what I told your wife when she asked the big question."

Tom wondered if the answer had satisfied Paula, and what else she and Mrs. Toomey had talked about.

"We're going to Alaska," Mrs. Toomey said. "Our kids bought the tickets."

"It's supposed to be spectacular," Tom said.

"She always wanted to go there, and I always say be careful what you wish for," Mr. Toomey said, and then left.

Tom assured Mrs. Toomey that he'd have everything ready in an hour.

"He's scared," she said. "I keep telling him, what's the worst that could happen, and you wouldn't believe what he comes up with."

It might be the Ambien, he thought, that made him feel shaky, but he finished the contact sheet, placing it beside the Toomeys' wedding picture, pleased with the results. The Toomeys looked dignified, and Tom wanted to tell Paula this tonight when she called, but he'd probably sound like a needy kid, eager for attention and praise, and she'd be justified in being impatient with him. Hadn't he always been impatient when she tried to describe her sessions with her clients?

Mr. Toomey returned alone, explaining that Esther was at the beauty parlor. Tom gave him the contact sheet, and Mr. Toomey held it close to his face.

"Hard to choose without Esther. They all look the same to me." He pointed to one in the middle. "OK, that one. Well, now I can say that I've made the papers twice. One more time to go, but I won't be around for that one, unless Esther goes first."

Tom felt a shiver, and waved goodbye to Mr. Toomey, as if they'd had a long history together.

"What's the worst that could happen?" he asked himself about rushing to Safe Harbor. He looked at the time. Paula would be attending a group session? Working in the garden? What's the worst that could happen? The Kiels scolding him for breaking the rules? The other residents seeing him and thinking, "So, this is the husband? He's older than I thought."

He dressed, studied the map, and grabbed the earrings and nightgown.

A light rain started soon after he got on the road, but then it stopped, and fog hovered meekly above the fields, as if to allow a view of the foothills. He turned onto a dirt road corrugated with ruts and surrounded by scrub country, nothing at all like the brochure images. And then he saw a wooden sign that said, "The Beaten Path." Other signs followed. "Off the Beaten Path. Entering Nature's Disneyland. Slow Down and Smell the Roses. You're On the Road to Recovery."

The air smelled metallic. He reached the top of the hill, seeing a humble ranch below flanked by a dilapidated barn, a chicken coop, and a corral.

The dog startled him. It lunged at his car, barking savagely, and then Tom saw a young, skinny bald man waving his arms frantically and trying to whistle through ruined teeth. Tom had never seen such a wasted-looking specimen, and figured he was a meth addict. The dog took off the minute the man tried to hug it.

"The dog gets excited," the man said at Tom's window. "Someone should medicate him. You lost?"

"I was heading to Safe Harbor," he said, the name sounding utterly preposterous. "Is this it?"

"Reservations only. You can't just drop in," the man said, as if describing an exclusive hotel and not a place that looked like a cult compound.

Tom felt queasy, thinking of Paula in the company of this man and others like him. "My wife," he said. "Paula Mays. I'm here to see her."

"We honor privacy and anonymity," the man said, peering into the car, an odd odor wafting from him. "I was in a sweat lodge earlier, ridding myself of toxins."

"Good for you," Tom said, and then saw a sight in the distance like something out of an old movie — a Conestoga wagon coming over the rise. Behind it were four people on horseback, led by a plump woman in a pink cowboy hat. Paula was in the middle, wearing the outfit she'd bought for her exercise regimen at the hotel last year. He was about to press the horn, but the man stopped him.

"You want to ruin everything?" he said, and scurried down the hill.

Tom stayed, watching the people below proceed into the corral, the sun folding itself away behind them. Then the residents entered the ranch house, lights came on, and smoke fluttered from the chimney.

He imagined Paula undressing in her room and examining herself in the mirror, probably feeling pleased with the positive changes. She'd take a bath, then write in her journal about all the pretty sights she saw today, and that she was smart to leave a camera behind so that she had a genuine view of everything.

He was glad he'd been spared making a fool of himself in front of her and the other residents, and yet felt this nagging pity for her that she'd been denied a first-class retreat. He knew that the meth-head would never mention his visit. And when Paula called tonight, he'd act like nothing had happened.

He felt a pitch of dread, picturing what it'd be like at home, and then realized he hadn't eaten all day, and was still feeling muzzy from the Ambien and the sense of being towed back underwater.

He was close to town when he thought about his mother. Maybe she'd really wanted Tom's father to find her. He'd never forget how guarded and tentative he felt, knowing that she'd been so miserable at home that she took off and only came back because of him. All those secrets, and to what end? He never told anyone that he'd gone to the motel a couple of times, hiding in the bushes, expecting to see his mother with another man; but he saw nothing remarkable, just his mother bringing takeout food into the room, and the homely light of a television screen flickering beyond the curtains.

When she came back home, telling him and his father about the pretty things she saw out West, he listened, feeling furtive and powerful, as if he'd suddenly grown up and had something over her, and could wait for the right moment to say, "Liar. Liar. There's nothing out there where you went."

He'd been doing homework at the kitchen table, weeks later, when his mother said, "I love you. I'd never leave you. You know that, don't you?" She touched his shoulder, the gesture so tender and real that embarrassing tears welled in his eyes, so he glanced away, ready to insult her, but surprised himself by asking her to tell him again what she saw on her trip.

He entered his house now and checked the time. This was when Paula usually called. She'd gush about Safe Harbor, just like before, and he'd get no satisfaction in knowing the truth, so he'd talk about the clients, and how he liked stepping into her shoes, working on personal portraits, getting to know people's inside stories. And then he'd ask the big question. "So, are you going to stay?"

"Sure," she'd say, and he could pretend that she was referring to home and to him, and he'd have to praise her for her commitment and determination to stick it out.

"Well, good for you. No disappointments this time," he'd have to lie. "That's the best thing I've ever heard."

Sovereign of the Sea   *Fiction*

In an exam room no bigger than a bathroom stall, the ship's physician spoke to Bob about chlamydia.

"It's treatable, not terribly serious, but an unchecked infection can lead to sterility. You'll need to take Jillian to a specialist when you get home."

Bob felt the cruise ship shift around him like the tremor of a high-rise in heavy winds. He backed into a retractable stirrup. What looked like white ankle socks warmed the footholds. The exam room's single flourish, a cartoon dolphin with zipper teeth, smiled from the ceiling.

"Bet they don't have this kind of set-up on Disney cruises."

The young doctor pushed his glasses to the red stripe on his forehead where he hadn't gotten enough sunscreen. "I wouldn't know." He looked Bob up and down and seemed to be waiting for him to say something.

What kind of medical professional worked afloat? Maybe the cruise line had gotten this guy from one of those non-accredited Caribbean medical schools.

"Perhaps I should be talking to your wife."

Bob explained that Jillian's mother, Caroline, was his girlfriend. He claimed, when he'd found the girl knotted on the floor of their cabin, that he'd assumed she was seasick. Food poisoning might have sounded better; passengers spoke of diarrhea as they would storm clouds or pickpockets in upcoming ports of call. Really, Bob had been waiting for something like this.

The doctor lowered his glasses. "I'll charge the antibiotics and Pedialyte to your stateroom."

"Pedia-what?"

"We stock it for dehydrated toddlers, but it helps with hangovers."

Bob pulled his shorts higher on his waist; pocket change settled beneath the velvet ring box.

In the infirmary's waiting area, he coughed to rouse the sleeping girl and told her they were done. Jillian draped her leg over an armrest and sighed. Bob feigned interest in a poster pushing the Aruba cruise while Jillian stretched and yawned. He should have offered her his arm as they walked, but Bob didn't touch her.

They could both stand in the 117-square-foot stateroom since a stewardess had stowed all three Pullman beds. Caroline slept under her daughter's. Bob's, on the opposite wall, unfolded below a cabinet holding T-shirts, windbreakers, shorts, and the sweater he'd worn on the plane. Jillian's things were everywhere. She'd left out bathing suit tops, used Q-tips, tiny sharp earrings crusted with blood, and colored rubber bands.

He didn't know what she'd done to the bathroom since he'd surrendered it to the women. He used a public one two decks below, a familiar concession. Bob's sickly mother had camped beside their home's single toilet. Young Bob stopped putting his ear to the door at ten. In the house in Madison, Donna (before she was his ex-wife) had installed a vanity table, rain shower, and soaking tub. The substantial room, a former bedroom in a home older than indoor plumbing, had a heavy oak door with a warded lock, to which Donna had the only key.

Bob pulled down Jillian's bunk and saw that she'd tacked pictures of boys with stupid haircuts on the wall above her pillow.

"Stop the rocking," she said kicking the sheets off as soon as she'd climbed up. She booted Bob's right shoulder but didn't apologize. Jillian rolled onto her stomach, and he took in the length of her legs, the creases behind her knees, before looking away toward the portal: a permanent horizon, indistinct without islands or fins.

"This ship doesn't rock. You're hung over. I won't tell your mother about that, but this other thing — you'll need to tell her, you'll need to go to a specialist."

"Like I give a shit about fertility." He could see the elastic bands attached to the metal braces that fought her overbite.

"You will."

"I'm fourteen."

"Don't remind me."

With narrowed eyes, she propped herself on her elbow. "If you tell her, I'll I tell her what you did to me in the bathroom last month. You violated me."

As of recent, public school health classes had provided precise, arresting language. He backed away for the door.

"Be careful."

"*You* be careful," she called after him.

An elevator adjacent to the room waited, but Bob took the stairs, descending two flights. On the Empress deck, he made his way toward the restroom.

"Hey!" someone hollered from a doorway behind him. Bob turned to find a gray-faced man wearing sock garters and boxers with a cell phone clipped to the waistband.

"Jesus Christ, where's the fire?" He smiled, more lonely than angry. A pair of electrodes patched the man's sternum, some kind of heart monitor. "You chasing something? We're too old to chase anything."

Finally alone, Bob put his hands, almost too large for the small basin, under the faucet. The water pressure was worse than in airplane bathrooms. He patted his hot face with water that smelled funny.

Somewhere on the Serenity deck a band plunked out pop melodies on steel drums. It sounded too precious. Caroline watched a boy change a block of ice into an angel while humidity undid her hairdo. Bob touched curls darkened by perspiration that had fallen onto her neck. The sculptor cut wings with a chain saw.

"I had my money on it being a mermaid," Caroline turned to say.

"Too obvious."

"No, really. Then when they tossed her over the side it would be like setting her free." Caroline mimed a throw.

"Actually, they just let them melt." At around four a.m. the night prior, he'd watched a guy push a slushy puddle across the deck with some kind of a broom.

As they walked, Bob had to adjust his shorts, which were at least a size too small. Caroline had packed for him. He'd watched her shake pennies and toothpicks from the pockets of clothes purchased by his ex-wife. Caroline had said, "It's weird to see things you wore before I knew you."

He'd dated enough women but hadn't gotten so close to anyone since the divorce. Bob spent most nights at Caroline's condo on the spreading side of town. When Caroline would come to his place, it could be uncomfortable; she asked him all kinds of questions while she went through his record collection and reorganized his pantry. But he'd decided he loved her when she'd put her ear to an oak column in his living room, as if she'd been listening for the house's heartbeat. She'd said she would like living in such an old place, to wonder about everyone who'd lived there.

Bob didn't remind Caroline that his ex-wife and daughter had been the last ones to leave. He didn't tell her that he and Donna had bought the place cheap in the mid-eighties because it had been trashed by renters, probably college kids, who'd covered all the oak trim with flat, purple house-paint. Caroline didn't need to know that a possum had once lived in the basement or that his ex-wife had picked out the wall colors and retiled the bathroom.

Bob had only helped Donna with the renovations in the evenings and after three on Sundays when he'd close his small import shop. He sold olives, sardines, and aromatic sea salts among other things, but Donna had never taken to the place and stopped helping out altogether when their daughter was born. The store did OK, but since the divorce, everything he'd made went into child support and trips (more like vacations) overseas to meet with distributors.

He hadn't wanted to take this Caribbean cruise. Really, neither had Caroline, but they figured they'd be able to relax with Jillian under the supervision of energetic but unfortunate cruise-line employees running the "teen program" they'd read about online.

But they were having a good time. Bob didn't like the heat as much as Caroline but was happy to be far from the Wisconsin winter. By the third day they were done making fun of the campy decor and would follow the masses of passengers to auditoriums, cocktail hours, and meals. At the evening buffet, they drank sweet wine and ate cream puffs shaped like swans. Caroline said hers tasted OK but didn't seem to really enjoy it. Bob went back to the dessert table to bring her mango sherbet and a small slice of Key lime pie, which she liked.

Caroline had gotten pregnant with Jillian as a college freshman and was much less insecure than some of the other thirty-somethings Bob had dated. She didn't diet, wear silly oversized jewelry, or paint her face as the younger woman she'd been. Nothing embarrassed her. Bob was familiar with the way she fastened her bra, hooking it in front and then pulling it around.

He reached for the ring box in his pocket but stopped when Caroline said, "I should bring Jilly something. She didn't eat anything at lunch, and she's been so quiet."

Bob tapped the table. "Does she ever have much to say?" He tried to smile.

"That's true. Thanks for always checking on her."

"You deserve a break."

"She can be handful," she said.

"She's a good kid; she can't get into too much trouble in the middle of the ocean."

After they'd had enough to eat, they walked the deck.

In front of the steel drum band Bob scrutinized deeply tanned musicians and tried to seem imposing. They'd been sniffing around Jillian since boarding. Though they were scrubbed clean with matching floral shirts, segments of serpentine tattoos showed beneath their short sleeves. The tallest one had bands of inscrutable writing — either ancient or Russian — on his wrists and fingers.

They banged "Blue Bayou" on their cans.

Bob and Caroline lay out on chaises on the Lido deck. Children splashed and yelled in a pool surrounded by sunburned retirees. The drummers had set up beside the bar but were on break. Waiters pushed blended cocktails. The ship was chartered for a chunk of the Dominican Republic called Labadie. On the starboard, they passed an empty Cuban beach.

"Did you bring an explosive cigar?" Bob asked.

"Jillian could probably take out the entire regime in a couple hours," Caroline said and they laughed.

He was studying the floral pattern, elastic lilies, on her bathing suit when Jillian, belly button exposed, showed up after her daily run around the exercise deck. She jogged toward them in a bikini top so small that her breasts peeked out beneath.

"You should have come with me, Mom," she said, sounding neither winded nor ill.

"Hey, kiddo." Caroline removed her sunglasses. "We got our exercise hours ago while you were still in bed."

Bob pretended to read his magazine. Jillian slid her shorts down before perching herself on the edge of her mother's chair to untie her sneakers. Caroline told her to take her hair out of "that tight ponytail" and then rubbed Jillian's back with her left palm, just for a few seconds.

"She gets headaches sometimes," Caroline told Bob.

Jillian frowned at her mother and stood up.

A man drinking a Bloody Mary three chaises away shook his head but then watched her cross the deck and make her way down toward the pool.

Caroline leaned over to pick up Jillian's sneakers and put them in her bag; she didn't catch her daughter's dive.

The girl's recent transformation made it difficult to believe that she was Caroline's. Jillian stood tall with a smooth aquiline nose and stark cheekbones, but she wasn't beautiful. Something about the closeness, or the meanness, of her eyes prevented that. Narrow-hipped and -headed, with a mouth that usually hung open.

The band started a song Bob didn't know while Jillian posed by the edge of the pool with her back to the couple. She might have made eyes at anyone. A small sunburnt crevice winked at Bob above her suit bottom. The weather seemed warmer to Bob than it had the day before.

Before her growth spurt Bob and Jillian had gotten along well enough. When they'd first met, two years before, she'd liked horses, lisped, and leaned across the booth at Doyle's diner to whisper to her mother. Not secrets. Caroline listened, laughed, and then reported to Bob that Jillian was curious about his age. Bob was only forty-six that day. He'd ordered her another orange pop, complimented her ability to tie cherry stems in her mouth, and claimed he liked horses too. Twelve was an easy age, really. He remembered his own daughter, Alex, at twelve.

Just after Alex's thirteenth birthday, she and her mother moved to Tempe to live with Donna's sister, whom Donna never seemed to even like. First she'd claimed that Bob spent too much time at the shop — even though they'd agreed that they needed the money for

Alex's college fund. Then it was that she was tired of living in a house always under construction. Donna didn't know how to lie because she probably never had; she'd loved the work almost as much as the home itself. When she confessed to having met someone, Bob relented. Donna had always had this look like she was about to say something but never did. She'd been a silent woman.

In the pool, Jillian floated on her back.

"Why so quiet?"

"I'm reading," Bob said. "The next cruise, let's do an Alaskan: polar bears and glacial bays."

"You mean pay to go somewhere cold?"

The cocktail waiters and the towel boys dawdled on the pool's perimeter. A maintenance kid checked the pH on all sides. Jillian kicked off the pool's wall, arched her back, and somersaulted beneath the surface. When she climbed out a short guy, in a uniform Bob couldn't identify, said something that seemed to stop her from diving again; Bob couldn't hear.

Jillian wrung out her hair and then ran off in just her bathing suit.

"She really needs to start wearing that jog bra," Caroline said.

"What about her shoes?"

"She can't get into the casino without them," Caroline said smiling. She thumbed the spark-wheel of her lighter and got her cigarette burning at what must have been nineteen knots.

Maybe Caroline was right; maybe Jillian was just trying to hit slot machines rather than rendezvous with crew members. But Bob didn't know what a normal amount of trouble meant.

Alex, pretty in a purple sweater, with shiny lips and a missing front tooth, could stay young in photos in the small office behind the shop. Over the phone he'd instructed her to behave and do her homework. He'd visited Tempe once before being told that just sending checks was better. Donna hadn't remarried but had become strange after joining her sister's church; she insisted on staying with them throughout the entire trip. By then, though, Alex had quit playing basketball and was a soft, shy young woman who blushed when waiters took her order. Bob didn't know her. Not that he ever really had. When they'd all lived together in Madison, Alex and Donna had talked behind locked doors and could communicate with just their eyes across the dinner table.

Bob liked to remember Alex on the basketball court before her mother had taken her away. She'd played center as a seventh-grader on a team called the Lady Tigers, but Bob had a hard time keeping his eyes on her among all the other girls. The galloping throng of pre-teens and swinging ponytails — wild enough for his heart to speed up. Their sneakers would screech on the polished wood.

At twenty-four Alex was overweight, unmarried but living with someone, and still out in Tempe. Only recently they'd begun talking. Frosty phone conversations limited to weather and terse gratitude for the checks he still sent.

But now he had another chance with another woman and another girl. Caroline was suggesting that they take a swim.

Bob held the railing and followed her into the pool. Moving through water, he passed small children wearing water wings and old women in white rubber bathing caps. He came up behind Caroline and touched her waist. Droplets fell from her hair as he lifted her, light in water. They'd become especially affectionate among strangers.

Bob plunged downward to kiss her big toe, like a pink shell, at the bottom. Beneath the surface sunlight rippled and twisted the pool's floor. Four girls in bright bathing suits descended for a tea party. Kneeling in a circle, they mimed the pouring and sipping with their pinkies high until they needed air and pushed off the bottom. Despite the chlorine sting, he watched their headless bodies, spasmodic and slight. Their splashing hands broke the surface.

Bob ascended for air and Caroline. He reached for her again and pulled her through the pool like someone teaching a child to swim. In that hollow filled with water, high above the blue ocean, her legs trailed behind her and she closed her eyes.

The ceiling of the Gauguin dining room was a canopy of synthetic thatching. Copies of heavy-footed nymphets eyed Bob from menus, murals, and embossed dinner plates.

"Paradise, huh ladies?" Bob shook his head.

"Gauguin would probably think this is as funny as we do," Caroline said. Her blouse had patches of resplendent disks that reminded Bob of fish scales. Dots of light refracted onto the tablecloth. Caroline usually dressed conservatively in dark colors; he wondered if she was being ironic. Maybe she'd gotten it at the "on-board boutique" that ran ads every ten minutes on the small television in their stateroom. Bob hadn't slept much, but Caroline and Jillian could sleep even when he left the volume up.

Jillian pretended to eat her salad. Bob and Caroline had snapper fillets that didn't taste as bad as they looked.

"You need to eat more, kiddo; don't worry about getting stuff stuck in your braces," Caroline said.

"No," Jillian said and set down her fork. She was staring at the diners at the center of the room, the captain and people whose staterooms had picture windows and beds that didn't fold from a wall. Bob watched the way she tilted her head toward busboys, waiters, and the crew of kitchen runners who replaced metal bins of indistinct food at steam tables.

After asking if anyone needed anything, Caroline went back to the buffet.

"I see that you're feeling better," Bob said.

Jillian picked at a small pimple on her chin.

"You need to tell your mother that you were sick. If you don't, I have to."

"You know what I'll tell her if you do."

"I don't care; nothing happened."

"If nothing happened, why haven't you told her?"

Bob smoothed his breast pocket. "Where have you been going?"

"Wouldn't you like to know?"

Caroline returned with slices of chocolate cake, but no one wanted any.

After dinner they went to the auditorium on the Riviera deck for some kind of musical theater production that didn't make any sense. Most of the dancers had been frequenting the buffet, too.

As soon as Jillian ran off, Bob took Caroline to the Sky deck, ordered a bottle of champagne, and asked her to be his wife.

Back in their cabin, they made love. The humming elevator adjacent to the room might have delivered Jillian at any moment, but she didn't return until Caroline was asleep.

"Are we sure that the Dominican Republic is safe?" Caroline asked as they advanced in the procession moving down a long ramp. Bob glanced over his shoulder at the ship that looked very much like a giant white ant-farm.

"It's not the Dominican Republic, it's Labadie," Jillian corrected. She'd slept through breakfast and didn't appear to have showered. She hadn't seen the ring, either.

"Well, technically it's the Dominican Republic, but it isn't. It's leased by the cruise line," Bob said.

"Then it must be safer than Disneyland," Caroline said.

Bob bought them wooden jewelry boxes shaped like tortoises from the open-air market before they all reclined on sagging chaises and dug holes in the sand with their feet. Elderly passengers under umbrellas slept beneath the afternoon sun. Just as the smell of a pig roast began to overtake the beach, Caroline put out her cigarette and announced the engagement.

"No fucking way!"

"Watch your language," Bob said, but it sounded flat. Would it ever feel right?

"He's a pervert. He walked in on me in the shower."

Bob remembered feeling warm even on that cold Madison morning. He'd been waiting for the girl to get out of the only bathroom in Caroline's condo. Jillian's floral soaps and lotions stayed in the steamy air. The hinges on the crumby hollow-core door didn't hold it straight. The lock was busted, but Bob never got around to fixing it. He'd put his unshaven cheek to the warm wood. The smells were peachy and then powdery. Something she used reminded him of strawberries even though it smelled nothing like an actual berry.

"What's this?" Caroline asked.

"It's nothing." His face felt hot.

"What's nothing?"

"All right, then, let's put an end to this. A few weeks ago I accidentally walked in on Jillian in the shower. I thought it was you in there."

"He saw everything."

"For a second, but I didn't look."

"What the heck does that mean?" Jillian asked revealing her braces.

"Jillian, it was an accident," Caroline said.

"He watches me all the time, Mom. I think he's even been following me around on the ship."

"Don't flatter yourself," Caroline said.

"Screw you both!" Jillian took off into the mass of people.

Caroline told Bob she would "handle it" before following her daughter.

An hour later everyone had left for the roast. Bob was alone with a thousand chaises and the sunset. When he closed his eyes he saw Jillian's shoulders and jagged hips. One nipple was more erect than the other and her skinny legs bowed. These things were precise in his memory.

After boarding, he stopped at his bathroom on the Empress deck and let the little faucet run. He washed the back of his neck and felt somewhat better. But then, in the hallway, while he dried his hands on his shorts, he recognized the doctor who'd treated Jillian standing before a narrow doorway. It was the man's cabin, the one with the sock garters. The doctor nodded at Bob before he stepped aside for two stewards removing a black body bag. It seemed light. As they passed, he told Bob that these things happened on cruise ships.

In the dining room Caroline sat alone over an empty plate. Bob took his seat and drank an entire glass of water.

"Where is she now?" he asked.

Caroline said that Jillian was in the room. The penalty for leaving would mean the permanent loss of her cell phone, which her mother had already been keeping due to high roaming charges. In the girl's absence the waiters neglected their table. Bob's mouth was dry. He repeated that nothing had happened in the bathroom back home.

"Relax, Bob, of course I don't believe Jilly." She reached for his hand over the table, but he didn't let her have it.

A Tahitian Eve on the wall caught his eye for a quick second.

"You weren't even a little worried?"

"Are you trying to be funny, Bob? I know you."

"Enough to marry me?"

"I know you as well as you know yourself." She captured his hand.

A waiter interrupted with Bob's whiskey. They finished the meal in silence.

After dinner they wandered the decks looking down at the black ocean. Bob remarked on how it was a wonder that gravity could hold so much water. Caroline took a picture of him looking over the railing. They were walking over shuffleboard grids when Bob looked down to the deck below to find Jillian pressed between a spool of rope and a drummer; Bob recognized the floral shirt. Evening breezes carried off whatever sounds they made.

Caroline had not seen.

"We should go in, it's getting cooler." He took her hand and led her back across the shuffleboard lines.

The polished wood made him think of the basketball court.

Through wired door panes, away from cheering parents, he'd watched them play. All those spastic creatures who couldn't control their downy limbs. Some wore white T-shirts under their jerseys and had to keep clutching their shorts. But others were flushed and unbound; they yelled and let their braids and ponytails come loose. At the end of each game he'd search the court one last time for his favorite player: number thirty-three, with long arms, little breasts, and red hair. Willowy thin, but tough. Sometimes he called her Cindy, and other times she was a Kimberly. She'd get so wild. How much time did she have before she'd turn soft and silent?

When they got back to the room, Jillian, to her mother's surprise, was gone. Caroline wanted to wait up to punish her, but after two hours she'd fallen asleep.

Bob waited, but he didn't want Jillian to return safely.

He could find the girl down in the lower corridors that stunk of marijuana. She had to be beneath him in the hive of engines and employees. She'd want him to keep her secret. Bob wasn't sure what would happen, what could happen, but he needed to see.

He re-dressed without turning on any lights.

"Where are you going?"

He could smell the lanolin Caroline rubbed into her hands every night.

"Can't sleep."

"Then come here. I'll make room."

"No, I need to go."

"OK, Bob. I love you," she said, and closed her eyes.

He stopped on his way down and was sweating hard in front of a few occupied phone booths on the Lobby deck; most passengers were aware of roaming charges. He could make out his vague reflection in the folding glass door, his ears that seemed to be getting longer as he aged.

Caroline really did love him, and he felt sorry for her. He felt sorry for them all. His ex-wife. His daughter. She'd grown up to be as serious and silent as her mother. But after Donna died of breast cancer two winters back, Alex surprised him; she'd dialed the phone number on one of Bob's checks.

He'd sent so many, he didn't feel bad about calling her collect. He chose the farthest booth. Alex's boyfriend answered, didn't seem to know who Bob was, but then accepted the charges and told him to wait while he woke her.

"What is it?" Alex asked.

"How are things?"

"Bob, please."

"I — I've been meaning to ask you about Tempe, when you and your mom first got there."

"What about it?"

"What was he like?"

"What was *who* like?"

"The guy your mom left me for, the reason she left."

"What? There wasn't anyone. Not ever."

Bob had always suspected this.

"Can I hang up now? I have to get up for work in a few hours. Where are you, anyway?"

"Nowhere. Did I ever make you uncomfortable back then?"

"What do you mean? You were never around, always at the shop."

"Did your mother ever say anything strange about me?"

"No, Mom would never say anything bad about anyone, you know that. What's going on, Bob?" He could hear Alex yawn.

"Nothing. I'm sorry." He hung up.

Bob put his forehead against the glass and wondered what should happen in the world beyond him.

When he returned to the room Jillian was asleep in her bunk above Caroline. Even though he knew he wouldn't sleep, Bob closed his eyes.

At an early breakfast he told Caroline that he could not marry her. She set down her juice and asked, with a smile, "Is this a joke?" Bob shook his head and watched her face change.

A waiter approached with a coffee decanter, but Caroline waved him away.

"I know you think you're smarter than me, but you won't find anything like this again. This is the real thing," she said, and Bob agreed.

It hurt more than he imagined it would. He would miss her, but right then it seemed worse to disappoint her.

Caroline's mouth tensed like it would when she drove on snowy roads, proceeding with fear or hope.

"Then this is about Jillian."

His heart beat harder.

"You're ruining this because I have a kid who's kind of a pain in the ass."

"You aren't a mother to that girl. For Christ's sake, she had chlamydia, and I didn't tell you."

She looked at her hands and was quiet for a little while before saying, "It'll be different when we're married. You can help me get her under control. She'll listen to you."

"I can't help you with your daughter," he said and got up from the table.

Caroline followed him to their room. She sat on her bed, and Bob took his suitcase from the cabinet. Jillian had left a mess of colorful clothing, lip-sticked tissues, and other junk but was gone again.

"You're really leaving me? Right now?"

He nodded.

He wanted to tell Caroline that everything would be OK, but something small and lightning-white sparkled from the floor. A fiber from the carpet? No, an earring. Caroline was speaking, asking questions, but Bob couldn't hear, already submerged, descending to retrieve Jillian's star-shaped earring. It pierced Bob's closed hand but didn't hurt or bleed. He buried the glass jewel deep in his left pocket.

The cruise line offered the empty room at a reduced rate. The former occupant had died on board the day before, but that didn't bother Bob. The ship, the world around him, disappeared behind his locked door. This space, smaller than the first, was windowless and could have been below the surface of the water. He imagined that fish swam past just beyond the wall of the ship, close to his head on the pillow.

CHAD HELTZEL

from **The Hunter's Moon Over Chicago**

4.

Someone has discarded a rose
on the beach. Only one side
of the corolla remains: the petals
dried and wine-red. Next to it,
a dead tree branch sprouts
from the sand — pieces of sea grass
hang like Spanish moss
from the limbs. I can feel
the sand between my toes,
even though I am wearing
both socks and shoes.
My clothes are seaweed:
I can feel every grain.

CHAD HELTZEL

5.

The shells of zebra mussels cluster
in the sand. They are native to Europe's
inland seas, traveled so far on the sides
of ships like barnacles or in the mouths
of water birds. All the northern lakes
in the country are filled with them now.
They have formed piles here. On the pier,
a man is performing a dance: one foot
forward, a bend to the side, other foot
in front. He is not dancing, in fact;
he has no partner. I walk to the end
of the beach, and the man is at the pier's
edge, swaying as if bowing to the waves.
I walk back, and he has made a circle,
a slow waltz down the planks.
I must be the other dancer.

CHAD HELTZEL

11.

Once, my apartment was a city politician's office.
In an archive somewhere,
there is a short film of him at work,
a film called "Favors." One by one,
district residents enter his office
to ask for a recommendation letter for a promotion.
A hole in the sidewalk, refilled without support
underneath, must be fixed. The concrete will not
hold, will sink if not reinforced.
Only so much can be done, we are told.
The film ends.

In my living room's worn red tile floor,
four white squares bear his monogram
like markings on a tomb.
When I moved in, my cat disappeared —
only to emerge two hours later
from a small rectangular hole under a cabinet.
Who knows where she had been
or what she found — some dusty tunnel long
abandoned except by the spiders or centipedes
occasionally emerging from cracks under walls.
Fissures in beams. Mortar eroding from masonry.
Some nails and a book. A small rodent's skeleton.
The blueprints sketched in sand.

CHAD HELTZEL

14.

I walk down Ashland Avenue
on one of the summer's last nights.
Office windows blaze in a white building,
and all the pedestrians are speaking
languages I cannot understand.
At the corner, a Christian mission offers
blood tests from the back of a van.
Amid stacks of pamphlets teaching God's Word,
men sit on black upholstery, tubes taped to their arms,
their blood welling into the clinicians' vials.
Across the street a neon sign hangs
over a building's entryway, lights the name
of its first occupant over the lintel.
I see my face in a storefront window.
Once when I was very young, I looked
into a mirror, pointed to myself, and said
the wrong name. My mother believed
in reincarnation, said blue eyes suggest
ancient souls. But my eyes are not wholly blue.
The iris's inner rim is green.
And on certain days and with certain clothes,
they turn a shade of gray.
In my eyes, the city's language.

How We Pain
Nonfiction

My niece Mia swung her leg back. Like thread across a bow, it was taut in anticipation of the strike. Her target, her brother Nate's head. Seconds later he began wailing and Mia was nowhere to be found. Nate rolled around on the carpet of the living room floor like a snake trying to shed its skin. He seethed and wailed and moaned, crying out, "Mia kicked my inner ear! She kicked my inner ear!"

His ear turned quickly from healthy pink to blistering red. I suspected blue and yellow would follow.

I liked his choice of words. *She kicked my inner ear.* Not the outer part, as far as he was concerned. Not the lobe, but the ear canal itself.

I've taken a kick to the ear before. Hot blood shoots to all the areas just below the surface of the skin, and if you scratch it, you can relieve the pain a little, but the itching is its own pain, maybe a redistribution of it. More likely than not, you just hold your ear gently, covering it with a cupped hand to defend it against another onslaught. Nate held his like he was listening for the ocean, for white noise, for falling snow.

When I was Nate's age, I spent a thousand wintry days climbing to the tops of banks created by plows, and I burrowed my way through all that snow. Building tunnels with my brothers and sister, we were little beavers. Sometimes I fell from these heights, succumbing to all that snow and ice and landing on my chest with a thud. *To have the wind knocked out of you.* The chest tightening, veins constricting. I could not breathe for a few panicky seconds. But when my heart remembered to beat again, the pain was instantly gone. My sister pulled me up from the ice-covered cement by my pink mittened hand, and we returned to the tunneling with no echo of pain to remind me to be careful next time.

Our bodies work well, defending our most precious insides. There seems to be a direct correlation between how much something hurts and what it's protecting. I am thinking of this as I stand over my nephew Nate who has stopped writhing on the floor and who is covering his tears with the crook of his elbow. He is eight now and embarrassed a little for how much it hurts, for letting Mia, who is only three, know how much she can hurt him. I worry that he has already learned to hide his pain.

To be kicked in the shin or to feel the shinbone smack into a large piece of unyielding furniture as we move through life hurts, but not as much as a stubbed toe. The shinbone is not so precious to us. But the toe is another story. In fifth grade, I dropped a bowling ball on a classmate's foot. Her face not only changed color, but shape, too. It contorted from heart-shaped to an upside-down triangle of pain. I disappeared like Mia did.

My best friend Sue scrapped her way toward adulthood by fighting off her three older brothers, all of them mean. So mean they'd salt worms, as the expression goes. Only they'd really do it, just to watch the worms contract and dry out on the cement at their feet. Once, one of them held his BB gun to her arm and shot her. You can still feel the BB just below her skin, an unwanted souvenir.

Little sisters have their ways of getting back at older brothers. Sue had long fingernails, and if one of her brothers got mean, she'd chase after him, wait for the advantage, sit on top of him, and drag those long nails down his back until he bled.

This is anguished, on both sides, a sibling pain that seals us together or rents us apart. Speaking mathematically, the relationship we have to our siblings is the longest in duration of all our relationships — unless a sibling dies early, rendering an unyielding pain.

Mia returned to the room and was sent to the naughty chair, where her howls competed with Nate's. She was not crying because she hated the confinement of the chair, though she did hate it. She cried because she loved Nate and she didn't mean to hurt him. When her time was up, she drunk-stumbled over to Nate and fell into him, clumsily throwing her arms around him in a tackle of remorse. Fresh yelps erupted from him as he reached for his groin, newly injured. Mia, once again, ran.

One of my brothers says groin pain is enough to make you want to throw up, that you can experience it just from watching it happen to another guy. I can only watch in fascination and what nears empathy, though I have no ability to truly empathize.

I have never kicked a man in the groin, or if I have done so, I was innocent of it like Mia, probably in the throes of some similar tackle. But I have seen its aftermath, that return to the fetal position, childlike again in the unremitting pain. There is no female equivalent. It hurts to get a sharp elbow in the breast, no question. But it is more of a dull ache, a deep bruise that contracts and then dissipates quickly.

I cannot think of empathy without seeing Audrey Hepburn dressed in a black leotard, flitting her lithe body around a smoky Montmartre

Café in *Funny Face*. When I was eleven, my sister Andie and I watched this film, we two girls home sick with some ailment, real or imagined.

Over popsicles, we watched Hepburn's character explain to the homely Fred Astaire what empathy meant and how she wanted to be more than a fashion model.

"I am an empathicalist," Hepburn proclaimed in that blue-blooded voice of hers. "I want to feel intimately what all others feel."

My sister and I pursed our lips and stuck out our chins like her. "I'm an empathicalist!" We tried to imitate, to *feel* what her character was feeling.

Astaire laughed at Hepburn, at the supposition that understanding another person might have anything to do with dancing around in a black leotard. Astaire had to know about empathy, about what it meant to be in someone else's shoes for a time, that man with the awkward looks, that unusually long face, those droopy eyes, all of which we'd forget about when he danced — my sister and I seeing only his feet, that grace, those quick-stepping, free moments.

Our brothers were not interested in this movie. They teased us, called us names. We punched their shoulders with feeble fists. When you punch someone, it also hurts your hand, the act reciprocal.

One of my friends was punched between the eyes in high school. It knocked him flat on his back, and for weeks he saw everything through a black-and-yellow checkerboard that kept opening and closing, *like a flower*, he said. Different parts of his face felt the hit at different times. First his right eye, then his temple, then his other eye, his sinuses, and from the looks of it, his nose, which went from blue, to green, to yellow.

Color indicates pain and the progress of healing. The brain is gray matter, and also white matter, which is responsible for communication. How long does it take for the force of impact to travel from the nervous system to the white matter, telling the body, *You are now in serious pain?* How long does it take the heart to tell the brain, *Hide this in the crook of your arm?*

When my sister Andie died, I do not know if she felt pain. She could not breathe, or was breathing like a fish, my brother-in-law told us. The night Andie died, my dad guided my mom's arm, led her forward through my sister's house. My mom walked like one of the cutout dolls she used to buy my sister and me that we would play with until the knees tore and we'd need to tape their paper bodies back together. The renting apart of things is never so easily repaired as it is in childhood. So many words for snow and none for this.

Andie's husband Brian gave me her shirt to wear that night because the house was too warm for a sweater. It was an oversized T-shirt with a tiny satin bow at the collar and a stain on the sleeve's edge. The house was soft with morning light, and in the living room, my family — mom, dad, brothers, niece, nephews — we all sat in a circle against death. I lifted my sister's daughter to hold something warm. On the way up, her foot snagged the hem of my shirt, pulling it up and exposing my stomach, maybe the edge of my bra. My brother-in-law saw. The embarrassment of it — of Brian seeing me so exposed, of seeing his wife's shirt lifted and not her underneath it — this I have not found the right words for.

Mia rarely cries and almost never when she's hurt. To hurry her on their way home one night, to double the width and quicken the ambulation of her little legs, my brother led her briskly by her arm. It is a move one who has spent any amount of ordinary time with a child has done. Then he swung her up, his two-year-old daughter, in a playful gesture. There was no sound, or none he remembered. Only that Mia would not use that arm for the rest of the evening as she squatted on the carpet pushing a truck across the grain of it. In the morning, she could not reach up to be pulled out of her crib. My brother took her to the doctor and learned Mia's arm was out of its socket.

If we pretend it's not there, maybe the pain will go away. If I keep telling my mom she's fine, maybe she will be. If Mia runs away, Nate will not be hurt anymore. If I pretend there was no bowling ball — what bowling ball? — I will not be guilty of dropping it on that girl's foot.

In the crook of an elbow where the saline of tears dries, we think of the wound — our elbows rarely hurt, though we expose them often enough. Elbows in or elbows out, both positions hurt us. Oh, how we pain. Oh, how we pretend. Oh, how we sit in the corner and howl and mean not to hurt and mean not to get hurt. But our memories punch pain down, or worse, push it forward. The relationship of memory to pain is liquid and shifting, remembering pain all too well or not at all. If I ask Nate all these years later, he likely will not remember that kick from Mia. He won't know how much it pained me to watch him suffer. What he'll remember is what he already knew. That when you are hurt, you hide it. When someone kicks you, you cover your eyes so even if they can see you in pain, you cannot see them see you.

When someone dies, you stop saying their name. You don't speak of the night they died because these things just do not happen and because pain is reciprocal. If I promise not to tell you what happened, you won't have to dance around in empathy. If I promise to pretend and to use my elbow as a shield, we will be fine. If I promise to hold my leg and never let it swing into action, pain will never strike us. The right word is hidden right here where you cannot see it. I will hide it, I will never say it out loud, it will never find your ear.

GAYATHRI PRABHU

She of the Cryptic Clues   *Fiction*

This story begins in Varanasi on the banks of the river Ganga with its iconic ghats, the jagged steps that run from temples to river, and its abundant stereotypes of saffron-clad holy men, wandering pilgrims, and smoldering funeral pyres. Varanasi, where you go for salvation, for tourism, or both, and home to the hero of this story, a prince named Vajra. He was charming and brave but like most of his ilk was not much of a brain. As prince, he could afford to pay for the thinking, his father made sure of it. The minister's son and Vajra's childhood friend, Buddhi, was also his advisor in matters both personal and professional. But as young men are wont to be, the subject of women occupied them more than public policy, and here one can surely spot the beginning of trouble, the making of a story.

She was gorgeous, no matter what your idea of beauty. She had come there with her friends, but had drifted a little away from them. Her hair spread like a fan on the turquoise waters of the great river, she floated like a water nymph further and further away from the bank, her breasts rising above the ripples, a pert mouth opened in ecstasy, one hand spread out, the other dipped into her own folds. Perhaps she knew she had an audience, after all there were people as far as the eye traveled, but on this balmy spring afternoon she did not care.

Vajra and Buddhi were there by sheer chance, as part of their idle wanderings. One glimpse of the water maiden and Vajra was unable to look at anything else. Then the young woman, her face radiant as a full moon, languidly stood up to return to her friends and felt herself captured in the gaze of the prince. The garment across her shoulders slid down her shapely figure but she did not gather it back. Two could play this staring game and she was not one to be coy. She raised an eyebrow, as if to say — well, are you going to say something?

Rejection, a terrifying possibility, silences the best of men. Vajra continued to stare as the beauty reached out to a lotus near her and tucked it behind her ear, her eyes steadily on him. *Say hello, you dumb idiot, say something*. He had forgotten how. She then twisted the lotus in the shape of a leaf. He watched her fingers, mesmerized. *Her name, all I need to do is ask her name*. She picked up another lotus, placed it on her head, and then laid her hand very slowly on her left breast. *Gasp*! The prince nearly swooned from the lust that was swelling up in him, tying his tongue into knots. And then she was gone.

Vajra had met a woman who had moved him like he had never known before, and he had known plenty of women. He stood there, transfixed by her confidence, petrified by the intensity of his desire, not saying a word, not even when her friends swarmed back around her and whisked her away into the dust of the afternoon.

Since first there was attraction, now there must follow pining. Buddhi watched his boyhood chum brood and click his tongue in impatient regret, but thought it one of those brief engagements of the hearts that he would soon recover from. Vajra only continued to sigh deeply and punch fists into an imaginary self. "I can't believe I said nothing! Oh, if only I could see her again. But who is she? I know neither her name nor her address. And all I had to do was open my mouth and ask. She was ripe as a mango in late July . . ."

"But she did tell you. I was watching too," Buddhi finally spoke up seeing that his friend's affliction was probably a bit more than a seasonal crush. "By placing the lotus in her ear, her *karna*, she told you that she lived in the kingdom of King Karnotpala; by making it into a *dantapatra*, an ivory ornament shaped like a leaf, she meant you to look for her in the colony of the ivory carvers; by lifting another lotus, she let you know her name was Padma, and by placing her hand on her heart, she wanted you to know it belonged to you."

Really? It sounded too bizarre, this sign language, but somehow vague enough to border on probability. Or, Vajra thought, Buddhi must be imagining things, giving the mystery woman credit for being a lover of cryptic clues like himself. Sheer transference. And if the woman were indeed so smart, would she be worth the chase? He knew from experience that wooing a woman with his good looks and royal privileges was one thing, but continuing to keep her interested by wasteful things like riddles and conversations was quite another.

But the chemistry! Oh, that indescribable chemistry! And that decided it. Vajra and his faithful friend set out in the trail of the clues, of a woman as lustrous as a full moon and possibly as transient. They left a note for the parents, packed light, and hit the road before second thoughts arrived.

As with all romantic adventures, the big leaps of faith took precedence over boring little logistics of travel. The prince and his intelligent friend-cum-employee reached King Karnotpala's kingdom and quickly settled as paying guests in the house of the oldest woman in the colony of ivory-carvers, a natural inhabitant in the realm of gossip. And yes, indeed, she knew all about Padma. Why, in fact, she was her ayah, when the fair one was a little girl.

The boys were delighted. This was going even better than they had presumed. "In wooing a bold woman, one who invites you to find her address, it is important to be equally bold and send a direct message," said Buddhi, and the lovelorn Vajra eagerly agreed. They plied the old woman with presents and cash, and requested her to take a message to

Padma in secret. "Say to her: the prince whom you saw at the river has come here out of love for you and has sent me to tell you."

Keeping a secret will work for a tattletale only if she does not have to keep it for too long. So off went the old woman and came back within minutes, nearly in tears. "I did as you told me to. But as soon as that slip of a girl heard your message, she scolded me and struck me on both cheeks with her two hands smeared with camphor. Look, my humiliation is marked on my face! You boys are surely brewing trouble! I'll keep the cash, but you had better start packing your bags."

Vajra's spirits sagged. Who did this Padma think she was, anyway? A woman with the smarts was scary enough, and now she revealed a temper, too. This was not worth any amount of beauty and chemistry and all that nonsense, he declared, but his friend had a different view of the events. "She is sending you another clue! By sending you ten fingerprints in white camphor she is telling you to wait for the remaining ten moonlit nights of the white fortnight because they are unfavorable for a meeting."

Both Vajra and the old woman looked at Buddhi incredulously. How very farfetched! But the hypothesis offered Vajra hope and he gave their agitated host enough money to tide them through the next ten days. The old woman turned out to be as skilled in cooking as she was in chatter, and between eating and idling the young men did not feel the strain of time. Ten days later, they sweet-talked the old woman into returning to Padma's house.

This time the old woman said nothing of her guests and their message, but Padma brought the matter up nonetheless, taunting the old woman for pandering to such ruffians. The old woman returned home in a huff to report, "And then the slut dipped her fingers in red ink and struck me here on the chest. Look!" she pulled down her shawl to show her sagging breasts. The young men cringed and looked away respectfully.

"More clues?" whined Vajra.

"Of course! She cannot receive you for three more days. The days will fly by. This woman is worth the wait!" his friend assured him. Vajra's ardor was starting to fade, and his royal pride began to smart. There would be plenty of nymphs frolicking in random waters in the future. He was willing to put this entire misadventure behind him like men must do with youthful follies. His friend, on the other hand, was unwilling to give up now, as happens between word-lovers and word-puzzlers, managing to find enough distractions to keep them there for three nights.

Three days later the old woman nervously set out for Padma's house. This time she was greeted with respect and joy, treated to a banquet and honored with presents. In the evening, when the old woman wished to go back to her own home, they heard uproar from the streets, cries of a wild elephant on the loose attacking bystanders.

Padma said to the old woman, "You must not go by the main street, which is clearly unsafe. We will lower you on a chair supported by a rope down this window here into the garden of the house; you must then climb up that tree and cross that wall, and let yourself down by another tree, and walk though the back alleys to go to your own house." Even before the old woman could think it through, Padma had enlisted the help of her maids and lowered her visitor into the garden. The poor woman had to rouse her old bones, climb up a tree, cross a wall, and clamber down another tree, all the time cursing herself for getting into this muddle.

The young men, waiting anxiously for her return, began to fear the worst when the old woman came in sweating, rubbing her joints, and spitting profanities. Buddhi, however, guffawed as soon as the details of her visit were out. He clapped his friend on the back. "She is ready for you! And she has just informed you how to get there — two trees, a wall and a chair hanging from a rope from her bedroom window, that's all that keeps you from your lady."

That evening they sneaked over to Padma's house and saw that there was indeed a hefty rope hanging down the window and two maids on the lookout for their secret visitor. Buddhi embraced his friend, wished him well, and watched till Vajra reached his beloved's bedroom. Relieved, and knowing that there was nothing more to do for the lovers, Buddhi returned to the old woman's house.

Inside Padma's bedroom, Vajra was alone in the presence of his water nymph, lovelier than he remembered, draped in transparent silk, eyes looking at him boldly, invitingly. His heart trembled. What if there were to be more clues to decipher? On his own with a woman of such wiles, he was as lost as a bat in daylight. The only way to survive the situation, Vajra thought, was to get by as the strong silent type. Strong. Silent. Silent. Silent.

As it turned out, neither silent nor strong would matter. Padma thought he had been smart enough to unpack her clues and proactive enough to locate her. More importantly, he was easy on the eyes, his muscles toned, his height inviting, promise of perennial youth in his face. She let her guard down. A prince had arrived in moonlight when the night jasmines were in full bloom. Why waste time on small talk? She was in his arms, or maybe he was pulled into hers. He surrendered to her swaying body, let her lead him around her edges, sinking his head between her legs, feeling her ankles lock around him, released only when her body arched with loud moans, then flipped on his back as she straddled and worked him into a frenzy. Her fingers were searching him, finding spots that gave unnamed unfamiliar pleasures.

He wept into her hair, wept that bodies held such glorious possibilities, wept that it might never end.

The first light of morning revealed the lovers on the floor of Padma's bedroom, naked, damp in each other's fluids, limbs entangled, exhausted.

"Marry me. Be my wife."

Padma smiled at Vajra and ruffled his hair as if indulging an errant child, gathered her clothes, and unhurriedly got dressed. "Marriage is too big a promise to make on too little. It's sentimental mush. Anyhow, don't you know that what happened last night is how the Gandharvas get married? What is good for celestial beings is good for us! You can leave now, if you want to, but if you want to stay, we can hide you from everyone else in the house, and make you my little nightly secret. You can pretend you are my husband."

A pretend husband? All the benefits and none of the complaints? It was a good deal, and Vajra had wits enough to appreciate that.

Padma and her retinue of domestic help cleared a section of her cavernous closet to create Vajra's living quarters, where he could disappear when her parents came around. There was something indescribably erotic about being inside a closet that smelt like this woman, like burrowing his entire self into her insides. It felt like a charmed life to Vajra.

The first few days drifted like clouds on a windy day. Padma turned out to be adept at keeping secrets, her lover never discovered by the rest of the family. The happy couple made love in every nook they could fit into and at all times, licked each other's fingers over delicacies that arrived fresh from the kitchen at regular intervals, spent hours playing and listening to music, both of them content in the flush of new romance, missing nothing of the outside world.

One night, after the sex seemed a tad routine, and Padma began to talk about her favorite book in bed, Vajra found himself longing for long walks and fresh air. The closet turned slightly claustrophobic. His belly felt bloated, his muscles wobbly. And then he thought about the loyal friend who accompanied him on adventures, his forgotten ally.

"My darling," he gently broached the topic, "I'd rather live in your closet than in the fanciest palaces, but I just remembered something I need to do. My friend and personal assistant, Buddhi, came with me from Varanasi and is presently staying in your old ayah's house. He must be worrying about me. I'll pay him a quick visit and be back soon, I promise."

Maybe it was the strain in his voice, or maybe it was how he longingly looked out of the window, or maybe that blank look he had started to wear when she whispered her deepest thoughts. Padma propped herself up on her elbow. Something was amiss.

"Of course, my sweetheart, of course you should go. It is so hard to find good friends these days, even harder to find skilled staff. Tell me, did you decipher all those signs I made for you, or did this Buddhi help in some way? In my experience, brilliant friends are usually loyal only to themselves, and you are lucky if you found both qualities in one man."

Vajra felt a pressure valve open in his chest. Finally an opportunity to confess the truth! "Oh, I know what you mean! You are so clever, my dear, but I am better with my hands than with words. Being a prince would not have helped me pass out of school but having friends who let me cheat from them certainly did. No, I did not guess any of your signs, not even one, but it was my friend all along. He is good at this sort of thing, and how very fortunate for me, I get to be with a goddess like you!"

Padma's face gave nothing away, not her realization of the falsehood behind this romance, not her steep tumble back to reality, not her regret that the one man she thought possessing of both looks and intellect was traveling with a brain-on-hire. "Darling, you should have told me the truth long back. It is so unfair to the poor man to be ignored and forgotten like this. Any friend of yours is like a brother to me, and I would like to honor him. Don't keep him waiting anymore. Go now and come back soon." She needed to think this over and without the distraction of his good looks. How could she have been so dense? No, it was not her fault, but theirs, these halfwit boys. She had been outsmarted, humiliated, cheated, and there ought to be some consequences for such diabolic deceit. It was a cold kiss she planted on Vajra when he descended from her window, but he was too intoxicated by the prospect of escape to notice.

Buddhi was delighted to see his friend return in good spirits. They stayed up chatting all night, Vajra bragging about the good life in his woman's house and his sexual prowess. "She is very understanding. I even told her that her clues had been deciphered by you, not me, and she was cool about it. I have no idea why men grumble about wives and marriage. It's a good life."

"You should not have told her that. Some secrets are secrets because they are not meant to be shared, especially with women."

Vajra laughed away his friend's worries. He knew his Padma. And he was proud to be proved right when one of her maids arrived with the dawn bearing a tray of gifts that included a bowl filled with creamy kheer cooked by Padma herself. It was all for Buddhi, said the maid before leaving the house, and Padma was waiting for Vajra to dine with her. Vajra beamed at his friend, "What did I tell you? Isn't she quite the find?"

Buddhi smiled back sadly. "Now, let me show you something equally wonderful." He took the bowl of kheer and set it down in front of the mangy squirrel outside the old woman's house. The squirrel greedily took a mouthful, licked his lips, and fell down. Dead, there was no doubt about it.

Vajra was shocked. "What? What? Another clue? What does it mean?"

"It is a clue all right, but quick, not cryptic. She wants me dead."

"Why would she do this? Such a sweet, loving woman. Why? Why?"

Buddhi patted him consolingly on the back. "Such is love, my dear prince. It wishes to possess. She now knows she is dealing with my intellect not yours, but she does not know me, nor can she take chances with the kind of influence I might exercise on you. What is to stop you from leaving town with me, leaving her behind? She must also feel cheated, for not telling the truth can be called falsehood. But if I were to die, that would leave only one puppet master handling the strings . . . "

Just then a neighbor hurried in looking for the old woman, stepping over the dead squirrel as if it were not there, bursting with news. King Karnotpala's infant son had died. They had lost their little prince. Such sorrow! Hai! Hai!

Buddhi now had a counter-plan. He convinced Vajra not to give up on this woman he enjoyed so much. What is a little misunderstanding, a little poison between lovers? A woman with spunk is worth the trouble. "Go back to her. Buy a big bottle of liquor on your way. Get her drunk tonight, as drunk as possible. And when she is senseless, leave some sort of mark on her, any kind that does not come off, even if it means heating a piece of metal. Then take away all her ornaments, and return here. I will make sure everything turns out just right."

Buddhi rummaged in the old woman's storeroom and emerged with a small iron trident. Vajra took it with tears in his eyes, the cold iron conjuring up a heart of dark iron that had ensnared him, willing to do anything his friend tells him to atone, hoping there was a happy outcome to this twisted love story.

When Padma saw Vajra climb through her window heaving a couple of bottles of alcohol, his eyes red with grief, she presumed he was mourning for his dead (poisoned) friend. A streak of remorse ran through her. How vulnerable he looked, like a lost boy. She really needed to learn to control that temper, she admonished herself. Padma eagerly reached for the drink he held out to her and then again for every quick refill. By morning, Vajra had accomplished his mission, branding the inebriated Padma with the trident, and fleeing with all her ornaments.

When Vajra returned to the old woman's house, she redirected him to the cemetery where his friend was waiting for him, dressed as an ascetic and holding out some borrowed clothes that would turn Vajra into his pretend disciple. Buddhi riffled through the ornaments Vajra had stolen and held out a rope of large pink pearls. "Now go back into town and try to sell this. Make sure you go to as many jewelry stores as possible and hold it out conspicuously. Someone is bound to report you. When they do, tell them that your guru asked you to sell it."

Vajra had barely flaunted the pearls at the third jeweler's shop when he was arrested. Padma's father had connections in high places and had called the Chief of Police five times since that morning wanting to know what was being done about locating his daughter's stolen jewels. It was the news of the day, repeated over and over again — rich man's beautiful daughter's big treasure gone. Terrible publicity for the police force. Emergency meetings were held to discuss how the case could be cracked and closed as soon as possible. No sooner did they haul Vajra in for suspicious activity, the trail led just as quickly to Buddhi, who was waiting for them in the cemetery dressed as a holy man.

The Chief of Police personally turned up for the interrogation. The whole matter had to be handled delicately, first the high-profile theft, and then this holy man holding the evidence. Even though he was in mourning for the loss of his only child, King Karnotpala had asked to be briefed and updated on the case every hour. He released statements promising the public that the administration was on its toes to ensure their safety. The Chief asked for the newsmongers to be kept at bay while he respectfully asked the holy man how these precious pearls came into the possession of his pupil. Religion and crime was a potent mix; all it needed was a bit of politics to blow up in their faces.

"Well, I am a man of God, habituated to wandering about in the wilderness. The city and the cemetery are all the same to me," Budddhi said in his fake pious voice, "and I happened to be passing here last night when I saw a gathering of witches. One of them was holding a glowing orb in her hands to sacrifice to the Lord of Darkness, and I knew it was the life of the king's son. I chanted my prayers as loudly as I could, hoping she would release the life of the little prince, but one of the witches swooped down on me. I picked up a trident that was lying on the coals of one of the funeral pyres and stabbed her hips. While she screamed, I grabbed these pearls from her neck. God saved my life, but what is a man like me to do with fancy pearls? So I gave it to my disciple to sell it. I meant to donate the money to charity, of course."

It was a tall story and they bought it, not only the police, but the king too, still distraught at the sudden death of his infant. If the necklace belonged to Padma, and she did indeed identify it as hers, then that meant she had been present at the cemetery the previous night celebrating the death of his dear child. It also meant she was a witch! King Karnotpala sent one of the old women in the royal harem to examine the maiden for any trident marks. And there it was, exactly where Vajra had imprinted it. Padma was in great pain but refused to talk about her wound. She had been deceived yet again by her secret lover, her husband of the closet, branded like an animal, then abandoned. The night's revelries had left a hangover that did not improve her outlook. She seethed in silence.

The mystery was announced as solved in the royal court. This time King Karnotpala personally went to the cemetery to consult with the brave holy man who had branded the witch. What should the punishment be for such a dastardly crime? The noose would be nifty, but having never been tried on witches before its efficacy was in doubt.

"Banish her," Buddhi suggested. "From her parents' house, from the city, wrench her out from where she has taken roots, take her to the forest and leave her there."

"Well, that is no punishment at all!" protested Karnotpala, "What is to stop her from coming back, from taking more lives, more black magic?"

"I'll take care of it for you. The important thing is not to anger a woman of such power, but to keep her deceived. Don't you know what the scriptures say on this? You don't want to spill the blood of a witch in your kingdom, I shudder to think of the consequences. Banishment is the way to go, a fit retribution for the woman who complained falsely about stolen jewels. I will follow her to the forest and take care of the matter for you, a don't-ask-don't-tell situation, really."

Padma's parents' protests fell on deaf ears. Had King Karnotpala lost all his reasoning? How could their only child, this bright and wonderful woman, be a witch? How could they abandon her? How could they live without her, knowing she was being tossed into the wilderness? Stop this injustice!

That morning Padma had been one of the most admired scholars in the land, one of its famed beauties, and by evening she had been dragged out of her house, her clothes ripped off (if the public was going to have its spectacle, they wanted it racy), and then left alone on the outskirts of the forest without luggage or weapons. She trembled from the cold wind on her exposed skin, and from the fury of this injustice. She decided to march right back to the court of that harebrained King Karnotpala and let them finish her off in a decent way, with some respect, some dignity.

Padma ran back a few yards when she bumped into Vajra at a sharp bend in the road. His friend was by his side. Vajra clasped her tight before she could say a word and Buddhi threw a stole around Padma's bare shoulders. Tears of rage flowed down her face and the men thought it tears of suffering, perhaps even remorse. Vajra showered her with kisses, apologized for being a rat (it was just a temporary show, my love), promised to never let her out of his sight again, and began to describe this new life they would have. A luxurious life in the palace, marriage, a dozen children, annual vacations. What more could a woman want?

Padma listened to him, but her eyes were on Buddhi who politely looked away. She dried her tears. She had been betrayed and abandoned by everyone she had ever trusted. Months later she would find out that her father had died from a heart seizure as soon as she had been banished, that her mother dwindled away in grief a month later, but right then she did not have a home to go back to or a planned destination ahead. She silently accompanied them to Varanasi, the cryptic clue hid by a stoic front this time. Padma believed she was meant to have an exceptional life and she was going to have it. Retribution, as well. Someday. For now, just for now, she was going to let Vajra believe in his happily-ever-after.

Padma's story can be found in the eleventh-century Sanskrit text *Kathasaritsagara* composed by Somadeva. The present retelling has taken detours in the spirit of Indian oral traditions.

MOLLY LOU FREEMAN

Snowfall and Aftermath

This will take time.
Iota, dust mote, fragment,
Each rapid droplet beginning, of course, to end

At the river. And the river — that claim —
Twig, in time, also taken in.
Why say each thing?

So each flake,
Each marvelous branch, each glittering
Stick set apart.

So spacious — snowfall comes down —
Mid-note and its aftermath
Always unfinished, unsaid, undone,

As in this meadow
Along the snow fence. Daylight is silting slowly over
These asides — each, we are told, is different —.

Consider —— the river's surface —— how elisions will happen:
(*There is nothing now to expect.*)
Events put away, events remembered differently —

Why say each thing?
Why say all you heard?
In the blizzard let sound be softened.

Bird of black (bobolink, hid),
And the sky it divided
And the unlit sky behind.

And the modern gongs
So softened now.
All matter held still.

Now the pines take it also — snow.
There's always something unsaid, subtended —
a place beyond permission —

Kingdom, we say, or horizon —.

LINDA BIERDS

Darwin's Mirror

He placed a small mirror between his study windows . . .

Through reflection, he could watch me approaching,
down the curved lane from gate to door, as I,
looking back, imagine him rising from his wide chair,

and a bit of the hearth and foot cushion.
Whenever weather mottled the mirror, Comfort —
then Lettington — polished it, clipping back the foliage

to a living frame that held us equally. And then
I was in, walking behind him down the wide hall
and across the back veranda, then out

toward his sandwalk copse. The mirror bent down
from the outer wall much as the mirror at St. Bartholemew's
bends down from the organist's loft. And I told him this,

as we moved past the phlox and portulacas
and the ghostly rattle of the well's flywheel circled
behind us like locusts. From my pew in the empty church,

I knew that the mirror carried signals
up from choirmaster to loft — and didn't reflect
the organist's fingers down to the congregation, although

I imagined both, their seamless display cast down to me
through a slender cone of dust. Descent with modification —
but that is his phrase, not mine. And this

is his making: a long and narrow oval
shading a meadow's outer rim: a copse of hazel,
dogwood, hornbeam, birch, their leaves, as we walk

through the seasons, first a rasp then a rattle.
History is closer now, I say. And did he know that crows,
perched in the northern regions, gather

a little arc of ice on — what is it called? Just under
the throat? Gorget, he says. Yes, on the puffed gorget.
The ice looks like a queen's ruff. Or half ruff,

nothing at the back, of course. In the hazel
just over our heads, the bird waits for a moment, regal
in its ruff of ice: a dark shape

we fashion together, gorget, black eye in a membrane
of lid. And although we know the ruff ends
where breath stops, we finish the circle anyway.

BOB HICOK

Atlas' poem

My mother can't remember me. My father can't remember
my mother. The family dog thinks he belongs
to the neighbors. The neighbors moved to Spain
decades ago. Spain refuses to recognize the rebels.
The rebels have forgotten if they hate money
intrinsically or have a problem with capitalism
alone. The sky is getting farther away. Soon
it will forget where it belongs and wander
the universe, looking for a ball to cling to.
I can't recall if I kissed your navel. I think I did,
but to be sure, I'm going to kiss your navel.
If I've already kissed your navel, don't tell me
after I've kissed it again. Particularly don't tell me
if one kiss was better than the other. I want all
my kisses to be equal. I want there to be a socket
so I can plug into the larger mind of the forest.
I don't know who you are, but you have a lovely navel.
In the book of navels, your page is dog-eared.
Someone wants to remember your navel, come back
and look into it as if into a well, throw a stone
into it, make a wish, draw water from your navel
and live forever. Such a simple aid to memory,
folding a page slightly over and naming the act
for animals who've come from the wild to sleep
beside our nightmares with their large breaths
and noses that never forget. They were wolves once
but I don't remind them of that, as I don't want anyone
to remind me I could lift the world once
on my shoulders, no back pain, no nostalgia. Just me
and the weight of everything, at least I think
that was me in those pictures I've seen in books,
though years have passed, centuries, eternities
since I've sat with a book and forgotten
that anything else exists, in those lovely moments
when nothing else does.

An observer of the affair

The actor had a kind face.

I found a block of wood and carved his face into it.

I gathered the wood chips and praised their letting go.

I put his face on my pillow and my wife
fell in love with the kindness and the grain of the tree.

That was years ago.

The actor died.

The carving became a shrine people travel to to cry.

I heard of a woman who had ivy tattooed
around the blue number tattooed on her wrist
and only wore short sleeves and told little children
the truth about the accounting her body was meant to be part of
when they asked.

The actor looked like that.

Like someone walking in the morning
who just noticed her shadow take two steps to her one
and is more curious than afraid
of when the line between the two
will snap and what that will sound like
and will there be time to repeat the sound
on the telephone to her brother, who killed himself
decades ago but still takes her calls.

When we make love, my wife turns to his face,
to the memory of the tree
beside us and tells them both
she loves them and I love her
for having found this ménage à trois to be
one leg of the triangle of.

The actor looked like that.

Like the geometry of a clear blue morning after storm.

BOB HICOK

How we came to live where we live

The movie was over except the credits,
music like but not Satie, I don't remember
if I felt the loss of the child deeply
or needed people to think I did,
as when you stand before a painting
in a museum for as long as you hope
says something good about you, even
when you're not sure what that good thing is,
that you're considerate of red or appreciate
the historical significance of the brocade
or know that the woman in the foreground
holding the scythe was the painter's lover,
Mary Blake, who went on to swim
the English Channel twice, once forward,
once backward, but the vision was clear, I wanted
to carry tiny people around in a box, actors
who longed to perform "Our Town"
for an audience of any size, the numbers
didn't matter if their attention
was complete, *you would feel like the sun,*
wouldn't you, when they applaud, I longed
to ask the tiny actors in my arms,
and to feed them like the grasshoppers
I believed as a child only needed grass
in a jar to thrive, then we had cocooned
ourselves in our coats and were outside
with the gargoyles on the library, a gray sky,
I was carrying the box of actors
in how I believed the world was trying
to be perfect, nothing has to be real
to be real, like love, how often it makes me want
to eat you, not figuratively but actually
devour the hours you fill, one by one
or fill you, however that works with time,
and we walked until we couldn't, so far
there was no more light from the city,
and built a bed there, a garden,
a perspective, what you might call
the staples of a life, and stayed.

JOSH DENSLOW

Stay Awake

After sustained begging, his mom wore the sweater he got her for Christmas. There was no doubt it was ugly: bulky and beige with a deep maroon stripe across the front. Noah had employed his most strident voice, even misting his eyes by remembering the time his mom left the gerbil cage open and Baron Von Whiskers crawled into an uncertain future, never to be seen again.

Noah had taken a keen interest in keeping his mom covered since she'd attended his holiday recital in a black skirt and low-cut floral blouse. Rick Gold turned to Noah after what was basically a dirge of "Frosty the Snowman" performed by twenty-two scared fourth graders and said, "Your mom is hot," thus breaking the rule that the popular kids don't talk to the unpopular kids. It was that serious.

Noah knew his mom didn't want him to accompany her to the party. The girl who normally sat with him, Jessie from Apartment 4B, had laryngitis, and Noah's mom couldn't find anyone to replace her. She stood there with that horrible sweater hanging halfway to her knees dialing everyone she knew in their apartment building.

Jessie was over so often that she had her own key. When Noah got home from school she'd be on the couch, her knobby knees hanging over the armrest and *Wheel of Fortune* blasting from the television.

She was a fountain of information.

"You know your mom has a vibrator?" she might say as a greeting.

Jessie had straight red hair that hung limply over her shoulders. Once, after she'd fallen asleep on the couch, Noah wondered how long it would take him to lightly link the freckles on her cheeks and nose with the tip of his finger. She was the only girl in high school he'd ever talked to.

His mom turned to him, her slightly upturned nose suspended over a pout. "Guess it's you and me, kiddo."

Whenever she called him kiddo, things weren't going her way.

A week ago, the snow had sparkled on the ground like his grandmother's wedding ring. But when they left that evening for the party, the snow was plowed in brown, sludgy hills along the curb, and the grass along the sidewalk poked through the crispy layer that covered it.

His mom wore her baby blue winter coat with the shiny silver trim that wound along the sleeves like roads in the future. The beige sweater poked underneath it in a frumpy bulge that made her look like a puppet on *Sesame Street*.

She'd slicked back all of Noah's hair until it appeared that a shiny beetle had died on his head. She made him wear the charcoal dress shoes that hurt his pinky toes, and he had to tuck his green button-up shirt into his jeans.

Steam swirled in front of their faces as they waited for the Nissan Sentra to heat up. "Whose party is this?" Noah asked.

"A friend of Linda's. His name's Frank."

"Was he the guy that bought us doughnuts that morning?"

"No. But his name was Frank, too."

"Oh, OK."

His mom blew into her hands and then shifted the car into reverse.

"Who was the guy that watched the football game and kept licking all the cheese dip off his fingers?"

"Eric."

"What about that guy who snored real loud?"

"Noah, can we please not talk about this now?"

The car wheezed through the parking lot and out onto the street, the snow crunching loudly under the tires. Last year, Noah kept a snowball in the freezer until the sun returned and the leaves began sprouting on the trees. One afternoon he took the snowball out — a hard, oblong piece of ice — and carried it out onto the stairs leading into the building. While all of the other tenants came home from work carrying purses, briefcases, and groceries, Noah watched the snowball melt slowly into a dark patch on the cement.

The turn signal pulsed like a dry cough, and the light flashed on his mom's angular face. Noah loved how long and thin her fingers were, as if a skeleton were driving the car. He knew his dad's enormous hands must look like that in his box underground. His dad liked to tell jokes, and Noah wished his dad were there to make his mom laugh, a high-pitched tinkle that sounded like the tiny bell around the neighbor's golden cat. Every time it ran past his window or darted out in front of their car, Noah thought of his dad and how his voice made everything better.

"You think Dad would like that sweater?" Noah asked.

His mom grinned. "He'd say it looks like a trash bag."

"Yeah. He probably would."

His mom turned into a neighborhood full of houses so big they could be castles. Each driveway was immaculately shoveled as if snow was forbidden to fall there. The houses were draped in brilliant Christmas lights. Ten-foot trees remained decorated behind enormous front windows. He and his mom had set up a three-foot plastic tree with two strands of lights on the kitchen table. The day after Christmas, his mom had tucked it back into its box and slid it into the hall closet.

"Keep an eye out for six thirty-seven," his mom said.

"You're looking on the wrong side, Mom. That's all the even numbers."

She turned her head so she was looking over Noah to the houses slipping by. She stopped in front of a dull brick house flanked on either side by two twinkling Santa's Villages. The lights were on inside and cars lined the driveway.

"Please don't be rude, Noah. Make sure you eat whatever they offer you."

"What if they want me to eat celery? Or fish sticks? Or hot dogs?"

"One bite won't kill you. Besides, they won't be serving fish sticks and hot dogs."

"They better not be." Noah stuck his hands into his gloves.

He remained a few steps behind his mom as they shuffled up to the front door. Noah could hear voices rumbling inside and the light tinkle of a piano. She rang the doorbell and then crossed her arms in front of her. Noah wanted to tell her that he smelled fish sticks, but she'd lost her joking mood.

The door lurched open to reveal Frank, a squat man with a pencil-thin goatee wearing an immaculately pressed black suit. He looked like the villain tasked with hunting down a cartoon mascot in a cereal commercial. He smiled broadly and winked at Noah's mom. "You must be Denise. I'm so glad you could make it." He didn't notice Noah.

"Why thank you," Noah said.

Frank furrowed his brow and paused, not wanting to make a bad impression. "Hi there, little man."

"This is my chaperone," Noah's mom said.

Frank lifted his eyebrows and then winked at Noah. "Fancy," he said, and then whistled lightly.

"The sitter was sick."

"The more the merrier." Noah wondered what it was about Frank that he got to keep walking around while someone like his dad would never see the sun again.

The three of them stepped inside to find twenty people mingling in the large living room with the rest spilling into the glowing kitchen. The house looked fake, as if it had been assembled for a catalog. Everything was brand-new and white. All the men wore suits, and the women wore festive dresses. If he could, Noah would have stopped Frank before he peeled off his mom's jacket and displayed the hideous sweater Noah had begged her to wear.

"What a lovely sweater," Frank said as he draped the blue coat over his arm.

Noah's mom flushed and reflexively wrapped her arms around her midsection, ducking her head. "Noah gave it to me for Christmas."

Frank turned to Noah and smiled. "You have great taste." And that's when Noah realized how nervous Frank was. His jaw was slightly clenched, the muscles knotted above his jawline.

"Would you do me a big favor? Could you take your mom's jacket upstairs?"

Noah's mom smiled and rubbed the back of his neck. "Of course he can, right Noah? He's quite the gentleman."

Frank draped the jacket across Noah's outstretched arms. "Second door on the right. You can put yours in there if you'd like." He then turned to the room and said: "This is Denise."

"And Noah," his mom added quietly. The partygoers raised their glasses and then commenced talking. Noah tried to catch his mom's eye, but Frank had already whisked her into the kitchen. His first thought was to walk around the room and knock drinks out of hands to prove that he was there. Instead, he began climbing the stairs, his dress shoes slapping loudly on the hardwood flooring.

At the top of the stairs he encountered a large painting of a nude woman wearing a red and white flotation ring around her waist. She was pale, almost translucent, with skin dripping over her hips. Noah didn't notice the parts that made her different from him. Her eyebrows curled up into her forehead and her dark eyes followed Noah as he walked down the hall.

Whispering emanated from the second door on the right. Noah shifted his mom's coat to his right hand and leaned around the doorjamb. A hulking boy was digging through the pockets of each of the jackets piled on the ornate double bed, whispering over and over again, "What do we have here? What do we have here?"

He must have felt Noah's presence because his shoulders tensed and he turned to the door, his forehead huge under his curly black hair. "You got a crush on me or something?"

"No, I was looking for the coat room."

"Well, maybe your eyes stopped working. I see a shitload of coats here."

Noah quickly checked the pockets to make sure there was nothing in his mom's coat that this beast could steal.

"Are you in second grade?" the boy asked.

"Fourth."

"Same thing." He grinned and slapped himself on the chest. "I'm in sixth."

Noah walked into the room and dropped the blue coat on top of the pile.

"What do you think of that?"

"Of what?" Noah asked.

"About me being older than you."

"It's fine with me," Noah said, deciding to keep his own jacket on.

"Well, I'm like the boss of you."

Noah's dad always said that a bully just wants a hug, but the idea of hugging this behemoth was disgusting. He looked moist all over, as if he never stopped sweating.

"Have you found anything cool in the pockets?" Noah asked, trying to act approving, maybe even complicit.

The boy held up a small square-shaped silver wrapper. In the middle was the outline of a small ring. It looked like it came out of a gumball machine.

"This is a condom," the boy said.

"Oh."

"You don't know shit, do you?" He ripped the corner of the wrapper and pulled out a balloon. He unrolled it until it resembled a limp banana. "You put this on your pecker."

That couldn't be possible. It was too big for that.

"I forgot how stupid fourth graders are." He immediately started tugging at his pants, fumbling with the button. "Stop staring."

Noah turned his back to the large boy and heard the sound of his zipper. A little more fumbling and then: "OK." Noah took a deep breath and looked over his shoulder. The boy had his yellow-stained underwear pulled almost to his waist and the top of the condom stuck out of the band. "See."

"Yeah." Noah wished he was back in the apartment, at school, at the cemetery — anywhere but in the coat room.

"You probably don't even know that boys make baby juice. It goes inside girls and turns into a baby."

Noah's mouth went dry. There was no way that's where he came from. His dad would never do that to his mom. He still hadn't figured out where he was before he was born and where he would be after he was dead, but he was sure that this boy didn't have his facts straight.

The boy pulled up his pants, leaving the condom inside. "Get out of my face, second grader."

"No problem." Noah backed out of the room. He could hear the light murmur of voices downstairs punctuated by bright bursts of laughter, like fireworks at a funeral. He tried not to look at the painting as he made his way to the stairs, but he could feel the nude woman's eyes boring into him.

There was a creak on the stairs followed by his mom's friend Linda.

"Noah! Check you out. You're looking more and more like your dad." Her voice was too high-pitched to talk about anything serious, like she was doing an impression of someone instead of using her normal voice. But she was also the only person he ever saw who had known his dad.

"Really? You think my hands will get as big as his?"

"Of course they will." She patted him on the head. "Have you seen the bathroom up here?"

"No. Is Mom still downstairs?"

Linda knelt down in front of him and put her hand on his shoulder. "I want to tell you something, since it's just the two of us. Frank's a really good guy, Noah. I think you'll like him. Give him a chance."

Noah stared at the skin stretched over her knee, the light blue veins that traveled up her thigh into her wool skirt. She dabbed her fingertips on his cheek and smiled, her front two teeth crooked and yellow. "Trust me." Then she got up and proceeded down the hall.

The boy in the coat room poked his head out and grinned. "My dad is totally going to fuck your mom."

Noah was roasting in his puffy coat. He'd found a spot in the corner of the front room between a recliner and a potted plant. A few minutes after Frank offered everyone an appetizer on a serving tray, a rotund white cat puked up something hairy and red on the white carpet behind the plant.

Noah looked around the room and attempted to listen in on the guests' thoughts. The man with the big nose carrying a drink in each hand was thinking, "Even if I drink both of these, it won't make anyone like me." The woman with the tight dress: "I have the biggest butt crack in the world!" His mom's friend Linda: "I'm better than Cupid. And much taller, too."

His mom walked out of the kitchen holding a drink, looking small next to everyone else. She was thinking: "Can I be happy?" Frank sidled up next to her, so oily that it looked like his suit might slide right off him. His thoughts: "I will devour this woman and send her pesky son to a boarding school."

Noah tried to imagine what his dad would add to this round of the thought game. He would probably say that his mom was thinking, "I'm the most beautiful woman here."

And she was.

Every time Frank lightly placed his hand on Noah's mom's back or leaned in to whisper in her ear, Noah shot daggers from his eyes and watched them pierce Frank in the throat, the brilliant magenta blood spurting onto all the guests. Not one drop landed on his mom.

She frowned at him and made her way across the room. She always knew when he was thinking terrible thoughts.

"I thought that green shirt was your favorite?"

"It is."

"Then why do you have it covered up?"

"This jacket makes me invisible."

She frowned at him. "I think hiding in the corner is making you invisible. You know Frank has a son your age."

"He's two years older than me. And he's a pecker."

"Noah. Watch your mouth."

"Sorry, Mom. I don't sugarcoat the truth."

She smiled. "There's a lot of nice people here that I'm sure would really want to talk to you. You're making a strange first impression, standing here with your jacket on, refusing to talk."

"OK. First, tell me what I'm thinking," Noah said.

Her eyes narrowed and she pursed her lips, creating a slight dimple on her chin. "You're either thinking that Frank doesn't like you, or how that lady has a huge butt crack."

A laugh jumped out of Noah's throat and coated the room like syrup. "You're good."

"I know. I invented the game."

Noah put his hands in his pockets. "You can be happy, Mom."

She smiled sadly and tousled his hair. "When you're ready, come look for me and we'll find someone interesting to talk to."

When his dad was still around, Noah used to wake up as soon as the sun poked through his window. He'd jump out of his bed and run down the hall to his parents' room. He'd fling the door open and launch into their bed. His heart racing in his chest, his dad's beard scratching on the pillow, he'd curl up between them with the smell of soap and sweat.

A year ago, Noah found a man snoring in the spot where his dad used to lie. Noah had no idea how he got there. His mom had come home the night before and given Jessie ten bucks and tucked Noah into bed. The apartment was quiet, and Noah dreamt of his dad. He could feel the warmth of his dad's arms and smell the mint on his breath. In the morning, for the first time since his dad moved underground, Noah scrambled out of bed and ran into their room. He almost jumped into the bed before he noticed the man. He was lying on his back, unlike his father, who slept on his stomach. The snores rumbled out of him like a brewing storm. His mom was curled on the edge of the bed, as far as she could get from him. Had a burglar entered their home and fallen asleep? Noah's first thought was to smother his birdlike face with a pillow. Then he realized his mom was awake. She put a finger to her lips and waved him gently from the room. Without his even realizing it, tears had curved down his face. He backed out and slammed the door as hard as he could. It vibrated in the frame until he was safe in his room. He never saw that man again, but from that point on, Noah's mom began locking her door. Sometimes, in the middle of the night, Noah would creep out and put his hand on her doorknob and give it a slight turn, hoping that she had forgotten.

He spotted his mom across the room talking with Linda. The beige sweater hung on her like a curtain, and Noah felt a surge of love for her, as if his feet had been magnetized. He pulled off his jacket and emerged from the corner. Linda was tying up her thick blond hair in a tie. "Here comes your son now."

"Frank's cat puked on the carpet," Noah said.

"Frank has a cat?" Linda said.

"It's disgusting." Noah scrunched up his nose like his mom did when she disapproved of something.

His mom wrapped her arm around him. "I'm glad you found me."

Frank walked up with two glasses of wine and handed one to Linda. The other sat in his hand waiting for Noah's mom to take it. "I'll just stick with water," Noah's mom said.

"You have a cat?" Linda asked.

"I do indeed. A Persian."

Linda gave Noah's mom a baby face. "That's so sweet."

"I know. Peel back the layers, and I get better and better. Like that sweater."

"Noah, why don't you tell Frank where you got it," his mom said.

"I don't want to give away my secrets."

Linda snorted a laugh. "He's got his dad's sense of humor."

"And his temper," his mom said.

"I'm curious, though." Frank grinned at Noah, trying so hard to be nice that he looked like he might pass out.

"They did a clothes drive at his school. For the homeless. Everyone brought in clothes, and Noah was the only one to take some home."

"Maroon's her favorite color," Noah said. "Also, I asked my teacher first."

"That's a lovely story," Frank said. "My son never thinks about me during the gift-giving season."

Linda giggled and suppressed a belch. "And it's not like Noah has a job."

"Maybe you'll rub off on Toby." Frank punched Noah lightly on the arm.

Of course his roly-poly son was named Toby. Might as well have named him Fatty. Noah laughed and his mom pinched his ear. Noah squirmed out of her embrace.

"You should really talk to Toby," his mom said.

"I'd rather eat the cat puke."

"Noah!"

"Did my cat puke somewhere?"

"Over by the plant," Linda said.

Frank tapped Noah on the back. "Why don't you give me a hand?"

"Go on," his mom said.

"But it's not my fault."

"Of course it's not. She does it all the time. I even have a special cleaner. Follow me." Frank gave Noah a thumbs-up and set off into the kitchen.

His mom clamped her hand around his bony shoulder. "If you do this, I'll forget about your rude outburst. And when you imagined shooting arrows into Frank's eyes."

Linda's mouth opened into a slight O. With her deep red lipstick, it looked like one of the Fruit Loops Noah ate every morning.

"It wasn't a bow and arrow. It was knives in the throat."

"That's a new one."

"I know. I was pretty proud of that one."

"Did you hit an artery?"

"Yeah. Blood went everywhere."

"Go help Frank."

"OK." Noah walked past a few people into the kitchen.

Everything was stainless steel and smudged with fingerprints. Empty glasses were littered across every available countertop. Frank had a door propped open, and Noah could see a blue BMW parked on the other side.

"This way," Frank said.

The two of them stepped into the garage.

One whole wall was lined with cabinets, hanging tools, and rusting toolboxes. Noah's father had always wanted a place to use as a workshop. He told Noah about the huge house they would have one day and the furniture the two of them would build. It was hard to imagine that Frank could have anything in common with his dad.

"You're the man of your house, Noah. And I respect that."

"Thank you."

Frank knelt down and opened a small cabinet. He pulled out a dirty white spray bottle. Still in a crouched position, he turned toward Noah. "My wife died. I don't know if your mother told you that."

"She didn't tell me anything but your name." Noah watched particles of dust hover above Frank's head.

"It's been hard on Toby. They were very close. And I know he can be a bit rude." Frank looked him in the eye, as if they were both adults. "I'm not expecting you two to be friends. I'm not expecting anything. I'm just taking each day as it comes."

Noah thought about what his life would be like if his mom had moved underground instead of his dad. His chest shuddered.

"Can I ask you a question?" Noah asked.

"Absolutely."

"Do boys make a baby-making juice that goes inside girls and turns into a baby?"

Frank stood up, the spray bottle dangling at his side. "Toby told you that, didn't he?"

"Yes."

"Do you want me to tell you the truth?"

"Yes."

Frank opened the door and the sounds of the party washed over them. "Yes. That's what they call fucking." The door shut behind him as he disappeared into the house.

Linda was asleep on the couch with her mouth wide open. Noah counted four fillings in her top row of teeth from where he sat on the floor. Frank put a small quilt over her and then called upstairs to Toby. Noah's mom was picking up glasses.

"You don't have to do that, Denise," Frank said.

"I don't mind."

"Toby will do it. Please, sit down."

She sank into the couch and put her head on Linda's shoulder.

Toby stomped down the stairs wearing Noah's mom's coat and Noah jumped to his feet. "I'll take that."

"Whatever, second grader." Toby pulled off the coat and threw it on the floor. Frank didn't seem to notice. Or he didn't care.

"Get these glasses into the kitchen," he said.

"How come he doesn't have to help?"

"What do you say, Noah?" Frank said. "Feel like chipping in?"

His mom yawned loudly. The sooner he got this over with, the sooner they could go. His eyes were threatening to close and he was daydreaming about his bed.

He grabbed two glasses and walked toward the kitchen. Frank sat down next to his mom on the couch. He leaned in and whispered something into her ear. Her face didn't change.

Toby shouldered him as he barged into the kitchen, and Noah almost dropped the glasses he was holding.

"My dad has girls sleep over all the time."

"Well. My mom has guys sleep over all the time."

Toby laughed loudly, wispy for his big frame, like the sound of an eraser on a chalkboard. "Your mom's a slut!"

"Your dad's a slut."

"Guys can't be sluts, dumbass. Only girls. She's probably too gross for my dad to hook up with."

As far as Noah knew, only that one guy had slept over. "She doesn't have lots of guys over."

"You can't take it back. Your mom's a slut."

"Well, at least my mom isn't dead." Toby's face crumpled. Noah imagined a giant knife dropping from the ceiling and landing directly in the middle of Toby's head, the hilt glinting in the track lighting.

They just stared at each other, neither of them breathing. And then Toby's hands were around his throat. Noah tried to yell but no sound came out. Toby's face turned purple as he squeezed harder. Brilliant flashes of light popped in front of Noah's eyes. His legs gave out and he slumped forward. Toby loosened his grip and attempted to get better footing.

Noah belted out a scream that tore through his throat like gravel. "Dad!" he yelled. "Dad!"

Toby pushed him to the ground and sat on his back. He slapped Noah on the back of his head until it felt like it was on fire.

Frank and Noah's mom burst into the kitchen. "Get off of him!" Noah's mom yelled. Frank grabbed Toby around the midsection and hoisted him to his feet.

"He made fun of Mom!" Toby kicked his legs toward Noah, who rolled away from him.

Noah's mom knelt down next to him and cradled his head. "You OK, sweetie?" She smelled like the cheesecake that they had eaten earlier.

"What did you say?" Frank demanded.

"I'm sure Noah didn't say anything about your wife."

"Let him speak for himself."

Noah propped himself up and leaned against his mom. His voice was barely a whisper. "I only pointed out that she was dead."

Another spasm shot through Toby, and Frank dropped him to the floor where he began to cry loudly.

"Noah. Why would you do that?" His mom looked concerned.

Frank glared down at him.

"He called you a slut, Mom. He said his dad had girls sleep over every night."

"That's not true." Frank's face reddened.

"What's not true? That I'm a slut or that you have a lot of girls over?"

"Both."

Toby choked on his tears, no discernible words escaping from his mouth.

"Toby would never say something like that. Noah's making it up." Noah's mom got to her feet.

"I didn't make it up," Noah said softly.

"Your son is obsessed with sex. He asked me about it earlier in the garage."

"My mom only had one guy sleep over. He snored really loud."

Noah's mom took his hand. "We don't have to explain anything to them."

They walked out of the kitchen. Linda was still passed out on the couch, a small amount of drool forming on her chin. Noah's mom picked her coat off the floor and put it on.

Frank followed them out and leaned against the wall. "Can I call you?"

She opened the front door and pulled Noah into the cold. Noah grabbed his gloves from his jacket pocket and put on his hat. His mom's hand shook as she slid the key into the car. Noah kept twisting around to see if Frank would open the door. But everything was perfectly silent. Snow whispered in the air.

They sat in the car for five minutes waiting for it to heat up. They both stared at the door. The front lights went off, followed shortly by the lights in the house.

His mom's head kept dipping forward, her eyes staying shut longer each time she blinked.

"Mom? Are you OK?"

"Everything's great, kiddo. Just you and me."

"I wish Dad was here."

She put the car in reverse and pulled into the street. The engine clanked under the hood. "Thank you for my sweater. It's so warm."

"I thought it might be."

"It's like being in a big hug."

"I'll give you the biggest hug when we get home."

She smiled, but Noah knew it wouldn't be big enough. Her head tilted forward and the car drifted toward the shoulder.

"Mom!"

"I'm going to need you to keep me awake, Noah. I'm really tired."

"How am I going to do that?"

"Just keep talking to me."

"What should we talk about?"

Her eyes drooped again. Noah pictured both of them flying through the windshield and landing in the shape of perfect snow angels on the side of the road.

"Maybe you should talk to me, Mom."

She looked at him, her eyes two slits in the dark. "This sweater is so warm."

"Tell me about the snoring man."

Her eyes opened a little wider. "He doesn't matter, Noah. He never mattered."

The heat mixed and twirled in the air between them. "Will you leave your door unlocked so I can visit you sometimes?"

"Of course. I'm sorry."

"You don't have to be sorry."

"I'm sorry your dad isn't here anymore. I feel all alone."

Noah looked out the windshield as the snow began to fall harder, like the car was going into warp drive. "What should we talk about next?"

One day, Noah would buy a big house. He'd have a workshop where he could make furniture. He'd hear his mom laugh again.

One day, he'd be able to stand up to people like Toby. One day, he'd be old enough to drive his mom home.

MARY BUCHINGER

New Year's Eve Afternoon

Avon Hill lifts its houses again,
always again, up and over the shoulders
of other old houses, each household
strange as mine walled within.
This salmon pink Victorian
with its sturdy door, stucco exterior
beginning to crackle, creeping
green at the edges — let's walk
by it again, Dover. I tug her leash,
redirect her fervent pursuits,

and the house unfolds
like a revelation, something here
about the new year, or the old one,
in its turret, bubbled glass,
garden entry sinking sideways,
staked roses wrapped against winter,
gray granite cobblestones
in the walkway, bucking up
against each other, against
original intentions, but

following laws, particles acting
how they must, patches visible as
interruptions, efforts, a series
of cuts and stitches — what we
inherit, what we work ourselves into.
There are lives in that house
accumulating in its moldering
darkness, and I will never know them,
will barely know my own. Dover nudges
my palm, proposes we move on.

IMPRESSIONS

Quick! Father's Back Has Turned!
Petra Ford

The Original Polish
Petra Ford

4 Sunglasses
Petra Ford

Left-Handed Encounters
Petra Ford

Trained Monkey & Audience, Marina Beach, Chennai, India
Sriram Ramgopal

Two Boys and Two Dogs, Cairo, Egypt
Sriram Ramgopal

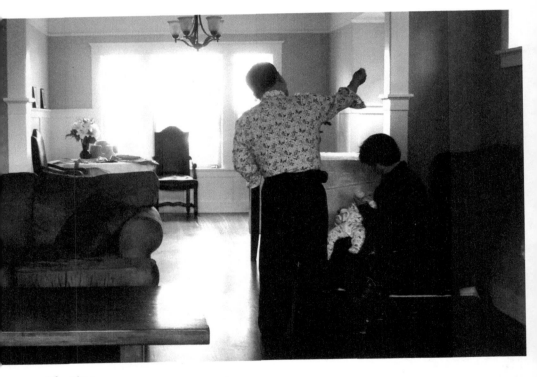

Blessing
Savannah Clement

Zoom By and By
Rob Shore

Nun
Stacy Simmering

A Moment of Silence
Stacy Simmering

Elizabeth Strout Takes the Fifth

Photo credit: Daniel Libman

On a pleasant March afternoon in New York City, I got to sit down with writer Elizabeth Strout in the reception room of her apartment building overlooking the East River, just a stone's throw from the iconic 92nd Street Y. We talked about the writing life and her three novels, *Amy and Isabelle*, *Abide with Me*, and the Pulitzer Prize winning *Olive Kitteridge*. Strout is a slow, deliberate writer, who creates messes in rough draft form and cleans those messes up as she revises, turning chaos into breathing characters and memorable stories. Shy about reading reviews and an avowedly private person, Strout spoke to *Fifth Wednesday Journal* as a way of acknowledging her love and debt to the literary journals she devoured as a young writer, which she said helped shaped her both as a writer and as a reader.

FWJ: *Did you conceive* Olive Kitteridge *as having such an intense, omni-inclusive structure when you started, or did that come organically during the writing?*

Elizabeth Strout: Once in a while something happens and it just happens accidentally and I'm so grateful, but I understood that form immediately. I think it's because I wrote one of the Olive stories quickly, which for me meant maybe a couple of months. To me that's an amazingly fast story, and I might even be making it up, but I mean it didn't take me years. Some of those Olive stories took me ten years. But that one, the first complete Olive story where I saw her, where she was the main character, didn't take me that long, and I thought, ah, OK, I'm going to write a book called "The Olive Stories." Right away I understood that Olive would have a book to herself. Every story would be about Olive. As I started going I understood that nobody, including myself, would want to see Olive on every page. She's just a lot to take. Rhythmically you have to let her fall down and rest, and the reader can rest. I love point of view and I love towns, so I thought, OK, she can make an appearance in every story, but she won't be the main character in each story. That happened pretty naturally, which was wonderful.

FWJ: *Did that first Olive story you finished make the final cut into the book?*

ES: Yes. It's the one where she steals her daughter-in-law's bra on her wedding day. And there were a number of stories — because I write all the time and I write bits and pieces, there were lots of small-town stories with an older woman protagonist, and they kind of weren't working. When I found Olive I looked back at these three or four stories and I thought, wait a second, this is an Olive story.

FWJ: *Which was the toughest one to write, the Olive story you really had to struggle with the most?*

ES: The hardest one to write was the one where they're taken hostage in the hospital bathroom. That was one I had been working on for years, and the woman in the story's name was Evelyn because I hadn't yet found Olive. I had this woman stopping in the hospital with her husband and I wasn't sure how it would play out and I couldn't get someplace with it. Then Olive showed up and it was like, sorry Evelyn, you're not the girl. But the form of that story was very difficult. It took me years to write because I couldn't find the form. It wasn't until I realized that she'd been traumatized, so her memories of it are the memories of someone traumatized. And when I came up with that image it seemed to me like the inside of her head had been painted with a sponge, the way kids do in kindergarten or something, sponge painting. Then I could visualize it thinking that her memory took the shape of these splotches, and I could present them in some kind of forward-leaning narrative.

FWJ: *She casts such a big shadow on everyone's lives around her, and I thought more than once when reading Olive about Rabbit Angstrom.*

ES: Yes! I love *Rabbit at Rest* — the final one. I just recently went back and read them all again to see how Updike does things. It's great how awful Rabbit is.

FWJ: *They both put their sons in therapy.*

ES: Right. And especially in *Rabbit at Rest* he's so awful — going to bed with his daughter-in-law. That was the point my father-in-law put the book down and said, "This is disgusting, I don't want to read this anymore." I talk about it sometimes when I give a lecture; I find it so amazing that he's my favorite Updike character. He has this heart problem and he's driving back down to Florida or something and eating all those electric orange Cheetos and trying to play basketball, and every time he shoves more junk food in his mouth I keep thinking, don't do that, you're going to die. I think isn't that interesting that I have such a response to him while at the same time he isn't even remotely what you would call a good person.

FWJ: *Updike squirreled away that little coda to the Rabbit books, a little novella about Rabbit's son in a collection of stories.*

ES: I think it was called Lick of Love. Or *Licks of Love*?

FWJ: *You also did that with the characters from* Abide with Me *making a surprise appearance in an Olive story.*

ES: Yes. I couldn't help myself.

FWJ: *It was fun to find them back again. Do you have any plans to bring Amy or Isabelle back?*

ES: I was playing around with that the other day, with a story about Amy and her mother. But I wasn't comfortable with it. It's funny.

FWJ: *There's so much potential now there at the end with the new family. Have you ever gotten pressure from an agent to write a sequel or do something more* Amy and Isabelle *like?*

ES: No. Other than everyone hoping that *Abide with Me* would be much more like *Amy and Isabelle.* People were disappointed.

FWJ: *But it is similar in many ways. You gave us another town full of people with lives and back stories . . .*

ES: I thought so too. But New York is not a place where . . . Let's just say my sense was the New York publishing world was not a place where people would be inherently interested in the struggles of a minister.

FWJ: *What do you write on?*

ES: I write by hand. I still do. I used to write on almost anything. But mostly notebook paper is what I like. Loose-leaf. I use a pen to write and then a pencil to go over a typed page when it finally gets messy enough to the point where I can't read it anymore, then I'll type it out.

FWJ: *Revisions by hand too?*

ES: Oh yeah. It's all by hand until I can no longer see what I've done. I really, really don't like to print things out. It seems so serious. It becomes more difficult then to get it back into a state of fluidity. I think of it as very malleable. I very literally like turning the page, you know, writing around the edge of the page, and then I make notes, "go here, and here, here, turn it sideways and then go here." I like mess. I'm also, maybe unfortunately, a messy person, and it's how I work. But then it reaches a point where I don't understand what that arrow meant, go where to what paragraph? I lose things all the time; I lose pieces of writing all the time.

FWJ: *Which part is most pleasurable? The first draft or those revisions?*

ES: I'm pretty much a scene maker, so my favorite part is the revision where I'm feeling like I'm finally getting there, figuring out what the scene should be and it feels right. It feels energetic. That doesn't happen on a first draft.

FWJ: *How do you store it all? In a box or just piled on your desk?*

ES: It's everywhere. It's terrible. It's terribly chaotic, I'm afraid. And there will come a point where I think, now wait a second, I'm getting a scene here and I'll need to be able to see it. Then I'll type it up, and then of course I'll immediately mess it up as fast as I can with a pencil.

FWJ: *So is revising for you expanding as opposed to contracting?*

ES: Oh no. I cut and cut and cut. I write tons of stuff that just never makes it. I've written hundreds of pages sometimes just to get one page.

FWJ: *Do you have a set amount of time for writing during the day?*

ES: I wish. I used to be more disciplined about that when I had a family, a daughter, and a dog, you know, going around in different circles trying to keep everyone organized. And I was teaching part-time so I had to be more disciplined about when I was going to do everything. I'm not that good about it anymore. But I also used to write first thing when I got up. I lived alone for a few years and I worked late at night. I think I'm just made differently. I get a real second wind around eleven o'clock and I'm able to go back over all the stuff that I've done. I've been reading the biography *Capote*, and he liked to write at night. I'm always glad to read something like that because then I can go, oh yeah, me too.

FWJ: *You find inspiration reading about other writers?*

ES: I do. In fact I was thinking, why am I giving this interview if I say — which I think is honest — that I'm not comfortable being in the public? But I love literary magazines. They've meant the world to me, and my sense of doing this is that there might be other writers out there who are on their own, and if there's anything I can say that brings somebody a sense of hope or comfort . . . I can remember being young and reading things that writers said about writing, and I was so happy. When you're a writer you live with such a private sense of alienation. And then I would just go to the library where they had them all lined up, and it was sort of like going to a bakery. You find out there are other people living like that. *Ploughshares* is one which never took a piece but just asked me to guest edit an issue.

FWJ: *Do you get a lot of moments like that, having been through the slush piles?*

ES: When *Amy and Isabelle* was published and did well it was like a dream come true. I happened to be in the basement of where we lived in Brooklyn and I had kept all this stuff. It was pre-e-mail, and I had submitted everything by mail then and I had all these rejection letters, a big box of rejection letters which I had perversely kept, maybe to keep track of who I was sending stuff to. But they weren't organized, of course, because it's me. But I thought, oh well, you know, now I can look at them and feel triumphant. But I couldn't. They made me sick. I started to look at them and they still hurt my feelings so much. I just threw them away. I did eventually get very nice rejections from Dan Menaker at the *New Yorker*. He wrote me bigger and bigger personal rejection letters.

FWJ: *Ah! The highly coveted, rarely sighted personal rejection from the* New Yorker*! That must have been thrilling.*

ES: Are you kidding? It was amazing. Twice he called me up. One time was when I just turned thirty and he called me and the first thing he said was, "This is Dan Menaker from the *New Yorker*, now don't get excited because we haven't —" And I was like, that's quite all right. I really was just as excited as if he had taken it. But he was basically calling me up to say keep going. That my stuff was good; he said better than eighty percent of the things that come across his desk so keep doing it. I couldn't even sleep that night I was so happy.

FWJ: *Did they ever offer concrete suggestions?*

ES: He would. Not for me to revise and send back, but he would tell me what he thought wasn't happening. And deep down I knew what wasn't happening. Once I got rejections like that — they still hurt — but at least someone was in dialogue with me. Someone believed in me. He was deeply, deeply important. Then he left the *New Yorker* when Tina Brown came in and I had started to work on the novel so we were out of touch for about five years — plus I wrote so slowly that I only sent him a story every year, every two years, anyway. Then I couldn't get an agent for *Amy and Isabelle* so I sent it to him at Random House, and he liked it. And that's how that got published.

FWJ: *Do you think of yourself as a funny writer?*

ES: You know, I do actually.

FWJ: *So do I.*

ES: Well good. I think I'm hysterical. I don't mean to be. I don't sit down trying to be funny. My mother thinks I'm a riot. She says, "Oh Lizzie, I laughed my head off; I just howled."

FWJ: *You did stand-up comedy.*

ES: Oh my God. I did. I can tell you what I did that for, and it was really, really scary because I do have stage fright. It was back when I was not able to finish a story. I had been writing for years and years and all of a sudden I was unable to finish even a single story — I was getting ready to become a novelist, really. This was right when Cuomo lost the election and Pataki became governor so many years ago.

FWJ: *Were you doing political jokes?*

ES: No. But it was just that night, election night.

FWJ: *So it was just one performance?*

ES: Well, I'll tell you: I took a class. I was having trouble writing, which is scary, and I thought to myself because I'd done it long enough, OK I can tell I'm lying about something. There's something I must be holding back. That's usually true. When you get writer's block it's because you're doing something false. There's a billion ways to be false. You can be writing a story one way when it really wants to be a different way. You can be trying to protect yourself — which is even worse. Or you can be showing off or whatever. So many different ways to be false. And I was really concerned because I couldn't finish a story. I thought, what is it? What am I doing wrong? What am I holding back? And I was interested in comedy because it seemed to me as I went to various clubs in the city — which of course we didn't have in Maine or New Hampshire or at least not the Maine or New

Hampshire I came from, nor would I have been allowed to go if there were — but here I was in New York comedy clubs and people are laughing when they hear something true. And so I thought to myself, what would come out of my mouth? Because you know as a writer we get to stay in the house, be real squirrelly. I wondered what would come out of my mouth if I was responsible — directly responsible — for making someone laugh. Strangers, not friends when you know what their funny bones are, but it seemed to me to be like putting myself in a pressure cooker. So I signed up for a class at the New School in stand-up comedy. Oh my God, it was so frightening. You'd see people outside of class in break times just eating cigarettes, and every week attendance would be smaller. But I made myself stick to it. And those of us who made it through that class — probably half of us dropped out if not more — those of us who made it through performed on the Upper East Side here. I wouldn't let anyone come who knew me. I've never been so frightened in all my life. It was horrible how frightened I was. But I did it, and I got laughs.

FWJ: *Do you remember any of the jokes?*

ES: Well, what I remember is that it worked. I made a lot of jokes about hair, about my hair. I hadn't yet written *Amy and Isabelle*, so obviously I have a lot of issues about my hair. I made a lot of jokes about my in-laws, who at that time were New Yorkers. And I made a lot of jokes about being from New England. And the truth is, honestly, until I took the class, this is how much of a WASP I am, I didn't know I was a WASP. I didn't even know that's what the jokes were about, really. I was just making fun of the difference between myself and my in-laws, things that they would say and do that my family would never say and do. Really, what I was doing was talking about huge cultural differences. And that's when I realized, oh, I really am from New England; I'd been so busy trying to run away from it. My instinct to do it was right, but I know it took years off my life. Afterwards the guy asked me if I'd come back and do a regular Tuesday night thing, and I said, "No. I won't." Because I'd be dead. Wasn't for me. It's on tape somewhere. Anyway, it worked for getting over writer's block, and I'll never do it again.

FWJ: *Do you carry a notebook around with you?*

ES: I do. I used to be better about it. When I lived in Brooklyn I spent so much more time on the subway. It was fabulous actually when I look back now on it. I would spend hours on the subway and things would come to me with an urgency and I would write it out. I'm not the kind of person who needs a magazine or music or anything. I can just sit and stare because I have so much going on in my head.

FWJ: *In the subway were you working out your ideas in your head or listening to people talking?*

ES: Both, actually. There's this story in *Olive* called "Starve" about a young couple. I was on the subway one day and that couple was there. The girl had on that denim jacket I used in the story — she didn't appear to be sick at all, that was something for the story, but I saw them and she was sitting on his lap and it was so cute. She said, "Stop smelling me, I know you're smelling me." And then she said, "We could take a nap and that way we could stay up all night." They were just so cute. I didn't write it down but I remembered it.

FWJ: *At what age did you start writing?*

ES: At least since I was about four. I don't seem to have a memory of thinking seriously about ever being anything else. My mother wanted to be a writer and she's a hugely important presence in my life. Always has been. She encouraged me from a very young age, and when I tell some people I was writing in notebooks at three and four, they say it's impossible because three- and four-year-olds don't write. But I really do think I did. I certainly knew how to write when I got to kindergarten. I loved letters. Now that I think about it, I can remember learning to read — we were driving someplace and my father said, "Now everyone read the signs." I remember I couldn't read them because I was so little, and so when we got home he taught me to read. What my mother would do is she would buy me notebooks and she would say, "Write down what happened today." One time we were buying sneakers, and I remember the person who sold them to us was a man, and he was very nice, and she said, "Write about that in your notebook." So all that started at a very young age.

FWJ: *Did she get to read your books?*

ES: She's eighty-three years old and has read my books and has always been enormously supportive. There was a long period of time where she didn't read anything I wrote. When I was in my early twenties and starting to get things published in literary magazines, she and my father when I sent them something would both be sort of quiet about it, so I stopped talking about it. And then eventually when *Amy and Isabelle* came out I sent it to her and she loved it. She's loved all of them.

FWJ: *Were you worried about her reaction at all, especially since it has such a troubled mother-daughter relationship in it?*

ES: No. Nothing I do is all that autobiographical. I'm the least autobiographical writer I know. I certainly use every single thing I've ever lived through. But I don't write — it would make me too nervous. I would be too self-conscious to write about myself in any way that seemed like myself, so I write about somebody like Isabelle Goodrow. I did work as a secretary in a shoe mill one summer back when I was in my twenties, and it came back to me when I was writing. I thought, wait a minute, here we are, back to that setting, which seemed very vivid to me, and here we had this uptight woman. She wasn't anybody I knew in my life. She just wasn't. She seemed very real to me and there was something very freeing about writing about her because I thought, well she's not me. I'm not this squirrelly little uptight secretary. But then of course as the years go by you think, oh, of course that was me. I mean they were all me.

FWJ: *You have a daughter, so you've also been on the other end of that relationship.*

ES: My daughter is an only child, and she does have the sensibilities of a writer, and we're just very close. It happened to be that way, that we're very similar in some ways. She grew up with me writing. She ate breakfast off manuscript stacks. And I used to think, I wonder what she'll think of me when she realizes I haven't done anything? That I've failed, only published a few small stories. But of course it never occurred to her. I was her mother. She just coincidentally turned sixteen when *Amy and Isabelle* came out. And I said to her, this is about a sixteen-year-old girl and people are going to . . . you know. And she said, "That's fine I don't care." But she's never read any of my work, which I think is great. It's a great choice. She wants to be a writer herself, a playwright, so it seems to me to be a very good choice since we're so close. She doesn't need to read my work. And she certainly wasn't Amy. Not at all. She grew up in a city — though she does have the wild curly hair like Amy.

FWJ: *Amy also has those big feet, which I noticed Olive has too.*

ES: I remember when I wrote that about Amy I wanted to write against the grain. I wanted her attractive in a certain way. That seemed necessary but I didn't want to write a stereotype, so I thought, let's have her have large feet and large hands. Conventional beauty is not interesting. At least it's not interesting to me. I gave her the great hair and that's enough.

FWJ: *Can I ask you about the movie? Did you know it's on YouTube?*

ES: *Amy and Isabelle* is?

FWJ: *Yes. I guess someone posted it on YouTube in little ten-minute segments. Looks like they just held up a video camera to the TV while it was airing. It even has the commercial breaks.*

ES: Strange. No, I didn't know that. I know you can't rent it — didn't go anywhere after being on TV.

FWJ: *Was it fun to have your characters interpreted for the screen?*

ES: I had to think a lot about making that decision. Most writers are pretty excited to get a movie from their work, but I had to think a lot about it because I had worked so hard on that book. I'm not a fast writer and I thought a lot about it. And it was my mother, she said to me, "Do it." Because it was Oprah's name behind it and more people would end up reading the book. She said, "People need that book. You will reach more people with the movie who will then find the book."

FWJ: *What was your involvement with the project?*

ES: They were very nice. The production company is terribly book friendly and that was one of the reasons — I mean everyone thinks, "Oh well, Oprah." You'll just jump at the chance to let her do anything, but it wasn't true.

FWJ: *Did she feature the book too?*

ES: No. She wouldn't feature the book. That was one of the things I negotiated, to have her feature the book on the show, and she could buy the rights. But she was like, no, I don't do both. She doesn't make the movie and also feature the book. But they really wanted it, and they were careful readers. The woman who produced it, Kate Forte, was really quite wonderful. They were very wonderful to me. They included me every step of the way. I honestly didn't want to be included because I don't know anything about movies and I don't want to know anything about movies. They sent me the drafts and I'd say, sounds good. What do I know? She'd call me up and say, guess what we put in her refrigerator? Or she'd call me up and say, what do you think if they're eating macaroni and cheese, do you think they'd have carrots with it? And I'd say, sounds good to me. So they were wonderful. But ultimately the film didn't feel connected to me. And it's OK.

FWJ: *Can you talk at all about your reaction to the film itself?*

ES: Well, television is interrupted every fifteen minutes, and then there was a snowstorm that night in New York so they kept cutting in. I think Elizabeth Shue is much lovelier than Isabelle Goodrow. The girl who played Amy wasn't the actress I would have chosen; I thought there was something too hard about her, which is central to me. And you know a funny thing about that is that I don't read reviews. I don't read anything about myself. And I was out in St. Louis doing something, and I was in a hotel room by myself. My father had just died. I was there for one night for some reason and I was upset and there was nothing in the room but *TV Guide*. And I looked and the movie *Amy and Isabelle* was coming out and *TV Guide* had this article about it and they interviewed the girl who played Amy. I remember looking at it and thinking: don't touch it. Don't touch it. But I didn't have anything else with me or whatever so I picked that damn thing up and I read it. And that girl said, "Oh, the clothes I had to wear were so ugly and it was so depressing, and I just couldn't wait to get back into my trailer and put my regular clothes back on." I was so mad at her. It really hurt my feelings. And I thought, if you don't get Amy you don't deserve to play Amy. Welcome to the world of a lot of girls out there, honey. And I should never read anything like that.

FWJ: *It seemed to me, and again I didn't get to watch the whole movie, that the tone was off. In the book, even though I had a sense that Mr. Robertson was probably grooming Amy, I wasn't entirely sure because it's all filtered through her adolescent perspective. But from what I saw in the movie he seemed obviously predatory.*

ES: Exactly. Exactly. Which is one reason I wasn't sure if I wanted to do it. That's a perfect example: Mr. Robertson. I must have written three hundred pages if not more just trying to understand him more and how much of his story was going to be in the book. Was he going to have a point of view? I eventually decided to just mostly have his actions, but I don't want to write a melodrama ever, and however the reader responds is fine because they're bringing their own stuff to the character. I just didn't want him automatically this bad person. I wanted him a person who finds himself in this situation. You know sort of like, I shouldn't have gotten myself into that situation. And it was very, very important to me that she kisses him first. Totally important.

FWJ: *But he creates that moment.*

ES: He totally creates that moment. And I don't mean to suggest that he's without responsibility, but I just wanted it messy because life is.

FWJ: *Do you believe fiction should be uplifting?*

ES: That's a good question, and I've thought a lot about that recently. I think literature should make you feel less alone. And I'm not sure that would be called "uplifting." I've received great comfort from some really dreary stories because they're truthful and they're engrossing and they give me a slice of a moment or a color that makes me feel included somehow. And I hate to dis other writers, but there's one I've read for years whom I love. She has sentences that are amazing, that go for a whole page, and she can sometimes change point of view inside a sentence, and she's very good. I've learned so much from her. But her books became very similar, very arid. What was being presented on the page became more stuffy and the characters were so lonely that the reader wasn't feeling better because you've just met another lonely person. I remember finishing the last book of hers on a subway and I thought, I don't know what to do with this book. I don't want to recommend it to a friend or loan it to anyone. I just wanted to jump in front of a subway train. It was the first time I ever consciously thought, I don't ever want to write a book that makes somebody want to die. I don't want my books to do that. I think life is amazing. It's a lot of other things too, but primarily amazing, and I just would like to not write about despair without a little something that also suggests we're capable of something else as well.

FWJ: *Olive at the end finds a little grace note with a man she meets while walking, someone she might not necessarily have imagined for herself.*

ES: The conclusion that I came to was that someone doesn't tear through life like Olive without learning something. That's not the end of the story just because she's learned a lot. She gets a chance to acknowledge, "I was awful to my son and you were awful to your daughter." Life is lonely and hard and at first I hated you and we can have a drink — well, she doesn't drink, but you know. The writer

Fredrick Bush was a friend of mine, and he said, you know Liz, you're a writer who has a really dark vision but you can't stop believing that people are fundamentally good. I think it's probably true. People will say to me, your work is so depressing, and I'll think, OK, my writing is just not for you. Because I don't think it is depressing. With *Amy and Isabelle* I wasn't planning for that ending.

FWJ: *It's amazing the way that family completely opens up at the end.*

ES: Yes, that claustrophobic situation they had been in. And now she's got family and her mother's letting her go and they're driving off . . . But that came naturally. And with Tyler Caskey [in *Abide with Me*] I thought this man is just going to fade away, this is going to be a tale. An old-fashioned T.A.L.E. This guy is going to disappear and fade off and no one is ever going to know what happened to him. But then as I got going into the book I thought, no, oh no, he's a real member of this community. He's a real guy and he's going to turn back and come back. And the community is going to feel bad about what they've done. I want to make people feel a little better, without being a Hallmark greeting card.

FWJ: *I love the names of your characters.*

ES: I love names. Names are very important.

FWJ: *I caught myself saying out loud Rosie Tanguay whenever she was mentioned. Quite often you refer to characters by first name and a last name.*

ES: I noticed that too. I don't know. I was just thinking about it. It might be a little New Englandy. A lot of times in New England, in certain towns, half the town will have the same name. The same last name. So you'll say, Dick Moody. You know, if you see someone? It was Dick Moody from so and so. It conveys more information. I'm kind of making this up as I think about it because I was wondering, why am I always referring to him as Avery Clark? It's a little more formal than Avery. The narrative voice gets to stand back a little more. Amy then is a little more intimate. It also has to do with sound, what's the sound of the narrative. I play around with it a lot and some of them come pretty easily and some of them just don't. I ask my mother, she's a New Englander from a billion generations back and she just has the best names. She loves all that history. Everything I ran away from she just adores. I have a list of names, but of course I lose them because I lose everything. My husband will say, do you need this? I'll be like, oh God, there's that list of old family names and relatives that go back to the seventeenth century, with names like Reliance and Experience. It's wild. Just amazing. The ear is important. I read a lot of poetry, Auden and Wallace Stevens. Czesław Miłosz. I just like sounds.

FWJ: *Do reviews affect you?*

ES: I can't say I'm completely ignorant of them, because you can't be. I get a sense of what's happening. Back when Dan [Menaker] was the general editor for all my books, I told him I'm a very excitable woman so you must not tell me. If something really great happens tell me, if something horrible happens don't tell me. So he calls me up one day — he was furious, and he said, "Did you ever read *Peyton Place*?" And I said, "I don't think so. It was passed around when I was a kid I guess, but I never read it." And he said, "Some woman's written an article that *Amy and Isabelle* just rips off *Peyton Place* and this and that." And I said, "Dan, now I'm upset. Why did you tell me this?" And he said, "Because I feel like killing her. I feel like driving out to Long Island and finding her." I said, "Now I want kill her, so don't do this." Once in a while something will come my way. I was in Iowa and about to go on the radio and some woman said, "Oh, I thought you might like to see this." And it was a review of *Abide with Me*, and it was terrible. It broke my heart. Obviously I know those things are out there, but I just don't want to know about them. The book is done, I did my best, and that's it. I don't want to know.

FWJ: *Tell me about winning the Pulitzer Prize. Is that the kind of thing you know is coming ahead of time?*

ES: No. No, I didn't know at all. Maybe some people do, I don't know. My agent and my publisher know me well enough to just "leave Liz alone. Don't get her involved in anything." Which is correct for me given my nature. When I won I was on the West Coast giving a lecture series, and when my agent finally got a hold of me she was mad. I had turned off my phone because I was giving a talk. And when I turned it on she was mad. She goes, "Where have you been? You just won the Pulitzer. Liz, you were the only writer in the country not glued to your computer at three o'clock." I had no idea it was Pulitzer day. I was amazed. I mean I was thrilled, I was absolutely thrilled to get it. And I had been nominated for a National Book Critic's Circle Award, and I didn't have any idea about that either. I was up in Maine and Dan e-mailed me and said congratulations, and I said for what?

And he said, "Don't you know you just got nominated?" I was really happy about that too.

FWJ: *Are there dinners for these things?*

ES: There's a reception for the NBCC, and then for the Pulitzer there's a luncheon up at Columbia. But you don't have to talk or anything, which is fabulous. I took my daughter with me. It was great. All these little tables with little flowers on them, and you just go up there and get it. I said to my daughter, "Isn't this wonderful? I get to walk in this room and I don't have to speak." I get so nervous.

FWJ: *How do you do those lecture tours then?*

ES: They finally, finally figured out to give me a beta-blocker. I don't have high blood pressure or anything, so I didn't know anything about them, but then a doctor, a cardiologist, finally told me, you know, we all take them. He said, "When we go to medical conventions to speak the first thing it asks on the questionnaire is what beta-blocker are you on?" It just slows the heartbeat. It helps tremendously because the psychological dread remains the same. You just think: I would rather die than do this. But the body responds — it stops the adrenaline from going full force. It's a life saver.

FWJ: *Can I ask you about teaching?*

ES: Sure. When I taught in Manhattan Community College I taught composition, and sometimes I taught a literature class. It was fun to get kids interested in reading — I shouldn't say kids. They were adults. Young adults mostly. I got to introduce them to Raymond Carver and John Cheever, whoever I was excited about at the time. If they like you, they get excited about what you're excited about. And I always changed it because you don't want to get sick of whatever you're doing at the time. It's a danger. But then after my books came out I started to teach writing at Queens University of Charlotte, the low-residency MFA program. I've spent the last ten years reading student writing, which is a mixed thing. On my best day I would almost feel like a radiologist. I felt like I could pick up a manuscript and pretty quickly understand what's going on. Like, "You sure can do landscape, you've got that down, but what is it with people? You have a problem with people." I wouldn't say it that directly. Maybe. And that was sort of helpful with my own writing, knowing what I'd say to my students.

FWJ: *Who are your readers?*

ES: I have these little made-up readers. We writers sit around all day and make things up and so you might as well make up a reader as well. I have kind of an ideal reader and I write for her. Somebody who is patient but not too patient. Open. Thoughtful. And who somehow needs the book. Especially *Amy and Isabelle* because I spent so many years of my young life walking through libraries pulling books off shelves, and some of them would be fabulous and some of them wouldn't be, and I just thought, what if there is some young girl in the middle of Kansas and she feels like a knucklehead all the time? She pulls this book down and feels less like a knucklehead.

FWJ: *Do you get a lot of reader response?*

ES: I do get reader response. It used to be letters and now it's e-mail. Especially about *Amy and Isabelle*.

FWJ: *Is it the mothers or the daughters writing you?*

ES: Both. About equal.

FWJ: *Do men write you?*

ES: Not as much. A couple of men wrote and said, you're just a man hater. And that was very painful for me because I don't think I am at all. I like men, it's just this book happened to be about women. And I actually like Avery Clark. It wasn't his fault Isabelle was hung up on him, it was just time and place. More men have written about Tyler and Olive. Mostly they write nice things. There are certain people who write and say, "I really liked the book, until I got to the last story and Olive called the president a cross-eyed cocaine addict. That made me think that you're a horrible person and I will never recommend your books." Obviously these are hardcore Republicans and they hate me and that's fine. Canadians got very upset with me because Olive says the terrorists on 9/11 came from Canada and down through Portland. Actually they had spent a night in Portland but not through Canada, but when 9/11 happened an awful lot of people in Maine thought that. There were all these false reports and Olive would have thought that. I can't answer those letters because I don't think it's my place to give a class in narrative voice. You know, why did Raymond Carver call the African American housekeeper colored? It's what the character feels; it's not what Carver feels.

FWJ: *Do you have a set of books that you tell young writers they need to read? Books that taught you how to write or inspired you in some way? This is that question.*

ES: God, I love Hemingway. It's something I don't even talk about that much anymore because a lot of women don't like Hemingway. He's out of fashion and what's the point of having the conversation except that I love him? Love Fitzgerald. I feel like I've learned so much from them and D.H. Lawrence and Virginia Woolf and all the Russians because they're not afraid of anything. And Updike, of course. John Cheever's journals. The stories and *Falconer*, but especially the journals are so gorgeous. They're so honest. And I have friends who say, "Oh, they're just the ramblings of an alcoholic depressive," or something. But they're beautifully written. You can learn a lot about weather. He's so observant he just knows the wind is coming off the east and this is what it's doing to the Hudson, and you read it and think, that's right! That's what it's doing. Alice Munro is huge — a huge, huge influence, and so is William Trevor.

FWJ: *You've set all three of your books in small New England towns. You live in New York, but so far you haven't set a book here.*

ES: No. Not yet.

FWJ: *Do you have a New York novel you're secretly working on?*

ES: I don't know what I'm writing at the moment.

Daniel Libman is a past fiction editor of *Fifth Wednesday Journal*. His debut collection of stories *Married But Looking* is forthcoming from The Livingston Press in the spring of 2012.

JANE MEAD

Like a Blind Man
I Crouch Down

My mother pots or doesn't pot the soil.
In the cold rain, I crouch down.
My ears are clean, but there's a boil
on my forehead, and soil
under my nails, crusty and blood-brown.

December rains gather, froth and boil —
the river runs brown with topsoil.
On the road the earthworms stretch and drown.
(My ears are clean but there's a boil
where my heart should be and soil
in the flashing waterfalls near town.
My lover tilled or didn't till that soil.)

Loyal, disloyal, loyal, disloyal,
loyal. I flip my penny to the ground.
My forehead's mud-streaked. There's a boil
where the icy waters rise and roil.

In the field, the field-mice drown.
My brother loves or doesn't love the soil.
In the field the narrow ditches boil.

Dorothy and Jane in Tesuque

Dorothy pretending to be water.
Dorothy pretending to be
sky. In the wide arroyo

under cottonwoods. With electrical
lines and without. With Forgiveness
and without. We were girls —

we were beautiful children.
For good measure, we stole apples.
We cut strands of barbed-wire

for our ponies' passage. The prow,
when there was a prow, cut through
green waters of the Indian

reservoirs where heron stopped
in spring. Sometimes the dream-mask
shifted: bone-bruise and blood-clot,

seepage. The cliffs were red clay —
folds of shadow and light, home
to small rodents. Mystery

with neither name nor notice,
brackish river, world of salt
cedar, a rot-out tree and nested.

Now, pour the honey down my throat —
thistle-ditch of darkness, dream-door
to the sun: ours, the pit and sink

to nowhere. And nowhere my blind body.

JANE MEAD

The History of Genetics

Wisdom you've forgotten —
garden of wisdom we've forgotten.
The bird in yesterday

almost the bird in tomorrow.

BRUCE BENNETT

Analogy

It's not a Cornell Box, but it is like one.
No. No. Give me a minute to explain.
What's most important is, it's all enclosed.
Everything has to fit, but be suggestive:
not just itself; itself, yet something more.
I almost said, the world. But it's a world
that's curious, peculiar, someone's life
that's odd, but recognizable, one's own.
For instance, I could mention here a glove.
A small one, black. A woman's. See? Already
you're thinking. But its story isn't here.
It's in the head, though, of the person speaking —
in this case, me. But it's a Cornell Box.
Or like one. So, *you* have that woman's glove.

BRUCE BENNETT

Ephemeral

Ephemeral? It's all ephemeral!
Suppose I write this great stuff in an email?
It's there, you read it, it will still exist,
but no one's going to see it or collect it.
It's of the moment, in the moment. Gone.
It served its purpose. That's what it was for.
Then someone will delete it. Never mind.
I've never been a great one for the notion
that we need all the intricate details
behind, about, the making of a poem.
In fact, I think we're better off without them.
The poem's what matters. It will live, or not.
The rest is inessential. We can skip it.
I mean it. Yes! You can get rid of this.

MICHAEL LEVAN

Pastimes

Nonfiction

Man may forget his Creator or hide far from his face; he may run after idols or accuse the deity of having abandoned him; yet the living and true God tirelessly calls each person to that mysterious encounter known as prayer. In prayer, the faithful God's initiative of love always comes first; our own first step is always a response.
— *The Baltimore Catechism*

No game in the world is as tidy and dramatically neat as baseball, with cause and effect, crime and punishment, motive and result, so cleanly defined.

— *Paul Gallico*

We nearly always walked through the left-most doors, the ones with the view of the blue spruce my mother had planted in memory of my aunt, her only sister, who always had cookies waiting for me and my sisters and had perfected the sugar-to-water ratio of the world's best pitcher of Kool-Aid. I'd stare at that tree as I grabbed the cold, black square of a handle and jerked the door open, propping it with my sneakered foot so everyone in my family could go in first, maybe even a few of the elderly men and women hobbling in just behind us, too, because kindness and peace were symbols for this place, or at least that was the idea. Since my parents were raised to believe in the Church, and their parents before them, I was brought up to be one more in the long line of believers holding the door open for others.

I don't remember when it was easy to walk through that door, whether it was much longer after my mom stopped bringing a sandwich bag of Cheerios, those perfect whole-grained Os, or a Matchbox car, all speed and shine with the black plastic wheels so easily bent or misshapen on our driveway after the gravel was replaced by concrete, brushed and marked off in rectangles my father would have to caulk yearly for protection from the midwestern winter or just for simple cosmetic reasons. I still don't know the cause for those repairs even now, not that I'd ever ask him, not that I shouldn't know these lessons about a driveway where rain would settle in small, splashable pools after a June thunderstorm, so many June afternoons and evenings that I spent barefoot and playing at something else, something so unquestionably childish and easy, something so unlike anything I remember about myself.

Each Sunday, after I dipped my index and middle fingers into the bowl of holy water and crossed myself, my father led us to a pew on the left, choir-side of the church, our shoes squeaking on the buffed floors while the priest was in the back organizing the slow, solemn procession of altar boys and lectors. We never sat close to the front and hardly ever in either of the center sections facing Father Baugh or Father Jaime or, God help us, Father John, whose homilies my father often fell asleep to. Sitting front and center, it was too easy to call attention to yourself and how Catholic you thought your family was, which as far as I could tell was an unforgivable sin in my parents' eyes since we were Catholic *and* from the Midwest, where modesty isn't just a virtue but an obligation.

So when my father picked a pew not too far back and not too far forward, we filed into the row. We slowly lowered the kneeler, its foam padding diminished under the weight of so many of the past fifty years' faithful that there might as well have been nothing under the black faux-leather cover. I knelt between my sisters and mother, again crossed myself, much more quickly this time, and bowed my head. When we were learning about the Mass's rituals in preparation for receiving our First Holy Communion, my second-grade teacher, Mrs. Heramb, told us we should pray for our families and ask that God fill us with His Spirit so that we could participate in the Mass fully and as a community of believers. We should ask that He help us focus our second-grade minds and hearts on the splendor and awe that was to come. Since I did have a second-grade mind and because I couldn't take much more of the padding-free kneeler, I closed my eyes tight and mouthed some serious-looking words that had more to do with debating whether the Harlem Globetrotters or the Three Stooges were the better guest stars on the *Scooby-Doo* episode I wished I was watching instead of being at Mass, pretending I understood something, anything, about the solemnity of prayer. I crossed myself again, which would not be the last or even the second-to-last time I had to do so, and sat on the lacquered wooden bench.

I got up and down as each part of the Mass demanded and mumbled through rituals I still didn't understand but knew the words to. When I wasn't doing that, I either flipped through the parish bulletin or the Saint William Church hymnal, looking for songs whose melodies I could re-create from memory after so many Sundays, and hummed them in my mind. I did whatever I could to pass the hour more quickly and to distract myself from that mix of Pine-Sol and incense that fills all Catholic churches I've ever been in, that cleansing scent floating high up to the rafters along with our Prayers of the Faithful: prayers for Our Bishop Anthony Pilla, so that he may lead his diocese with honor and grace; for peace in the former Yugoslavia and the local soldiers stationed there, that they may help to end turmoil and hatred; for the elderly of the parish, especially Noreen Murphy, for whom this Mass was being offered. So many people I never knew and never would were asking me for my prayers, whose power I never quite trusted or believed in, at least not without proof of their success, however that could be measured.

"Stay close," my father said. "And hold onto that bag."

I nodded and clutched the small, canvas duffel's two straps more tightly, but then eased my grip so I could unzip it and confirm all the contents were still inside. Brown paper bag of peanuts my father had just bought from a vendor in the parking lot we always used, check. Two rain ponchos, check. His two cheeseburgers and my hamburger from McDonald's that were all too easily sneaked in, check. My black leather mitt secured firmly around a ball with rubber bands so it would keep its shape after being neglected all winter, check. Everything was still there since I last looked a few minutes before, and another few before that.

We walked from the car and down the fifty-three steps to the pedestrian bridge we had to cross to get to Cleveland Municipal Stadium, a bridge where, here and there, I could see through the seams in the concrete to the trains rumbling underneath us. This was my routine. I didn't want to disappoint my father by forgetting anything, for one, but I was also scared of falling to the tracks below. Looking at the lake just beyond the stadium, the water reflecting the gray overcast sky, wasn't any help. So I clung to a ritual that kept me concentrating on something, anything, besides my imminent death and the smell the breeze off Lake Erie swept up, sulfur and tar with a hint of salt from the lakeshore warehouses' winter supply. Sometimes it was too much. I had to close my eyes, grab the back of my father's shirt, and get pulled into his wake as we and a modest few hundred others moved toward the Gate D box office to buy three-dollar bleacher seats. It wasn't until the salt and sulfur faded away, replaced by that too-familiar smell of popcorn and urine, that I opened my eyes. Only then was there a peace.

My father directed me to our right-field bleacher seats, though it didn't much matter what our tickets said. When a team routinely loses ninety games a year, there's not much clamor for tickets. That was the case in the early to late 1980s; the eighty-eight thousand-seat stadium only sold out for Browns games. For the Indians, an announced attendance of nine thousand was not out of the ordinary. An actual crowd of half that wasn't either, which meant the games suffered an unnatural silence. And since usually we didn't have much to cheer for, most games we could hear the beer guy over in the left-field seats call, "Beer here! *Beeeeeer here!*" from the top of the first all the way to the bottom of the ninth.

Tucked up as close to the blue, padded outfield wall as possible, eating our smuggled burgers, the bitter mustard loitering on our tongues as Joe Carter sliced an Oil Can Boyd fastball down the right-field line and chugged around first, digging for a double, there we were.

"Watch him cut that corner at first," my father said. "A good base runner is more than fast. You gotta know how to catch the inside of the bag so you can take a good angle into second. You see?"

After Carter slid safely into the bag, in the last row of the right-center field seats Jon Adams started to beat his bass drum to aid the Indians' rally, this time from a five-run deficit.

"He's been doing that since the early seventies," my father said. "I even remember him doing that when your Uncle Wally and I went to Nickel Beer Night, the game that ended cheap beer promotions in the Majors. The Indians had to forfeit after fans started throwing empties at the players and then dozens of drunks charged the field. Remember me telling you about that, right?"

I nodded slowly because, whether he knew it or not, I paid attention to what he told me about the Indians, like how on July 17, 1941, third baseman Ken Keltner caught two of Joe DiMaggio's line drives, including a screamer destined to be a double, which ended Joe D's fifty-six-game hitting streak. Or that he only took my sisters with us if Greg Swindell was pitching because he worked fast, and they had little patience. Or how the Indians' catchers had to use extra-large gloves when Tom Candiotti pitched because with a knuckleball, they never knew where it'd break. Each scrap was a fact that I thought I might be tested on later during our weekend visits to the stadium because school was still in or weeknights when summer finally came and I didn't have a game of my own.

I raised the brick-red seats on either side of me and slammed them in unison to the drumbeats, the paint falling in flakes to the discarded peanut shells and empty beer cups at our feet. My father, a man who preferred quiet, winced each time I banged the seats on either side of me, but he tolerated the noise I was making, understanding the necessity of heeding the call Adams's restless drumming made. It was part of the tradition, a way for all of us gathered to be one in our intentions, to become one in our hopes for an Indians win. When we saw Cory Snyder knock a single through the middle and then heard the quick *crack* of bat against ball meander to us soon after, we all rose and cheered as the Indians got another run closer to the Red Sox. No matter that they were still down four or that the bottom of the Indians' order was not known for its hitting, let alone its *timely* hitting, we followed custom and kept cheering as Mel Hall stepped into the batter's box, only stopping when he grounded into an inning-ending double play.

Regardless, I still believed in them. Although I hadn't been to many games, whenever my father took me, the Indians won. Not counting that one game against the Twins, of course, since we had to leave early and leaving early didn't factor into my own personal win-loss record. They were going to win. I just wasn't wishing hard enough yet.

There isn't much choice in the matter, so I turn the radio off and sit quietly in the driver's seat, while my girlfriend begins to cross herself. I hesitate at first, but after going to Catholic grade school and high school, the motion is always there, just hidden deeper in people like me.

"In the name of the Father, and of the Son, and of the Holy Spirit . . ." I trail off and let Molly direct our clearly defined appeals.

"Please, God, let us be safe and healthy and happy during our trip . . ."

I stare ahead and focus on the road, wondering if we are making good time on our way to Sand Lake for a weekend of camping with friends and waiting to put the radio back on. She knows I am someone who "grew up Catholic," the term for those of us who finally decide that the rituals, the sense of faith and community, the hour which cut into our teenage weekends wasn't worth our time anymore. Once I got my license, I didn't tell my parents I stopped going. I couldn't hurt my mother like that. Instead, the hour before I was to leave for Mass, I hid a book in the back hallway of my parents' house. When I put my shoes on, I tucked the paperback in the back of my jeans and under my shirt and walked out the door, not removing it until I had rounded the corner on my way to Jindra Park where I sat on a bench and read Zbigniew Herbert or Levis or Larkin, while, on the swings across the way, children pumped and pumped their legs, each arc sending them closer and closer to heaven with only their moms' calls for dinner able to pull them back to earth. Reading in a park was simple. Unlike so many things during that time, it didn't make me question myself.

Molly knows all this, and still she tries to get me to join her in prayer, settling at last for my silence, which could be prayer if she believed hard enough. I don't think she wants to know for certain, though, so when she says, "Amen," I cross myself again and half-smile at her. I turn the radio back on and hear the last few chords of "A Hard Rain's A-Gonna Fall," my favorite Dylan song.

I was at home the night the Major League Baseball All-Star Game was played in Jacobs Field, the Indians' new ballpark and part of the Gateway Project that led to a rebirth in downtown Cleveland. My father had tried to get tickets, but after the city spent so many years recovering from the embarrassment of the Cuyahoga River catching fire, suddenly we couldn't afford them for a game like that. Instead, we watched at home, my father spread out on the living room floor reading the paper, my mom at the dining room table, stirring her coffee as she looked through the week's ads, and me on the couch. I leaned forward when, tied one-one in the bottom of the seventh, Sandy Alomar Jr., the Indians' starting catcher, came to bat with a runner on.

As Shawn Estes paused in his windup, I whispered halfheartedly, "Wouldn't it be nice if he hit a home run?" I said it just like that, not really caring one way or the other if it actually happened, but thinking what it would be like for him, for us Cleveland fans who've suffered so long, if it did. When Alomar made contact, I knew it was gone. The ball arced just over the eighteen-foot wall in left-center and rattled around in the first row of seats. It was just about the same place my family and I sat three years before during the first season at the new ballpark when we took my aunt to her last baseball game. Manny Ramirez knocked one over the wall, and my aunt, with her easily bruised arms, ducked out of the way of the ball's parabolic trajectory, fearing the damage it would do to her body that had so quickly turned against itself. Now that I was older, I had stopped taking my mitt with us, but as the ball came closer, I hoped it'd take an unnatural curve toward me.

As Alomar rounded third and touched home, his hometown crowd chanting his name and applauding, I wanted to tell someone what I'd done. I thought better of it. My parents wouldn't have believed me, and I wasn't certain I did anything in the first place. I went over the sequence again: the windup, my *wouldn't it be nice*, the pitch, the quick crack of ash against leather, home run.

I hadn't wished hard or over and over again. I just softly spoke a question I didn't think would ever be answered.

The first time we watched *Bull Durham* together, Annie Savoy, as played by Susan Sarandon in a passable North Carolina twang, contradicted a simple truth Molly had known from childhood.

"I believe in the Church of Baseball . . . I know things. For instance, there are a hundred eight beads in a Catholic rosary and there are a hundred eight stitches in a baseball. When I learned that, I gave Jesus a chance."

"What is she talking about? There aren't a hundred eight beads on a rosary," Molly said. "There aren't!"

I trusted her faith in the rosary's workings. After all, when she was growing up, for fun, her mother quizzed her on the Baltimore Catechism, and of late, Molly had made at least a dozen rosaries for her mom, her nieces and nephews, friends, even my parents. The last time I said a rosary was years before, if not more than a decade. My mom had my sisters and me come into her room and say the Hail Marys, the Our Fathers, the Glory Bes, to help her sister recover, or at least to let her be at peace. I followed along, not quite remembering how it went. The last time I had prayed one before that, I think, was in class the week before I first had Communion. In my mom's room that day, I tried hard but could only think about how the last few times I had been asked to visit, I came up with excuses to avoid seeing my aunt, her bed sheet rising faintly and then falling over her disfigured chest, despite everything I had whispered to God in the dark of my bedroom.

I wasn't shocked by or curious about Annie's voice-over. Maybe this was because I never had a nun for a teacher, or because in grade school, class time for religion was usually spent making get-well cards for more people I never knew. We did this so often the cards became a formula: grab a black marker and draw several squiggly lines all tied together by a bow on the once-folded piece of construction paper's cover, trade the black for a blue and then a red, maybe orange and yellow if I was feeling adventurous that day, draw balloons sprouting from the ends of the strings, and fill in the inside with a generic "I hope you feel better soon. Love, Michael." I would knock out a few of these, if need be, in a matter of minutes. Though I didn't want these people to die or hurt, I didn't feel anything for them as I colored in the big, round circles. After I finished, I'd turn to my spelling book, fill in all the lessons for the next few months, and wait to be dismissed for recess and the kickball game to come.

When the number of stitches on a baseball came up, I nodded. I could have told Molly that a regulation major league baseball weighs no less than five ounces and no more than five and one-quarter ounces with a circumference of nine and one-quarter inches. I could have told her that a two-seam fastball sinks because only two seams grab hold of the light breeze it's rushing through and that, since all four of the ball's seams catch the air and generate lift, a four-seam fastball tends to float, rising higher and higher until the catcher has to pray he can get his glove on it in time.

I didn't think she'd care about any of that. "A hundred eight is way off, isn't it?" I said, faking my agreement reasonably well, I thought. I looked at her, the corners of her mouth turned down like when I hesitate answering if I'll go to church with her. Even then, I loved her, though I knew our priorities might never overlap.

Once my mom turned off the light and swung my bedroom door shut, there wasn't any more protection from the nightmares that kept me awake. I pulled the covers over my head and tucked them under my pillow, leaving only a small opening near my nose and mouth so I could breathe. I made sure every part of my body was wrapped up in the green flannel sheets my mother put on my bed during the winter or the summer's sheer cotton baseball sheets, the ones with the logos of every major league team positioned in closely packed diamonds, scenes of pitchers hunched over and following through their motions as the ball sped toward home, and others where batters watched some imaginary ball soar from the cotton on its flight to the darkness which surrounded me so cruelly and that I had to work so hard to keep out.

At eight, almost nine, I thought I was supposed to be too old to be afraid of the dark, and maybe for the sheets, too, but I didn't leave either one behind for a few more years. Each creaking of the stairs outside my door or the furnace's rumbling coming through the vents next to my bed was too much. Each night I pulled the sheet over me more tightly and went through my nighttime routine. I rushed through an Our Father and a Hail Mary, and then said the prayer to my patron saint. I kept repeating it, over and over, until I was too tired to be afraid, slipping off into a sleep that, if I had prayed right and hard enough, would be nightmare-less.

When I was old enough to need a clock radio to wake up, I prayed myself to sleep less and less. From April to October, I set the radio to "sleep," and for the next fifty-nine minutes, Herb Score and Tom Hamilton called Indians games from the Bronx, Minneapolis, and some weekends, even from Anaheim, which was so many miles away that the sun hadn't even set there yet. Sometimes, I fell asleep as Felix Fermin snared a one-hopper deep in the hole at short, turned, planted, and threw across the diamond to get Kirby Puckett by a half-step, or as the fireworks launched from the centerfield bleachers at old Municipal Stadium blossomed in red and blue asterisks high above the field to celebrate another Albert Belle homer, or, much less frequently, an Indians win. Other times, I wasn't as lucky, nodding off to a Pep Boys commercial or the hourly station identification break. But even those tedious announcements couldn't stop me from picturing each stadium's dimensions, how the outfielders shaded for the pull-hitters or the other less predictable batters who tended to hit inside the ball and shoot one to the opposite field, or all the boys and girls with their small, soft hands tucked into their mitts praying a ball, any ball, foul or fair, would come their way.

Then, like that, it was morning.

When my aunt finally died, I didn't cry. After I answered the phone and my uncle said that my mom's drive to visit my aunt was unnecessary, I just put the receiver back in its cradle. My mom had left a half hour before, and there was no way to get hold of her. I didn't tell my dad or sisters who hadn't gone with my mom either; I went back to reading the *Plain Dealer's* sports section and deciphering the previous night's box scores. The Rangers went zero for seven with runners in scoring position. The White Sox went scoreless for the first seven innings. Thirteen different cleanup batters went hitless. None of the fifteen games played ended in a shutout, but only the zeroes — the nothing they stood for — made any impression. All the anxiety and pain from seeing my aunt propped in a hospice bed in her mother's living room left me. I was hollowed out. It didn't even matter a month later when my mom, sisters, and I went to church on my aunt's birthday. Halfway through the liturgy, I heard Father Baugh say, ". . . and we remember in a special way Julia Klosowski, for whom this Mass is being offered."

My mom still wasn't cooking much, and she didn't have the energy for laundry, either. Since the funeral, she barely spoke in a whisper, and even though I didn't know when I would feel full again and that the reply being asked of me was not going to give us a tidy and dramatically neat solution for what we were all feeling, for my mom's sake, I joined her.

"Lord, hear our prayer."

"Here, Michael. Be sure to say that once a day, OK?"

I take the card from Molly's mother and examine it. On the front is a carefully rendered drawing of a young woman wearing a cream robe and a purple shawl, a gold ring circling her head. I turn it over and read, "Prayer to Saint Lucy of Syracuse, patron saint of vision and eye problems." I feel uneasy about taking the card, but I know I can't refuse it. I tuck the prayer into my shirt pocket and pat it twice. I smile and thank her again for thinking of me.

A week before, during a routine eye exam to get a prescription for new glasses, the optician had told me that the blood vessels in my right eye, and to a lesser degree in my left, were "tortuous." While I am busy setting up a second-opinion appointment with an ophthalmologist, Molly's mom thinks I should pray. I nod and thank her. She is a devout woman who has taught all of her children about faith, who goes to Bible study every Monday, and who doesn't work or shop on Sundays. Although she has never given me any reason to — in fact, she has always been especially kind and generous to me — when I am around her, I feel inferior. Only words like heathen, unbeliever, apostate come to me when I'm around her. Words that mean I am unworthy of dating her God-fearing daughter. I think of my First Communion photo my mom long displayed on the dining room bureau. Dressed in white shirt and navy pants, I am smiling at the camera, but my palms are not flat against each other in the holy pose I am instructed to keep. My fingers are bent, like I am waiting to hold something in my hands that could make me complete.

When I was sitting in the darkened examination room, red and green lights that made it easier to see the blood vessels at the back of my eyes flashing across my field of vision, it never occurred to me to pray. This is not how I deal with problems. I let them fester. Or I ignore them, hoping that they'll forget about me and move on to someone else. Or I go home and type "tortuous blood vessels eyes" in a search engine and find that, often, there is no specific pathology to the strained and twisted arteries. Sometimes, that's just how our bodies come, failing us in so many little ways.

The air is getting heavier and heavier, and I can see clouds blacker than the ones already rolling over us coming in from Lake Erie. Soon, the top of the Terminal Tower disappears, that building, my father told me, which hosted the breaking of a world record in 1938 when Ken Keltner tossed baseballs from the top floor to Pytlak and Helf, the Indians' steel-helmeted catchers, waiting on the street seven hundred eight feet below.

We are seated beneath the upper deck's overhang; I can watch the game without the worry of getting drenched. Down five in the bottom of the eighth, Travis Hafner comes to bat. Molly and some friends of ours are with us, so I am too embarrassed to say, as I usually do when the Indians are down late in the game, "Find some grass, find some grass, find some grass . . ." Since Sandy Alomar's home run, I've realized wishing for another is too much, so I only ask for singles now, maybe an occasional double, something to cut into the Tigers' lead. When Hafner flies out to center, I decide to risk it as Victor Martinez comes to the plate. "Find some grass, find some grass, find some grass . . ." I mumble under my breath, making sure that I say it low enough that each appeal will be drowned out by the last calls for beer and lemonade, the hot dogs that if not sold today will, I've been told, be held over until tomorrow's game. And then Victor gets a hit, as does Trot Nixon after him. I keep mumbling, a little louder than before, but Garko strikes out looking and Michaels flies out to center, killing the rally.

"Make a good pitch, make a good pitch, make a good pitch . . . " doesn't work either; in the top of the ninth, the Tigers tack on two more, stretching their lead to seven. When Borowski finally does get the last out, the thunderstorm begins, and the grounds crew races in from behind the center-field wall to get the tarp over the infield. Molly suggests we leave since the game's over anyway and get ice cream as we had planned. I hesitate at first. I want to stay and see how the game ends, maybe help get a few more runners across the plate. I want them to win this Sunday afternoon so that the team which has disappointed me so often over the years I should have abandoned it, if not for some midwestern sense of loyalty, if not for the love of a baseball team that's passed down from generation to generation, so often from father to son, so much of a tradition that keeps us feeling something close to whole and certain, might be rewarded.

Instead, since leaving now might keep away the hollowness I feel every time I'm part of another loss, I motion for her to get her jacket.

RACHEL FUREY

Stealing Scalpels   *Fiction*

When Mr. Lane asks if anyone knows where the scalpels are, Riley just stares back at him, at the bucket filled with frogs they would be dissecting now, if it weren't for the missing scalpels. He keeps them in the top drawer of his desk inside a small metal box. He has, or had, twenty-five of them. They are now tucked in the back of Riley's Captain Planet pencil case, under her colored pencils and crayons. She took them during lunch period, when Mr. Lane was out for a walk around the school pond, and after a fight had broken out in the cafeteria, leaving the hall monitors occupied. She could see her reflection in the scalpels. They were that shiny. She tested their sharpness, poking one against the edge of her pointer finger.

She rubs that cut now. It's not much larger than a paper cut, though a bit deeper. She rubs it while Mr. Lane stews at the front of the classroom, drawing his arms across his chest, staring out the window toward the pond, as if wondering if he could catch enough frogs from the pond for them to dissect. Riley can see it now: Mr. Lane leading them outside, giving them huge nets, telling them to wade into the pond, telling them that in order to get an A, they'd both have to catch a frog and then dissect it, successfully identifying all of the major organs.

Mr. Lane is tough. When they learned about the parts of the cell, he made Riley be the neurotransmitter, made her run all over the classroom, unaware that she had asthma. He simply told the whole class that they had to play their parts perfectly in order to get an A. Riley played her part so perfectly she ended up in Mr. Lane's arms, being carried to the nurse's office. He smelled like pickles. And fish. His chest was warm. Riley's lungs began to relax while she was in his arms, before the nurse even handed over the inhaler. Before the Albuterol flooded her lungs and left a metallic taste on her tongue. Mr. Lane had biceps so large Riley could feel the muscle flex and contract against her back when he lowered her to a chair in the nurse's office. He put a hand on her head, and smiled at her slowing wheezes. Riley wanted for him to stay and sit beside her, for him to push aside the nurse when she clamped Riley's hand over the inhaler and told her to breathe.

Now, standing at the front of the classroom, rubbing the stubble on his chin with one hand and slowly rotating a piece of chalk in the other, Mr. Lane looks just perfect under the fluorescent lighting. Not too pale. Glasses that are sleek and black, not too large the way Riley's are because her father picked them out, wanted Riley to see everything without realizing that Amanda had a designer pair in blue, or that Steven had a pair made of a special metal that allowed him to bend the frames and then watch them snap back to life. Riley's glasses are so heavy, the lenses so thick, she wears a strap around the back of her head in order to keep her glasses from falling off. The strap itches, especially in the summer. Especially on days like today, when sweat beads on her scalp.

Across the classroom, Riley's most hated classmate, Billy Miller, lowers his head to his hands and offers Mr. Lane a glare. Riley knows he loves destruction. He carves his initials into every desk he sits in. He broke the rotary saw in shop class by trying to cut a leg off one of the desks. And he always wins at dodgeball. This is probably the only day of biology class he has ever looked forward to.

Mr. Lane takes a step forward, away from the chalkboard he was leaning on, and calmly speaks. "Someone had to have taken the scalpels. I just want to know who. They're a dangerous thing to be carrying around."

Riley knows. They are tucked into her pencil case blade down. There is a piece of paper, the daily lunch note from her father, separating the scalpels from the colored pencils. Mr. Lane would be proud to see this. Deep down, he must realize that he brought this upon himself. The day they first studied frogs and he said *eco-indicator*, Riley fell instantly in love. An intimate sort of connection stirred within her. Frogs have thin skin, breathe through it. That's why they show signs of changing ecosystems before other animals do. And it's why they are dying off at alarming rates. Riley has asthma, allergies, and a poor tolerance for the cold that makes her lips and fingernails turn purple. She is lactose intolerant. She can't go anywhere without her medicine, an EpiPen, an inhaler, and a sweater. At a birthday party, a year ago, back when she was still invited to such things, more on the urging of the parents of the student rather than the actual student, she was the only girl to show up to the party with a nebulizer. Her father gave the student's mother a quick course in using it while all the girls looked on. Trina, the girl with diabetes, smiled. For the first time, she wasn't the guest requiring the most maintenance. Riley blamed her father for bringing the nebulizer, swore its presence was what brought on an attack in the middle of the night, after everyone had finally fallen asleep and the house was quiet enough for Riley's wheezing to echo through its halls. The lights flashed on. The birthday girl's mother went into action. While the chemicals drifted into Riley's lungs, taking effect at a slower rate than ever, Riley looked out at the faces of all the girls, their eyes wide. They slowly inched away from her.

"You look like an astronaut up in space. It's like you've run out of air," one of the girls said. And they all laughed, even Trina.

The frogs have taken the place of these girls that could never really be called friends. After school, Riley wades into the stream behind her house and watches them swim, their legs stretching out, their bodies easily drifting through the water. She envies the way they so easily slip out of sight under the mud, the way their shades of green range from that of a Monarch chrysalis to that of a dark pine. At night, she can hear them call, reminds herself they are small enough to hold in her hand, but sing out in chirps that carry for miles.

Mr. Lane looks from one student to another. When he gets to Riley, she keeps her gaze steady. She stops breathing, feels a trickle of sweat head down her back. But she is not who he suspects, not her — the honor roll student, the asthmatic, the gym class coward who sticks out a leg in order to get eliminated from a dodgeball game, saving her chest, her face, her glasses. Mr. Lane quickly moves on to the next student. When he gets to the last, and no one has spoken a word, he calls the principal.

When Mrs. Mitchells thunders into the classroom, her heels hit the floor so hard Riley begins to worry they might shatter the tiles. The vibrations shimmy up her chair legs and into her seat. All of Mrs. Mitchells sways to and fro under her black dress until she finally comes to a stop in the center of the room, close enough to Riley that she can make out the sweat beginning to bead on Mrs. Mitchells' forehead. The room falls silent.

In the corner, Billy Miller breaks out in a smile so wide it glows.

Mrs. Mitchells crosses the room to his desk and sets a hand on the edge of it. She grips the corner. "You want to fess up now? Or are you going to wait until we find incriminating evidence?"

Riley sinks into her chair. She plunges her hands inside her desk and fingers her pencil case. She wonders if maybe she should have buried the case. She could have walked out behind the school, stepped into the woods, and buried it deep beneath a maple tree. The rain and snow and freezes could have washed away fingerprints.

Billy doesn't budge and Mrs. Mitchells stares the class down. "Someone has to talk or I'll keep you here all day. I'll keep you after school. I'm not in any rush to get home. I have some monitors checking lockers, so if you have something stowed there, it's better to let us know now."

Her hands are still inside her desk, and Riley pops open the pencil case, slips a finger under her father's note, and tests the edge of one of the scalpels. She pulls the hand back out of her desk and squeezes the pointer finger against her thumb. She has drawn only the smallest amount of blood, but for good measure, she slips her pointer finger into her mouth and sucks.

Mrs. Mitchells fingers a silver bracelet on her wrist and continues her threats: she could take recess away from the class for the rest of the year; she could be sure they wouldn't be allowed to go on the annual field trip to the state park.

Riley supposes this should be the moment she stands, confesses to thievery, and dares to wander to the front of the room, climbing atop Mr. Lane's desk and delivering a speech on all that is wrong with dissections. At the end, she might hoist the bucket of bloated frogs onto her shoulder and lead a parade of her classmates out to the school pond where they would throw the frogs in, and Riley would hope against hope that they might spring back to life. When they didn't, it would just end up being a demonstration, like when they left a crashed car in front of the school to model the dangers of drunk driving. Herons and crows would swoop down and peck at the frogs. The organs would be eaten rather than labeled. Mr. Lane would have to acknowledge Riley in a new sort of way, see her as not simply a child with asthma, but as a strong young woman capable of standing up for what she felt was right.

But Riley can't move. Mrs. Mitchells has ordered Mr. Lane to open the lid on the bucket of frogs, and the smell of formaldehyde is filling the room. Riley's lungs begin to tie themselves in knots and she pulls her hands atop her head. She holds her breath, well aware that soon her wheezing will fill the quiet classroom and all her classmates will turn to her yet again with impatient and disgruntled looks. She squeezes her eyes shut and concentrates on making her lungs relax. She counts how many seconds she can hold her breath.

Riley has made it to eight when she hears sneakers stomp across the floor. Then liquid splashes to the floor. Amanda and Stephanie let out sharp shrieks. Riley makes it to eleven. Then drops of liquid spray against Riley's shin, the smell of formaldehyde intensifies, and Riley opens her eyes.

Billy Miller stands with one hand on the handle of the bucket, the other propping up the back of the bucket. One last frog slips out over the rim to smack onto the floor. Others are strewn across the floor, some belly-up, some head-up, their backs a slick green. The way the last frog falls makes it seem as if it's gazing right at Riley and she lets out her breath, her wheezing filling the classroom. She thinks of her inhaler on the top shelf of her locker and then how many frogs she would have to step over to get to it.

Billy makes the move to stomp a frog, but the thing is so slippery it slides under his sneaker and shoots across the floor, pinging up against Molly May's chair leg. She pulls her legs up onto her chair and lets out a small whimper. Billy goes for another, and this time makes contact. He grinds the frog into the floor and Riley watches its skin stretch out, its organs begin to spill onto the floor. She thinks she sees the liver ooze out onto one of the tiles. Frogs have large livers. She knows this the same way she knows that the small spheres spilling out beneath Billy's sneaker are eggs. Eggs that could have grown into tadpoles that could have grown into frogs.

Mr. Lane takes a step toward Billy, but when Billy peels the frog from the sole of his shoe and pushes it toward Mr. Lane, Mr. Lane backs up toward the front of the room. Billy's cheeks puff out and his face goes red. He licks his lips and sucks in a deep breath of air. "It was *me*," he says. "I stole the scalpels."

Mrs. Mitchells heads toward him and he starts picking up frogs and flinging them toward the girls in the front row. Riley feels it coming, sees it coming, but somehow can't manage to duck. The cold frog hits her in the space between her small breasts. It falls to her lap and looks up at her with dark eyes, seemingly panting out formaldehyde. Riley's lungs give up. Her wheezes become so loud even Billy stops his frog throwing long enough to stare at her. She reaches a hand toward her lap, hoping to knock the frog on the floor, but can't bring herself to touch it. She knows that to touch a frog is to endanger it; the oils on her skin can affect the frog's skin and, in turn, its breathing.

Mrs. Mitchells sets a sweaty hand on Riley's elbow, tries to ease her out of her seat. "Come on, let's go get that inhaler."

But Riley can't move. She's frozen in place, the frog cold in her lap — as heavy as a bowling ball.

The girl beside her leans over and says, "Where's your inhaler? I'll go get it."

Riley doesn't have enough air for words. If she did, she'd tell someone to lift that frog off her lap and give the poor thing a proper burial, but not anywhere near the football field, not where people spit and smoke and make out.

Mr. Lane nears Riley's desk. He pulls her chair back and then scoops her into his arms, the same way he picked her up after the neurotransmitter role became too much. The frog falls out of Riley's lap and onto the floor with a sickening thud. Mr. Lane smells like pickles again. The flannel of his shirt is soft against her cheek. She buries her head in his chest and feels her lungs begin to unknot themselves as Mr. Lane steps outside of the formaldehyde-filled classroom and into the hall. His heartbeat pounds against her shoulder. Its steady rhythm gives her hope that frog species might someday be carried like this, lifted into the arms of someone who cares, and escorted into safety, like she is now, being carried to the nurse's office where her spare inhaler will be pulled from a drawer. After two puffs, she will sit on a cot and drink a juice box, skipping gym class and dodgeball day.

After the chemicals have soothed her lungs and the juice box is gone, Riley begins to realize that Billy stole her show. She knows this should be her perfect cover. But with Billy as the perpetrator, the stolen scalpels will seem just another misdemeanor in his long chain of offenses, rather than an act of civil disobedience — a righteous boycott. While her classmates file off toward gym class, Riley takes a deep breath, heads to her desk, and grabs hold of her Captain Planet pencil case. She makes her way to Mrs. Mitchells's office. Along the way, she thinks of what she might say, wonders if she should have brought along some books from the library to back up her point about how cruel the process of dissection really is.

The principal's door is closed, and Riley knocks softly. When she receives no response, she knocks harder. Billy Miller opens the door. He reeks of formaldehyde and Riley tries not to breathe. Billy picks at frog parts stuck under his fingernails. "That was pretty good, wasn't it? I mean, that had to have been one of the coolest things I've done yet."

Riley gives Mrs. Mitchells a hard stare.

Mrs. Mitchells leans back in her chair and runs a hand along her dress. "Now, Riley, I know that dissection is important to you. You're very studious. Don't you worry. We'll get some new scalpels, since it seems Billy left them all out along the railroad tracks to see what would happen to them. You'll get to do the dissection. Now, I need to finish talking to Billy, and you should be moving on to class." She waves a hand toward the door and leans back over Billy's bulging manila file.

Riley stands in the doorway a moment, considers opening her Captain Planet pencil case to reveal the truth. She swallows. She fingers the opening latch on her pencil case. She runs her tongue along her lips, preparing to speak.

Mrs. Mitchells lets out an impatient sigh. "Is there anything else?"

Riley shakes her head, lets the hand holding the pencil case fall to her side. No matter what, there will be more scalpels. There will be another dissection.

Billy waves a hand toward the door. He breathes so heavily his breath feels like wind on Riley's face. She heads out the door, squeezing the pencil case in her hand, making her way toward gym class. As she walks, she thinks about the rainforest frogs that live high up in the canopy in order to avoid ground-dwelling predators, the way they get to perch on rubbery leaves, all the way up with the colorful parrots and toucans.

Mrs. Mitchells has told Riley that the girl's locker room meets all health standards, but Riley always feels sicker in there. Maybe it's the concrete walls, the lack of windows. Or maybe it's just the smell of prepubescent girls, some who haven't yet acquired the habit of showering on a regular basis. The floor is always cold on Riley's feet, sends chills right up to her scalp. She is always the last to change. She waits until the other girls have left and then pulls her clothes out of her backpack and stands on the wooden bench so that her feet do not touch the concrete.

Today, before she can change, she opens her Captain Planet pencil case, removes the lunch note from her father, and then takes a scalpel in her hand. It is cold in her palm, but she admires the way it shines in the overhead lighting. She gently presses it against her pointer finger and draws a small drop of blood. It makes her wonder just what the scalpel can do.

She lies back on the bench and pulls her T-shirt up. Mr. Lane said that when they dissect the frogs they have to start with the stomach. One clean cut down it, then two cuts, one on each side of the first, running perpendicular to the first. Billy Miller will only get suspended for a few days, and then he'll be back. Mrs. Mitchells will order new scalpels. The frogs *will* be dissected.

Riley slices into the skin just above her belly button. The frogs will be cut in this way, though Mr. Lane said they won't bleed the way Riley is now, the blood trickling toward the waist of her shorts. The cut does hurt, but the blood is warm and strangely comforting, and Riley is sure not to cut too deep. *You could nick an organ*, Mr. Lane warned. When she gets to the place in between her small breasts, where the skin seems thinner, she stops. She sits up and watches the stream of blood trickle toward her shorts. Against her pale skin, her blood seems bright red, the color of a radish. She wants to make the other cuts, try peeling back her skin to see what's inside of her, if there is really anything in there at all. She wants to hold her heart in her hand and feel it beat, to know it is large and strong and can carry her through anything. She wants to find her lungs and inflate them with the pump her father uses to put more air into her bicycle tires. She wants to tell her stomach and intestine that being lactose intolerant just isn't appropriate, and that a girl like her requires ice cream and chocolate to make it through life.

And then she could sew herself back up, the way her grandmother once taught her, Riley atop her lap, her grandmother smelling of lavender and tea, the pads of her fingers rough, the backs of her hands riddled with blue veins. She sewed the arm of Riley's old teddy bear back on. Other pieces of the teddy bear have fallen off since then: an eye, a leg, its nose. But that arm has held.

Riley can't make the other cuts. The blood smells sort of funny and is making her head spin. Her hands are unsteady. Her streak of bravery has run out and she wants only for the bleeding to stop. Nothing in her Captain Planet pencil case can save her. Not the glue stick, not the scotch tape, not even the small stapler, though she once saw staples in the stomach of her grandfather when she went to the hospital to visit him. They were larger, carefully placed in a way Riley knows she cannot do. In the front pocket of her backpack there is a first-aid kit, and she pulls out the gauze, running a strip of it from her chest down to her bellybutton, and then pulls out the tape and sticks the gauze in place. It doesn't take long for the blood to seep through and color the gauze.

She jogs to the row of bathroom stalls, balls up two handfuls of toilet paper, and presses them to the cut. She dizzily slips to the stall floor, blood trickling into her palms. She thinks of Mr. Lane and his flannel shirt. How good his arms would feel right now. Maybe he could lay her out on a desk, under one of those hot fluorescent lights, peel back her skin and explain to her how her organs worked, why, out of her entire class, she was the only one to suffer from asthma. Maybe he could show her the place the asthma grew from. Maybe he could begin working on a cure.

Riley balls up two more handfuls of toilet paper and stumbles back to the bench. She tapes the toilet paper in place and then pulls her shirt back on, blood immediately beginning to show through her T-shirt. She slips down the hall, one hand against the wall, leading her past the cafeteria, past Mrs. Mitchell's office and to Mr. Lane's classroom. Riley pushes open the door and is surprised to find the classroom full, Mr. Lane at the chalkboard, wildly scribbling numbers across it. It looks like the eighth grade class and one of the girls in the front row turns to see Riley first. She gasps and brings her hand to her mouth, her eyes going wide. Riley stands with one hand on the doorknob, the other on the cool metal of the doorway. Her knees begin to give way and she wants to turn and exit, wants to not have so many faces looking at her. The gasp from the first girl begins to travel the classroom until one of the boys says, "Hey, Mr. Lane, you better look at this," and Mr. Lane finally turns away from the board and his numbers.

He does not go to Riley. He turns a pale shade that reminds Riley of the underside of a toad. He slips back against the chalkboard, resting his hands in the chalk tray. The boy who spoke stands and says, "I think we should get the nurse, or call 911, or something." He turns to look at Riley. He squeezes his hands together and apart. "What the hell happened?" he asks, his voice soft and airy.

The girls shrink into their seats, some of them burying their heads in their hands.

Riley's lungs tighten. The room grows hazy. She slips to the floor. The boy who spoke rushes past her and off to the nurse's office and still Mr. Lane does not come to her aid. She presses her shirt to her chest, trying to slow the bleeding, the blood warm in her cold hands. She looks at the new white shoes her father bought her just last week, the shoes that are now spattered with small spots of blood.

When someone finally comes to sit beside her, it is Nurse Nelson. She smells like iodine and mothballs and cannot lift Riley into her arms. She pushes a large pad of gauze against Riley's abdomen. The pressure is so much that it reminds Riley of the time Billy cornered her under the playground slide and sat atop her until a monitor finally came to her rescue.

Nurse Nelson says they have to wait for the ambulance. It will be here soon. Riley's father will too.

Riley tries to gather words, but her mouth is dry.

"Ssshhhh," Nurse Nelson says. "No need to talk now. You will explain everything later."

Riley glances over at Mr. Lane. He has turned back to the chalkboard and is writing again, even though the entire class is looking at her and not him. He continues to fill the chalkboard while an ambulance pulls into the parking lot, while a team of medics roll a stretcher down the hallway, and even as Riley is lifted onto it, strapped into place, a needle poked into her arm, the world around her blurring and disappearing until the last thing she makes out is Mr. Lane's pointer finger and thumb squeezed against a piece of chalk.

KEVIN SPENST

Flutter-Stuck Flights

for Lara

Three crows perch around the rim of a basketball net.
If I stopped to teach them to fly through or just shut up,
I'd be of some use to our world so full of noisome complaints,
but I continue to walk along the path through Pandora Park.

If I stopped to teach them to fly through or just shut up,
my obsessions would leave me be and I'd relax in your company,
but I continue to walk along the path through this park.
I have an appointment with a therapist whose head angles like a bird.

My obsessions will leave me be and I'll enjoy your company,
for not all insights are reached on the mountain peaks behind me.
I have an appointment with a therapist whose head angles like a bird.
Epiphanies penciled in before lunch in a softly furnished office.

Not all insights are reached from the mountain peaks behind me.
Decisions made from within soon flutter their way without
epiphanies penciled in after lunch in a softly furnished office.
She draws a "thinking-feeling-acting" triangle that looks like a beak.

Decisions made from within soon flutter their way without
and I wonder why I'm paying a hundred dollars for doodles.
She draws a "thinking-feeling-acting" triangle that looks like a beak.
Her ever-present question chirps: does that make any sense?

I wonder why I'm paying a hundred dollars for doodles
but she wins me over within a gaze that watches with care.
Her ever-present question reassures: does this make any sense?
A problem is the world at an unexpected angle slipped into a knot.

She wins me over within a gaze that watches with care.
We must learn to fail towards perfection (if culture's taught us anything).
A problem is the world at an unexpected angle slipped into a knot.
With enough knots collected, they scaffold a fine nest.

We must learn to fail towards perfection (if culture's taught)
to be of some use to our world so full of noisome complaints.
With enough knots collected, they scaffold a fine nest.
Three crows perch around the rim of a basketball net.

Night Shifts at the Group Home

for Lily

The job was easy: I tucked
them in, kicked off my shoes, listened for
the floor to go quiet. Everyone

slept except one: outside her door,
she paced, she hummed, holding
the edge of her torn

nightgown — Pointing, I told
her: to bed. *Your* bed. But she would not
stay there. She was old,

older than my mother: manic, caught
up in gibberish, determined to sleep
on my cot —

That is how she
became a body next to mine
whether or not I wanted there to be

a body. She climbed
into my bed, and I let her
sleep hot and damp against my spine.

All night she rocked, she turned,
she poked her spastic elbows
in my calves and slurred

her broken noises in the dark. All the old
fans went round in clicks
those summer nights — and she rolled

in bed and kicked
me in the head and I was
happy. No words, no tricks,

I just didn't love
my loneliness. My mind
felt cooler
with her there. Beside
her, I could have been anyone.
She had no word for me and not the kind

of mind to keep one.
And if she kicked
me, some nights, just

for the fun of it — Who was I
to disappoint my one?
Sometimes I imagine I

was someone she won
at a fair as the wheel spun
under the floating, unfaltering sun

and clicked each lucky one
and one
until I was happily undone.

WENDY OLESON

Cotswold Cottage   *Fiction*

Every successful creature in nature respects certain laws of symmetry. A flower attracts bees with perfect petals. A red rose or a beating heart — both have reflections around one or more axes. But a Cotswold revels in its irregularity. Some rooms splay themselves open to visitors, while others, their walls sloping inward, crush the hands close to the body. Still, prospective buyers find them charming and often latch on to a particular detail — a stone chimney or built-in buffet — as though it marks the architecture with something truly homelike. "It's uncanny," they say: "I always pictured myself in a house with a fireplace like this." The imagination drops from the slate roof to the hearth; it lights a fire and conjures a family warming itself.

I thought I was lucky to have this Cotswold property listed under my name. I'd spoken to the owner over the phone, and even if the house wasn't all she'd described, she wanted far less than we could get. Money wasn't the concern, she'd said. And when I laughed she said it again, as though she sensed in my greed a Biblical offense. We decided I would visit that afternoon.

I encountered little traffic on the way and parked tightly against the curb, scraping the face of the rear passenger-side tire. I located the house number. From the safety of my car, I met tiny, reptilian eyes set in the windows' dry sockets; Cotswolds don't offer much light. After a moment, I realized someone truly was gazing back at me. The old woman watched me leave the car. She assessed my gait as I approached. Even from a distance, I saw her press the tips of her thumbs together, then touch the glass with her fingertips. Her hands could have formed a butterfly, but somehow I knew she was making a ribcage. With a chill it occurred to me that she was protecting something inside that house, and before I could push the thought away, I wondered how on earth she would manage to leave it.

A lovely commission, I consoled myself. A generous commission could more than make up for my trouble — whatever trouble a woman in her eighties could give a man like me. I did not consider myself greedy (not Biblically so); but I had a lover, and lately our bed had been cold. I sensed I might be participating in a relationship more triangular than I cared for. I wanted to buy a ring: white gold — a metal as pure as my heart, as true and polished as a mirror. I would buy rings for us both. I would give myself up and expect the same, and all I had to do was sell a perfectly charming Cotswold Cottage.

A gray dog greeted me. Only at first glance, I thought I'd seen a goat. I'd had a Labrador as a child, but this was not a Labrador. It was furless but for dark tufts on its head and along its tail. Slate-colored skin with terrible pigment-less legs — legs mottled like the skin of a burn victim. And haunches smooth as the stone of a gargoyle.

This is Rafael.

The old woman's voice calmed me at once, a clear stream in which I would have liked to dip my hand.

Usually, he won't let men into the house, she said, smiling. But you are a different kind, and I can already see he likes you quite well. She was tiny — the crown of her head reaching well below my shoulder. Your name? She cleared her throat. I've already forgotten.

I could have been anyone. I reached out my hand — her fingers were so slight, bones like the ribs of a chicken. Daniel, I said.

She had let me into this house to tell a story, to be unburdened by it. Once she opened the door for me, she thought I wouldn't be able to escape. It would bring me down like stones in pockets sewn shut. But I've done my best to record her words. Fear has opened my mouth. It moves my jaw and vibrates my throat. It unites paper and pen.

A beautiful house, she began.

I hope I can make you see.

A beautiful house, the kind that charms children in fairy tales — still, I'd like to be rid of it. He dropped it on me as though I were a witch. A fine thing to do to one's mother! Were the circumstances different, I'd stand an easel in the second bedroom. Or spend evenings on the porch. I would stay because I have almost grown accustomed to the neighborhood, and even the cottage's tiny windows, stingy with the light, don't bother me like they used to.

Let me take your coat, Daniel. I can show you the closet. (I do apologize for the boxes, but those things don't belong to me.) Notice the woodwork — not a single scuff. Do you plan to take notes?

How did I end up here? Lost in someone else's house? My husband died suddenly. My only son, Nathaniel, unable to bear the thought of his mother living alone, begged me to cross desert mountains to join him in his perfect Cotswold Cottage. The wheel turned; I sold the family home in Cleveland, and since I had never much guarded possessions — my life had always been about the living — I packed a suitcase and my late husband's Army canvas and boarded a plane for California.

I arrived with a dry mouth. Nathaniel found me at the curb. Because he hadn't bothered to meet me inside the airport, I had to carry my suitcase and my late husband's Army canvas. Were it not for a kind young woman who slung the canvas over her shoulder, I might not have made it to Nathaniel's car.

Perhaps that wouldn't have been such a terrible fate.

That's my Nathaniel, I told the girl. The gray car.

With the dog? she asked. That's when I saw it — in the passenger seat of the Honda — sitting like an Egyptian statue.

My son looked past the dog to me. I looked at him; I looked at the dog. The dog. A security officer stepped over, asked if I needed help. The man encouraged us to be quick. This was passenger loading, he reminded. At that my son scooped up my bags, thanked the girl, and put a thin arm around my shoulders.

I didn't want to embrace; I wanted to sit down. The animal, however, still occupied my seat. Rafael, Nathaniel said. To the back. But the dog intended to stay. It refused to look at me. I refused to sit in the back of the car as though I were being chauffeured by my own son! The security guard again reminded us to hurry. Nathaniel murmured into a leathery ear, and only then did the creature stagger to the backseat.

I watched the dog's reflection in the vanity mirror. Its brow and haughty snout so resembled my late mother-in-law, I'm afraid my own lip began to curl. The tuft of fur at the crown of its head was, of course, ridiculous.

You didn't tell me you had a dog, I said, folding my hands over the purse on my lap. I might have been warned. When he didn't answer I continued, still keeping my eye on the dog that was now watching the back of my son's skull. Nathan, you never seemed to get on with Cobbler. (Cobbler, our long-dead miniature apricot poodle, had always slept in Nathaniel's sister's bed.)

The dog belongs to Miguel.

Miguel was or had been Nathaniel's lover. He'd never said it, but that much I knew. Still, I hadn't heard him speak of Miguel in a while — neither at his father's funeral, nor his sister's. Well, if this is Miguel's dog — the dog snapped his head toward me, and our eyes met in the mirror — where is Miguel?

Look at me, Mom. Nathaniel took his gaze from the road. His eyes appeared more deeply set than before. Miguel's not here right now. It's possible he returned to Peru.

Possible? I asked. Without the dog?

The dog was honored there, back in Miguel's hometown. The people celebrated in his name every ten years.

Every ten years? Dog years, you mean?

Nathaniel shrugged his shoulders. He'd never been a fluent Spanish speaker. Certainly, something was lost in translation.

We drove until the sun had set, and when we arrived, the dog was pleased to be home. It did not, however, appear pleased by the scent of my luggage. I tried to ignore the animal long enough to appreciate all the cottage's stonework. Of course you knew to expect the beautiful exterior, Daniel. It's a Cotswold. It could have been transplanted right from the English countryside, wouldn't you say?

Anyway, once my son led me inside the cottage, he looked terribly thin. In the weeks that followed, I roasted chickens and stuffed peppers for my son. Unknowingly, I cooked for the dog. Now, come, Daniel, let me show you the dining room. The paper on the east wall is peeling, but this wall is entirely stone. Here, we ate well; Nathaniel gained some weight back, and I insisted we light candles during our evening meals. We learned to gorge, then rest languidly at the table. The dog relaxed his watch over me; he collapsed at Nathaniel's feet at night, and occasionally, I saw his tongue loll. Cozy and perfect were our repasts, save for a draft, which would announce itself now and then by blowing out our candles. I blamed the old windows — see, the panes are tiny as squares on a checkerboard — and draped myself in another sweater or blanket.

I suppose I should have found it queerer than I first did, but once, when I left the table to fetch a cardigan between courses, I returned to find the dog fully clothed. He stood right there in the limen, between dining area and kitchen, wearing a pair of purple silk pajamas. How Nathaniel managed to dress a dog in a man's clothes in the time I took to slip on a sweater I will never understand. Some things shouldn't be understood. The dog's barrel chest showcased the garment's monogrammed pocket: MCH. "Those aren't his initials," I managed, but Nathaniel just laughed. We'd been enjoying an inky Malbec — had even opened a second bottle (truly a rare indulgence) — and perhaps neither of us was thinking quite right. That was the evening I first noticed the hint of blue on my boy's lips.

But I'm getting ahead of myself. You're here to see the house. Come along with me.

Don't mind the creaking of the stairs — how this house aches and moans! I've taken the guestroom, here, at the top of the stairs. Dark curtains over a small window. I imagine the cream-colored carpet and walls will be a selling point — nothing too peculiar or loud — and perhaps it's fairly new? The ceiling reflects the slope of the roof, and though it takes away some of the space, it's been enough for me. That, next to the bed, is the dog's mattress. I believe my son purchased it from a catalog.

When — if — I sleep, I fall into bed alone. In the morning I wake with my body pressed against another. Not a crime, sleeping with a dog, still my hands shake to be telling you. Heavy and warm, he drools in his sleep, wet breath, a halo around his muzzle. He discolors the sheets, but I don't believe he would urinate there, not in the bed. Animals, even domesticated ones, know they must hide signs of themselves, their excretions and vulnerabilities. I often wake to a whimpering against my neck. Even large creatures whimper. It is a terrible sound that infects one's dreams.

The closet would be enough space for my clothing, to be sure, but I prefer to use this wardrobe. We had two of these in our family, twins. My father transported my grandfather's body from Algeria to Long Island in a wardrobe just like this one. It had been out of necessity, but I suppose it wasn't such a horrible box to lie in: carved mahogany, Rococo in its intricacies. Ripe after the journey, the wardrobe and my grandfather were never to be parted. I will leave my wardrobe (provided it doesn't contain my remains) for the cottage's future inhabitants. I am the end of the family line; I certainly don't have the energy or the means to take it with me.

As I ease on my clothes each morning, the dog watches me. His life has come unhinged, and change has the potential to drive creatures of habit mad. Living with me was not the arrangement he intended. I stand by the window to dress, turning away from him.

I left him outside one night. His crying had upset me. I hoped he would run away. But he waited by the door, even stood on his back legs to watch me through the window. Could I not be alone in my thoughts? The dog could smell the grief and fear on me, and I could see the way emotions weighted him. His back bowed toward the ground, something like grief swaddling his body like a wet undercoat. He can smell a million of Nathaniel's ancient footfalls. Layer upon layer of absence. He seeks Nathaniel in the mist of the shower. I think he sees him in the clouds against the mirror. He hears him in the whistle of the teapot.

In this corridor I steamed away the wallpaper and found a layer of flowers running floor to ceiling. Nothing filled me with a greater sense of purpose than when the paper began to wrinkle and sag, and I could pull away the delicate skin. When I removed the second layer of paper, I found nothing. Tired, I left a gash in the wall. That night the animal disappeared. I rustled the blankets without finding him. I walked around the bed but found only a bathrobe. I noticed shadows on the wall, my tired mind trading logic for whimsy. I lay in bed remembering the last months of my son's life. I called the animal's name: Rafael, what have you done with my son?

I've told you about the evening Nathaniel dressed the dog in silk pajamas? After that night, Nathaniel never returned to the dining table. As his mother, I saw he was sick; I smelled it. His health did not improve no matter how many pills I pushed to his lips. It was too late. He soaked his bedclothes when he slept. And he coughed, and the dog became a terrific nuisance, always underfoot in the bedroom, refusing to leave Nathaniel's side. A sorrow had descended over us, a mood matched by the unusually rainy summer. The roads often flooded. If we had wanted to leave that house, how could we? I didn't drive, Nathaniel was in no condition, and we certainly didn't trust the bus that careened past our window. While Nathaniel slept, I sat in the parlor. I stitched and rocked in the parlor because his constant fever drove him to hostility. Nathaniel angered at my presence. He preferred space and Rafael enforced this; he growled if I came too close.

I asked if Miguel would return. Could I contact him? Perhaps he could help us? I imagined the Peruvian mountains while I knitted. I imagined the Peruvian sky. I had no such frame of reference but nevertheless filled my mind with cloudless heavens, warm brown rock, and a sun turgid as a new bulb. And then I imagined Pompeii, where Nathaniel's father and I went for our honeymoon. We'd intended to stay in Rome, but the train took us further south.

Can't we find Miguel, Nathaniel? I will search for him.

My son told me I didn't know where to look, that I wouldn't be able to find him even if he was staring me in the face. He said this with anger in his voice; he sounded almost crazed, evil. It is a shame the way things end sometimes. I lost a daughter to the Atlantic — it swallowed her up — no chance to say goodbye. The abrupt endings for Nathaniel's father and sister hurt me both more and less. No final, living embrace, yet there was a rhythm to their deaths I could understand. I found a logic, tight as the stitches I made each night, that comforted me. His sister had salt water in her blood; she preferred that weightless underworld. His father died while rowing across the ocean of his love for me.

Let me take you to the brightest room in the house. Of course, it should be bright to inspire the chef. These counters are Venetian marble; I like to stare into their metallic stipple. There, I've found a galaxy — by the sink is the constellation of our family: my husband, daughter, and son, bright and sparkling as Orion's belt. Nathaniel used to grow plants on the ledge. It's a perfect western exposure for a pathos with all its sprawling hearts. But Rafael slips on the kitchen floor, a creamy tile, always cold. Shifting ceramic slabs, they challenge him as though he were a bear dancing in the circus.

His gaze peers level with the counter. He watches me slice tomatoes, apples, plums; they grow wild to my hands. Behind the house there's a garden you wouldn't believe. He watches me eat. The pantry door whines on its tracks, but it's large enough to accommodate one hundred pounds of dog food — were he content to eat it. *You are mine*, I say to him when I feel his nose against my hip. *We are the last of the living*, I reply, my fork touching the side of the plate. We chew slowly. He chews slowly — I never imagined an animal could. He chews and meets my eyes, and I might feel love for him if I didn't grow afraid.

At this kitchen table in the perfect breakfast nook, I take pills with milk and he with cheese. Nathaniel once told me the animal prefers Havarti to cheddar and anything to Swiss, but it unsettles me to indulge these preferences. If I've misjudged my appetite, I might lower my plate to the floor, ask him to take it. He sniffs at it, licks it with the tip of his tongue and turns his head away. You must be hungrier than that, I think. Just to survive, you must eat more than you let me see. But he is right not to show his appetite. It would anger me, his hunger, any desire to live and grow stronger.

Do you see how beautiful it is outside? A wall of roses to the east and birds-of-paradise growing against the stucco all around. And there are the flowers — green, succulent, and bursting at the heart — which I can't name. Maybe you've seen them before? Please, when we return inside, take one of the knives from the counter. Cut anything you'd like; we have vases to spare. This yard, though small, provides me with a perfect sanctuary. I can trust the foliage to bloom and die according to nature's design — a comfort.

About the neighborhood, however, I feel differently. We leave the yard because Rafael must walk. The dew is cold to his feet, and I sometimes catch myself thinking he is brave to step out into the world. From this street the sky is never blue. We live under a gray sky, and it matches the pavement. Our sky is littered with stones. In the early morning Rafael breaks spider webs spun between trees and front fences. A spider crawls up my coat sleeve. Webs cling to my arms: light, silky and sly, what one gathers from this world when passing into the next. The leanest webs are tethered from branches to branches, bushes to mailboxes. The ladies spin quickly when it's dark.

We turn the corner and see a young man standing in the street. I tell myself he's an apparition so I won't worry or wonder why he won't wait closer to the curb. His light, wavy hair meets his shoulders, his foppish arms akimbo. The strap of a black satchel twists across his chest. Rafael looks to me, imploring me to walk faster so he can approach the beautiful boy. He smells him in the distance, and he whimpers and oofs, turning his head back, showing me the whites of his eyes. Since the young man — is he yet eighteen? — is neither specter nor photograph, he reminds me of a poem. I close my eyes and the world drops dead. Only it is when I open my eyes that I feel death's tether leading me.

Even when it rains, Rafael wants to go out of doors. I put on a navy slicker and tie a plastic handkerchief around my head. We embark, but I'm wet even before we pass the orange trees at the end of the block. We return, and the animal gives off a scent: heavy leaves, wood soaked to breaking. His body curls. He even wraps his tail around his head. I sit in a wooden chair. I want to tell you that I always build a fire, that when rain penetrates us both, we sit by the fire to regain our civility.

I touch him with my ankle while I knit. The sound of the stitches clinging to each other sends him into sleep. While we rest in the drawing room, we do not appreciate the telephone's ring. It pricks our ears and waters our eyes. It beats our hearts too quickly. The shrill voices ask to speak with my dead son. They sound as though they have never spent a day staring at the ceiling. I ask them to stop sending things. More solicitations arrive.

Maybe you've seen enough. But you know there is another room: the master bedroom, the heart of the house. Nathaniel told me that last summer he found a white spider in the southwest corner. He blinked to be sure he wasn't seeing reality's negative image. He coaxed the spider onto his palm, cupped her, managed to open the window, and transplanted her into the dew-slick grass under the roses. Her life could be fruitful there, without Rafael nosing around her web. Nathaniel told me this the night I pretended he wasn't my baby. I was there for someone else's child, not mine. I sat outside his door waiting. My eyes burnished the gaps between the planks of the wood floor. I tried to erase my son from my memory: first as an infant, then a boy, and finally the man with death in the reservoirs of his brain. He'd gotten caught up in something I could not understand. My Nathaniel's soul was stitched with threads of silk, full of grace, though not strong enough.

Nathaniel died in this house. And the dog watched. I am sick.

The master bath. Wait, I won't open the door. Not yet. I've spent hours on my knees effacing trails of blood. Rafael bled all morning. Despite the bandage I fashioned with a green kitchen cloth, he painted a trail of blood from the bathroom to the bedroom and back again. I worried I could fill measuring cups with his spilled blood. My first instinct was to save as much as I could — I am a mother, above all. I told him I was sorry he was hurting. He gazed back at me, his eyes evolving into the perfect reflection of my own, the distinctly human marriage of sorrow and shame that prevents us from scrubbing our souls clean.

I had made him bleed. I had cut him. His nails were curling toward the ground; I'd found clippers in the cupboard and waited till he lay down on the rug. Easing my body to the floor took time — I imagined sinking into liquid, a warm bath. I held his paw in my hand. It weighed as much as the ruby grapefruits growing over the neighbor's fence into our yard. Even as I held his paw he slept. I imagined going barefoot like that, constantly pressing my soul to the ground. The blade snapped shut and he wailed — an unearthly pitch — his throat ripped away from a dream.

I coaxed him through the bedroom, over the blue tiles, and into the porcelain bathtub. I left him there and went to get the rags. A dog guides the soul through the underworld, I recalled. A dog helps the dead cross the river. When I returned to the bathroom, when I saw it, I crumpled to the floor. I couldn't breathe.

She opened the door for me. A white claw foot tub. But inside its belly — she pulled at my jacket with surprising force —
Look.
The crimson prints of bloody hands.
See, see?
She pressed her palm against the porcelain.
These are not my hands.

JASON ROUSH

Ezekiel in the Enormous Room

Everywhere that I'd seen him before
— in every restaurant, in every club —
he was the one treasure in a sea of trash;

in his pink polo shirt, he'd shone without
trying, age 21, lingering in the liminal zone
of early manhood, boyishly muscular. Now,

sitting beside me in the Enormous Room,
sipping a lime martini, his thigh against mine,
it's as if he'd been *poured* into his clothes,

blue jeans and navy blue polo, hugging
each muscled curve just snugly enough:
molten bronze that's cooled and hardened.

Studiously, he leans over to inquire about
the difference between modernism and post-,
his arm resting across the back of the sofa

behind me, and when I ease myself back
against it, he doesn't flinch, holding me up
intimately for a moment while I prepare

to propose an explanation to his question.
So much his strength is holding, and holding
onto — holding away, and holding apart.

The Faeries, Waking

Beneath the last lit constellation,
our tents pitched off-kilter drift

through the gently revolving night,
each one a starless satellite, unnamed.

We wake up early to watch the edges
of the eastern sky spread in blue bands,

radial above the summer tree line
an hour before daybreak. By sunrise,

the earth's paths will be more alive
than they've been for many months.

SHARON OARD WARNER

Whatever's Good Will Be Gone

Fiction

Jack breaks the news within minutes of making love, his words coming out between soft little pants: "Maybe . . . sweetie . . . we've . . . got . . . to . . . talk."

Both of us are stretched out on our backs, ample bellies rising and falling, eyes on the white ceiling. For a woman in middle age, I have good stamina, but Jack is heavy, and it only works for us when he's on top. Halfway through, I feel lightheaded, as though I can't suck enough air into my lungs; afterwards, I'm bushed.

"You still with us?" Jack asks me.

I say out loud what I've just been thinking: "Damned if I'm not alive."

"You sound surprised."

"I am."

This Friday afternoon tryst will go down as our eighteenth. I keep track in a cheap Hallmark date book, marking the days we have sex with a small round O. Why an O? Why not a J or an S or an F? I have no idea. It's certainly not an O for orgasm because I rarely have one of those. As an LPN, I was trained in recordkeeping. In my father's last days, I took notes on water intake and transcribed his last word, which was "boy." It doesn't do to rely on memory — memory is flimsy.

For instance, I remember that Jack and I met in the hallway of the apartment building in midsummer, but I can't be more precise because I didn't write it down. I was hauling in groceries as he was carrying in boxes, the kind you rummage for in dumpsters. The lids had been neatly sliced off, so the contents were heaped up and out in plain sight, no rhyme or reason to the packing, a sock draped over a sauté pan, that sort of thing. Right away, I figured he was running out on a marriage, or maybe just taking a breather because he was still wearing his ring.

My father had only been dead for a matter of days, and I wasn't feeling particularly sociable. So I closed the door and forgot all about my new neighbor, until he knocked on my door one Saturday evening in August. Wanted to borrow my microwave to pop some corn, he said. Afterward, the air in my kitchen smelled heavenly, and he invited me over to watch the Lobos lose their first game. According to my Hallmark calendar, that would have been nearly seven months ago.

Now, he clears his throat and tries again: "Something I need to tell you, Maybe baby."

I brace myself for what's coming — curl my toes beneath the sheet and tell myself an obvious untruth: *You were fine before he came into your life, and you will be fine afterward.*

But what he says next is entirely unexpected: "Sophie's pregnant." Sophie is Jack's teenage daughter, his precocious and smart-alecky seventeen-year-old.

Relief sweeps over me, more satisfying than any orgasm, but to show such happiness is unseemly. Instead, I ask how far along she is. Jack doesn't know. It didn't occur to him to ask. "Peggy must have some idea," he says. "She's the one who told me. At first I didn't much believe it."

"Of course you didn't," I soothe, "it's hard to think of your daughter as a sexual being."

"That's not it. I know that Sophie is a sexual being. I'm not blind. But I also know that Peggy is a worrywart. She concocts problems out of thin air."

"But not in this case," I say.

"No, not in this case," he replies.

When Jack dozes off for a few minutes, I return in my head to the classifieds. Fridays I scour the ads, looking for the likely sale. Estate sales and divorce sales are tops on the list, but part of town is important, too. By and large, I stick to the older, more established areas: the Northeast Heights, Los Ranchos de Albuquerque, and certain parts of downtown. February tends to be lean pickings. The only intriguing ad in today's paper is for a WIDOW'S SALE. The address is in the North Valley, where Jack's family lives.

"Feel like a movie?" I ask when he wakes.

"I don't know what to do," he grumbles, but he isn't talking about our plans for the evening. He's still on the subject of Sophie. "Should I give her some advice?"

"Well yeah, Jack. But I'm not the best person to ask."

"Why not?"

"For one thing, I've never been a parent."

"Count your lucky stars."

He rolls away, and my gaze roams over the naked expanse of his back, stopping at the nest of soft hair that sprouts from his sacrum before moving on again, to his shoulders, which are hunched and no doubt tight and sore. "Poor sweetie." I scoot closer, plant my strong, speckled hands to either side of his neck, and knead the knots with my fingers.

He sighs, then moans in gratitude. "Maybe, sweetheart. You always know just what I want."

"It's not hard," I reply. Men want touch and women want talk, as any nurse worth her salt knows. "It's not hard at all."

Then he's out with it: "If she's going to insist on this pregnancy — " his voice travels around the room before coming back to me — "I may have to move back home."

Right then and there, I want to wring his neck. "What did you say?" I ask, but I heard him; I heard him all right.

"Just for a little while."

I don't trust myself to speak. A tear trickles over the bridge of my nose and drops on the crocheted pillowcase, a beautiful piece of handwork that I would never have considered using if it weren't for Jack. Has he noticed the luxurious bed I created for him from the linens of dead rich people? Probably not.

We've gone from happy to horrible in a heartbeat. On his way out the door, Jack curses loudly, and I realize he's done it again: banged his hip against the corner of the claw foot table, my most recent acquisition.

Having started life in a hunting lodge in New England, the table is now wedged into this one-bedroom apartment in Albuquerque, New Mexico. We all have our come-downs to suffer, but the table has fallen hard. If retail space in Santa Fe weren't so expensive, I'm sure I would have placed it with a dealer. As it is, the table takes up every inch of my available dining room space and most of the hallway. For the time being, I make use of it myself; it's here that I spread the classifieds and take my meals.

When it comes to sales — garage, yard, or estate — early arrival is all. Don't bother to show up late because whatever's good will be gone. Pickers adhere to this rule, me included. But it's not fail-safe, you see. People don't necessarily recognize what's good or valuable. If they did, they wouldn't throw out their treasures in the first place.

As I head out the next morning, I cross the hall and press my palm against the varnished surface of Jack's door. As usual, it's chilly to the touch. It doesn't reveal whether Jack's inside or not, but I like to take a guess, and generally I'm right. This morning, I imagine him sitting on the toilet, reading one of his many issues of *National Geographic*, and am thus able to leave the building with a smile on my face.

Outside, the winter sky is a pale blue streaked by cirrus clouds, the air chilly but dry. Our mountain range to the east often gets snow when the city doesn't, but this winter Sandia has rarely been capped by white. It's been a dry year in a dry decade, and not for the first time I wonder whether human beings should build cities where there's not enough water to support them. My father called it tomfoolery, though he enjoyed the golf courses and blue skies as much as any of them. While he was dying, he would gaze out the window and remark, "Good day for golf," before drifting off to sleep.

Although the lot in front of our building is nearly full, the space where Jack parks his dusty Subaru wagon is empty — so much for my ability to take a temperature. This absence means nothing because I know he's not yet gone for good, but my heart lurches nonetheless.

When my father died, he left me his truck, and it's better for picking than the Dodge Caravan I used to drive. These days, I make more spur-of-the-moment buys, it's true, and some of them have been too big to fit in the truck. That's why I've made a rule for myself: whatever I buy and don't sell to a dealer must fit into my apartment. No renting storage lockers; no furniture hoarding, which is not to say that I haven't considered moving to a bigger place. The day Sophie knocked on my door I was scouring the classifieds for a two-bedroom.

Driving across town I recall what I can of that one encounter, which took place before the first O in the Hallmark date book, before I had any interest or investment in the Granger family. She was distressed. Her green eyes were bloodshot, and she sniffed loudly. "Need a Kleenex?" I asked. She waited at the open door while I pulled a few from the box in the bathroom and thanked me in the absentminded way of children. I'd already closed my door, but I heard Jack greet his daughter and Sophie's outburst: "Why don't you come home?"

The widow's house is within a mile of Jack's place, and when I reach the intersection of Fourth and Solar, I give way to curiosity and yearning. *What need have I for another piece of junk?* I ask myself. *None at all*, I reply. For a good half-hour I circle the bordering streets, getting a feel for the neighborhood. Stucco and pueblo-style homes mingle with the occasional brick colonial, all of them set back from the street. It's the sort of neighborhood that warms a picker's heart, well established, with mature trees and expansive front yards, most covered in dormant grass rather than gravel. The people who live in these houses pass down their possessions and tend to them with care.

In an effort to glimpse Jack's place from a safe distance, I turn into what I suppose is an alley and am immediately startled by a pair of longneck geese, stretching their snaky heads over a shambling picket fence and honking for all they're worth. That's the way of things in Albuquerque: roosters are common in the older neighborhoods, and so are goats. Given sufficient acreage, your next-door neighbors may have horses. I've seen llamas, and on the north end of Rio Grande, buffalo. Hell, Jack keeps bees, and he lives a stone's throw from Wendy's.

Full of potholes, the alleyway soon turns into the road that leads to Jack's house. It's set back from its surroundings and situated on at least an acre. What I notice first about the Granger place is its pitched tin roof, but then I take note of the long covered porch. Jack has told me about his home: the original owners were transplants from Dixon in northern New Mexico. Out of yearning for their own landscape, they planted a cluster of piñon trees at the east end of the house and a row of apple trees behind the garage. This time of the year, it's hard to see the point, everything so dry and dreary, but in the summertime it must be beautiful.

Next, I notice the wide-open door on the second floor, painted blue-green and yawning into empty space. Then I spot the telescope, glinting gold in the weak winter sunshine. I bid on and bought that telescope on eBay, a birthday present for Ian, Jack's son. Just now, it stands untended in the doorway, but Jack swears that Ian loves it.

The telescope came complete with the box and the instructions, absolutely as good as new. Certain things you should never pay full price for: telescopes, exercise equipment, and bridal gowns are all easy as pie to come by. You've got your pick of them. People like to imagine themselves as stargazers, but when it comes down to it, they aren't up to the task — getting up in the dead of night and screwing with a delicate piece of machinery, in the dark no less.

Too late, I realize that this gravel road I'm headed down dead-ends in the Granger's driveway. But I don't regret the mistake; if I hadn't gone the distance, I wouldn't have spotted Jack's wagon parked just off the gravel road, and he wouldn't have seen me. Really, we both needed to take sight of one another in the clear light of day. At least, this is what I told myself then and tell myself now.

He didn't need to come out of the house, but he did, and when he saw me there in his driveway, hunkered down behind my daddy's steering wheel, he stopped dead in his tracks. His sour expression was my cue to haul ass, but my foot slipped off the clutch, the truck bucked, lurched, and finally shuddered to a quick and noisy death. All the while I turned my key in the ignition and revved the engine, he waved me on, nothing friendly or welcoming. This was a shooing, get-the-hell-out-of-here gesture. I left as fast as I could.

A week passes, during which I don't hear a word from him, not even when I buy the armoire and stow it in his apartment. Our amiable apartment manager is only too happy to unlock the door for me, and, when he does, I can see that Jack is already in the process of clearing out. Once or twice I hear Jack coming and going with someone, maybe Ian. I consider poking my head out to say a simple hello, but the memory of his shooing me away keeps me hidden on the other side of the door.

On a Saturday morning at the end of the month, I return from my usual round of sales to find a slip of paper taped to my door: "Meet me for drinks at the Diner?"

Thank goodness, I think, *we'll have a chance at goodbye.*

The Route 66 Diner is down the road, a square white cinderblock building adorned with an excess of neon, most of it pink. The fifties color scheme — pink and turquoise and black — is offset with chrome, and I can't tolerate the place unless I'm seated in a window booth. There, I can watch the cars roaring up Central Avenue, headed east to the University of New Mexico or west to downtown. Most Sundays, the sidewalk is busy with mothers pushing strollers, homeless gentlemen wheeling grocery carts, and the occasional weekend student bent nearly double by a book-heavy backpack. No one walks empty-handed. Everyone has a burden of some sort.

Jack arrives ahead of me. I find him at our booth, wearing the red flannel shirt I gave him for Christmas. He's already ordered for us. I've no more than slid into the booth when the waitress delivers our malts — chocolate for him and strawberry for me. This is our version of going out for drinks. A little sweetness loosens our tongues better than beer.

"That's a nice piece of furniture you left in my place," Jack says, "but you're going to have to move it come the end of the month."

He doesn't use a straw. He prefers bringing the glass to his lips and licking the thick sweetness off his mustache with the tip of his tongue. He tends to make a mess. Myself, I bend to the straw and suck. Soon, I am rewarded with a mouthful of sweet cream and strawberries. Back when I was sixteen and miserably pregnant, I was especially fond of strawberry ice cream. I couldn't get enough of it.

"That armoire is not just nice," I say, "it's beautiful, and it would be really valuable if someone hadn't sawed off the feet. Can you believe people do things like that? Makes me think of the way people will chop off a dog's tail, cruel and entirely pointless."

Jack gives me one of his curious looks. "Like I said, you'll need to get the armoire a new home in a few short days."

I concentrate on the task at hand, sucking at my straw. Then, when I've had my fill of sweetness, I answer: "The armoire is for Sophie, Jack. An expectant mother needs a place to store things."

He peers at me across the table, uncomprehending.

"It's true I was never a parent," I explain. "But when I was a girl just Sophie's age, I was a mother for all of nine months and three days."

"You gave up the baby?"

"It was taken from me, Jack. Don't you remember what happened to girls who got in a bad way? They went to the Home. Mine was Catholic, and they preached forgetfulness."

"Forgiveness?"

"*Forgetfulness*. They knocked me out for the labor, and when I came to, the baby was gone. Out of kindness, they refused to tell me anything at all."

"You don't know anything?"

I think of my father's last word, neatly transcribed into my datebook. I could share it with Jack, but I don't. Instead, I reach across the table and grab his hand. He squeezes back hard, his fingers sticky. If I were to lick them right now, they'd be wonderfully sweet.

ROGER REEVES

In Adjuntas

The hen's breath still stuck to the down
beneath its wing. The boat attached to the fog
and quivering. The dead in the un-drunk coffee
forming rings on a red table covered in debt
and odes once sung to a morning bird in a boy's mouth.
If the dirt beneath this valley slides into the river,
as it surely will take the lives above and beneath it,
forgive your son's ghost for fighting the moonlight coming through the pines. He understands
very little of the fire you put his body in,
the ash tray you fill with sorrow, the priest
filling the church with smoke and tongues.
The dead are a rough animal with very little grace.

ROGER REEVES

Self-Portrait as Duchenne at La Salpêtrière

I carry no box of electric to shock the deaf
into hearing. I practice insanity to hold my sons
close. How many arch-dukes die at the hooves
of their own kingdom? I propose gunpowder
with every meal to stave off the mumps and war.
When treating madness, place a blindfold
over the moon rising above the nation.
If the asylum refuses you admittance, go
to the statehouse and call yourself the elect.
Carry nothing that cannot fail in winter. Often,
I carry the stars of madness home with a pinch
of honey. Bees are the only fruit of my kingdom.

ROGER REEVES

Sisters of Perpetual Indulgence,

The three coins of immunity bear no resemblance
to the three coins of hunger. Give the famished
what the saint refuses and watch a new saint rise
faster than the bearded monkeys climb the temple walls.
I have no wisdom beyond the boy who keeps his hunger
hidden behind his back and January on an answering machine.
Nothing goes on longer than a heron pulling its red
legs from the mud beneath a salt flat given over
to herons. When I kissed the old woman's cheeks,
I tried to leave what little honey I had eaten that morning.
Out beyond the pasture, the islands fell into the sea.
I have no way to explain the visions of an old man
feeding a box of crabs cups and cups of corn. *Sisters, be patient.*

CHAD SIMPSON

On Helplessness

Nonfiction

My first good bike disappears at dusk when I stop at a neighbor's and leave it propped on the sidewalk out front to roam the backyard jarring fireflies or shooting baskets on the dirt court until we can't see anymore, until when we look up at the hoop it's just another starless part of the night sky.

Before I get a replacement — this cruiser with a banana seat and gigantic U-shaped handlebars I'm embarrassed to ride even among friends — my brother has a birthday and acquires a slightly different version of the bike I'd owned just days ago.

The street we live on is paved with bricks and full of families with kids about our age. We are never not playing outside.

One night, my brother, who is seven and overweight and has been given by the older kids in the neighborhood the nickname Chunk, calls to us from the street, where he is on his bike. I am with Lynn and Mandy or maybe Mike and Lance, and we are doing something that is easy to look up from, so we look. My brother, Brent, is riding with his back straight, his neck turned to us. When he sees he has our attention, he refocuses on the road, pedals a couple rotations to speed up, and then lets his feet drift toward the street's jagged bricks.

He is almost past us now, gliding by at a pretty good clip, and in my memory of this, it is dusk, a dusk not unlike the evening on which my bike was stolen maybe a month earlier. It is an easy, beautiful summer dusk and my brother is hazy around the edges, indistinct, like the sky at sunset in the Midwest where we live, the humidity obscuring everything we see. My brother is fuzzy, but still I can see him lifting his right foot, the foot closest to us as he passes by from left to right, like reading words across a page, something that all of us in the neighborhood are pretty adept at, even if we prefer the things we do outdoors to sitting inside holding books in our hands.

My brother raises that right foot, and his bike has slowed down some, but not much. His hands are still on the handlebars, which are not embarrassingly U-shaped, and which are fitted with ribbed red handgrips as soft as the underbellies of mushrooms. Because I no longer have a bike with handgrips like this, I sometimes touch my brother's when he isn't around. I strum them with my fingertips, to remind myself of what the handgrips on my first good bike had felt like, to remind myself of what I have lost.

My brother looks down toward his front tire, which is filled with a mag wheel. These are the best kind of wheels, the mag kind. My mag wheels had been red. His are silver and not quite as nice to look at but I'd take them over the spokes in the tires of that cruiser that I don't own yet but will soon, after one of our neighbors wins it in a drawing at the fair and decides to gift it to me because he knows what happened to my bike. How one night I left it alone just long enough to let it disappear.

My brother looks down toward that tire, and we see him insert his foot into the bike frame's fork, so that the force of his foot jams the front wheel to a stop. There is science at work now, though we don't know all that much about science. But this doesn't stop us from observing, from learning empirically. This is how we learn most of what we learn in our small Illinois town in 1984.

The front tire of my brother's bike has stopped rotating, which means the bike has stopped moving forward, but there is momentum present, because just seconds ago he was calling to us, he was pedaling kind of forcefully.

If my brother was hazy before, a little blurry around the edges, and he was, I see what happens next indistinctly but in slow motion.

My brother's back tire lifts off the ground as if a rope is attached to it and someone high in the sky has begun hoisting it up. My brother is still holding the handlebars, and those handlebars are headed toward the street, just like his face. We see clearly what is about to happen, and we are a chorus of gasps, a perfectly timed soundtrack.

The collision between my brother's face and the street is soundless and miraculous. He is splayed there on the bricks, my overweight seven-year-old brother, a heap of flesh and bike metal, his bike's back black rubber tire still spinning.

I reach him no faster than my friends, whoever they are on this particular night. We arrive all at once and get close enough to touch him but don't. We ask him if he's OK, hoping he answers. We ask him what he wants us to do.

My brother begins to peel himself from the street and looks up at us, smiling with his crooked teeth, which are permanent teeth and seem too big for his mouth. "Help me up," he says, and he has this look on his face. Years from now, I will get drunk with him for the first time, and I will be reminded of this moment, how dopey and elated and out-of-his-head he looked.

I pull him to his feet, and he rights his bike, says without looking at any of us, "I'm going to do that again."

This becomes a thing for a little while, my brother arriving out of nowhere on his bike and face-planting in front of a group of onlookers.

One time, I am on Lynn's screened front porch, and her mom has just poked her head out the door to ask us something when Brent calls out from the street. Before he even lifts his foot from the pedal, before his bike even begins to slow down, Lynn's mom, Lorna, knowing by now, like the rest of the moms in the neighborhood, about this trick my brother has been performing, yells, "Don't do it, Brent! Please, stop!"

In just seconds, though, he is in the street, dazed, looking up at us as if unsure where we have come from, as if we are the odd ones.

I will forget for a long time about that bike of mine that got stolen, about how my brother used to smash his chest and face into the brick-lined street we lived on. There will be periods of time, in fact, when I pretty much forget about my brother, when we barely talk.

Before my brother finds a good girl, who has a job and is sweet to him, and who likes it when he is sweet to her, a girl who will become pregnant but who will not carry the baby to term, who will lose the baby after only five months, before all of this, things will be bad.

My brother will invite women to live with him who will rip him off. He will lose friends over petty shit like dime bags and stereo speakers. He will spend a couple — but not too many, he will get mostly lucky when it comes to this — nights in jail.

And I will be a bad older brother. When we are younger, I will excel at baseball and get good grades. I will become fairly popular and make fun of his strange friends, a crew of rotating misfits with bad acne and learning disabilities. I will be unsympathetic toward him, ignorant of much of what he endures on a daily basis.

When we are older, the years will pass much the same. He will work as a line cook at a country club while I go to graduate school, but then I will move back to west central Illinois, just like he and my parents did when I was a senior in high school. I will rent a house just blocks, technically, from where he is living. Technically, because it's true, distance-wise, but will never seem true in any other way.

Sometimes I will go over to the trouse — called such because it is part trailer, part house — to get high when I'm on summer break from teaching. I will let him borrow movies I will never see again. I will give him money I can't afford to give because I'm just an adjunct instructor, and he actually makes about twice as much money as I make.

Most of the time, though, we won't have much to do with one another. There will be a thing about his car that he will lie to me about for a couple months. He will let me know about the roommates and girlfriends that have come and gone, but mostly in vague and un-incriminating ways. One night, he will ring my doorbell at three o'clock in the morning, drunk and wanting to introduce me to a girl named Nora, who a week later will enter a bar with my brother and leave with another guy. She will do this three times before my brother finally breaks up with her. When I open the door for them at three in the morning, by way of an introduction, she will thrust her hands two times toward the ceiling and shout, "Skeet, skeet."

Despite all of this, on the morning after his good girl loses their baby, I will drive around town for an hour looking for them after they leave the hospital. I will find them in the Walgreens parking lot, where they are sitting in the front seats of my brother's truck and crying but trying to stop so they can go inside and fill the prescription lying on the truck's dash, a prescription the doctor at the hospital wrote out for them for anxiety medication, which will hopefully help them both to sleep away the rest of this day, week, year.

I will pull into the parking space next to the truck and see them crying, holding one another over the console, shaking, and I will think of my brother on that bike with the silver mag wheels. I will think of him lifting his foot toward that fork, about to flip face-first toward an unyielding street. I will think of how incapable I am — then, now, always — of doing a thing to help him.

JOSH CASEY

Tonight, When I Dream of Louie Berg   *Fiction*

We're in the checkout line at the Safeway in West Rapid City now, buying what Tom calls the "real food:" frozen pizza rolls, potato chips, three pints of Ben and Jerry's (a pint for each of us), and an assortment of Lunchables. "It'll be like a slumber party," Tom says. He's clinging to the end of our cart, squishing his face against the small bars there, playing a game he calls "Grocery Prison." Each time I see him now, Tom is trying out a new game. Just this morning, he showed up at my doorstep in a ski mask. "What are you doing?" I asked him. "Skiing," he said. His mask didn't come off for three hours. Half the morning, he didn't speak. I have to hand it to him. He's committed, even for a five-year-old.

He launched into "Grocery Prison" in the Asian Cooking aisle and, fearing another episode of masked silence, I followed along, jovially threatening to place him in the Hole for sharking cigarettes to Lucy. For disorderly conduct. For behavior unbecoming of a prisoner. "Lights out in cell block thirteen," I threatened, holding a megaphone made of air. "Turn them out," I said. People were staring.

"Warden," Tom calls to me now, swinging his legs over the bottom rack of our cart. He's watching me unload the food with criminal interest. "Haven't I been on good behavior?"

"No crime, no time," I say.

"Hey there, sugar," the cashier says to Tom. The name "Janice" is carved on a faded plastic badge pinned to her chest.

"Hey, lady," Tom says. "You got any shovels?" He squirms, dropping his feet to the floor. "I'm planning a dig-out," he tells her, "and I need to know if you can keep a secret."

Janice makes like she's zipping her mouth closed and then turns to my daughter, Lucy. Lucy is clinging to *People Magazine*, running her hand over Kendall Monson's paper face, his dark eyebrows and tanned teenage skin, his dimples. Below his photo — Lucy recognizes it instantly as a still from last year's *Kendall Wishes You a Very Merry Christmas* — sits the million-dollar question, "What Happened?" The big elephant, since late Thursday evening, in every parent's living room:

"Dad," Lucy asks, "why do you think he did it?"

"You getting that?" Janice wants to know about the magazine.

"No," I say, wrestling the thing from Lucy's grip. Janice looks over the cover before putting the magazine back on the rack.

"A shame," she says." He had so much going for him." Lucy sighs.

When Janice is finished scanning, I swipe my card in the machine and type in a PIN. Still behind bars, Tom asks if next time he can type it. I tell him maybe. "When you get out," I say. "When you're back on your feet again."

Janice hands over a receipt. "There's a coupon on there for the Salad Zone," she says, not letting go of the paper yet. "A free large Coke product with the purchase of any Family Salad Meal." Her fingernail circles the word "salad;" she frowns at the snacks laid out on the conveyor belt below her — the ice cream, the potato chips. A bagger starts to sack up all of our stuff, and when he goes to put the Lunchables in together, Tom corrects him.

"Separate," he says. "Please." He steps warily from behind the cart. "I'm on the lam," he tells the bagger.

Janice starts to laugh and I shrug my shoulders. *We're new at this*, I'd like to tell her. Except that we're not. We've been here before, just in a different shape, a different form. I wonder, "can any salad meal the three of us ever eat again be truly considered a Family Salad Meal?" My son has spoken for all of us. We are all on quite the lam.

Today is Trial Day. For the first time since the split, I have Tom and Lucy all to myself. Tomorrow, Sunday morning, Sheila will come back for them. We've decided to try a schedule, something regular, because as recently as last week I was showing up at our old house by accident. Out of habit, on my way home from work, I'd find myself gliding up the street in my car, my neck straining to take in the lighted windows of that old place that used to be mine. It was the crunch of gravel under my tires in the driveway — like I'd just stretched and something small was cracking, a tiny bone I never knew existed — that brought me back. That triggered the vertigo. I'd open the door anyway and fall out of the cabin of my car and wander onto the porch, in a stupor, half-expecting Sheila to come to the door, peer out at me, and then run for the dining room, screaming. I must have looked crazed. *Let me back in*, my eyes must have said. Or maybe I was just tired. Fearful.

"Hey, you," Sheila'd say whenever she found me there on the porch. Sometimes she'd kiss my cheek as a greeting. I'd come inside and watch them eat dinner, pick at the parts of Tom's plate he left unattended — the broccoli, the peas, bread crusts — and ask Lucy how school was going. "OK. Kinda sucky," she'd say. "Fine." Then we'd watch music videos or I'd read to Tom from the *Frog and Toad Are Friends* book, and after a few hours I'd end up at the door again, with Sheila, saying goodbye. She'd kiss me then, too, when I was leaving. If she'd had wine with dinner, her lips would wander dangerously close to the small border of skin around my mouth. On the last of these unannounced visits, I offered her my tongue.

"I guess you'd better start calling first," Sheila said. She had her hands around my waist.

"I guess so," I told her. "I don't know what I was thinking." She smiled and then took my hand, led me onto the porch. Before going down the steps, I tilted my head and tried to see past her, to look down our old hallway again, but it was much too dark.

"OK, Roger," Sheila grinned. "Get."

Back at the house, Lucy is working on a puzzle of Mount Rushmore I've laid out on the coffee table. I bought it, the puzzle, to keep my mind occupied, a five-thousand-piece distraction. I've since given up on the border, though, the base of the Black Hills. Where there should be trees, where there might be soil, there are gaps, spaces where the faded veneer of my coffee table peeks through.

When I ask Tom which of the ice creams he wants, he starts to cry. He goes to put his mask back on. "No," I say. "Thomas, don't," and at the sound of his full name, he freezes, arches his back. He floats a bleary, liquid glance over to Lucy. She starts laughing, and Tom, after a few deep breaths, follows her lead, snot bubbling from his nose. We all stare at my hand, hovering out in space, fingers stretched for Tom's shirtsleeve.

"Hey, Roger," he says. "You're shaking."

I take them to Blake's Lottaburger instead. "What is this place?" Tom asks as we're pulling into the lot.

"Hamburgers," I tell him. "You've been here before. You like it."

"I do?" he says.

"You puked last time, you liked it so much."

"Oh yeah," he says. "That was awesome."

"When?" Lucy wants to know. "When were we here before?"

We were driving home from the mall once when Tom started whining about his stomach. "I'm starved," he kept saying from the backseat. It was Sheila who suggested the Lottaburger. No one else was hungry, but we all went inside anyway, to watch Tom eat. Sheila unwrapped his hamburger for him. She held out a cardboard carton of fries. "See if this helps," she said. "See if this makes it better." When Tom finished his hamburger, he turned the carton of fries over and dumped them all into his mouth.

"I'm a dinosaur," he roared. "I'm a T. rex!" He flashed us his teeth, still stuck with small bits of mushed hamburger and fried potato. He took a gigantic pull from his Coke.

"Any of this ringing a bell?" I ask Lucy and she shakes her head. I look back at Tom. He gives me the thumbs up.

"Oh, man," Tom says, disappointed. "You don't remember the dinosaur, Lucy?"

"I remember telling the dinosaur to take it easy," I say to Tom. "But what did the dinosaur do instead?" He drops his head to his chest, the pain of the memory crystallizing for him. He moans.

Instead of taking it easy, Tom stood on his seat and made claws at the teenage girls working behind the counter. "Feed me Stegosaurus!" he cried, and when a burp rose from his chest and escaped his lips, a paleness fell over his face. "Uh-oh," he said, after a long, searching pause, and then he emptied his entire lunch out onto the floor.

"That's so gross," Lucy says. "I don't think I was there. I'd remember something like that. Freaking sick. Are you sure we were there? All of us?"

Tom unbuckles his seatbelt and opens his door. "I wonder what will happen today," he says, grinning.

Inside, I give Lucy some money and tell her to order for me. From the bathroom, I call Sheila. "Hey there," she says into the phone. There is some sun in her voice.

"The ski mask," I tell her. "You could have given me a heads up." I immediately feel bad for snapping, for raising my voice. "Tom's acting weird. He's calling me Roger. They're *both* acting weird," I say. "Things are different here."

"Isn't that the point?" Sheila says. She laughs.

We have a history, Sheila and I. We met at college in 1989, in Lincoln, Nebraska, of all places, at the end of what was an otherwise bleak fall semester for the both of us. It hadn't gone above freezing since Thanksgiving break, and I was addicted to cigarettes. I was also failing Intermediate Spanish, and Sheila'd just been stripped of her financial aid. She was, for all intents and purposes, squatting in our dormitory, the population of which had been slowly dwindling since midterm, thanks to a theatrical pair of freshman suicides. The first one was mildly forgettable: some stressed pre-med student stepping in front of a city bus. The second happened just before finals. Dead Week, they called it, when Sheila met me and I met Sheila, and an economics major from Denver named Louie Berg jumped from the thirteenth story of Abel Hall and landed on his head.

"It only started last night," Sheila says now, about Tom's mask. In the nineteen years I've known her, I've never stopped expecting her to get defensive, to snap back, but she never does. It makes me feel worse, her deliberate calm, both angrier and guilty, and in the current, unsteady footing of our marriage, I've begun to recognize it as Sheila's version of the low blow. Her secret attack. In October, when I floated the idea of separation, she was just as agreeable. We'd been deep in a bad patch, and I'd just spent two weeks in the guest room of my sister's house in Deadwood. "I sort of forgot about us," I told her when I returned. We were watching TV when I said it.

"I guess I'm unhappy too," she said, and then she changed the channel, falling asleep with her knee tucked into the small of my back. I moved my things out in November. I found a tiny place in Box Elder with an extra bedroom for Tom and Lucy to share. "It's what Tom wanted," she tells me now, on the phone. "I asked him to pack for a weekend at his dad's. He insisted on the ski mask."

"You said that? 'A weekend at his dad's?' Christ, Sheila," I say. "You make it sound like the title of a Kendall Monson movie."

"Hah," Sheila laughs. "By the way," she continues, her tone growing serious again, "how's the wake going?"

"Don't ask," I tell her.

Kendall Monson has the number one Billboard song in the country. Thanks to Lucy, I have the lyrics to "Kendall Kicks It" lodged deep in my brain. Whenever there is a blank moment between thoughts, Kendall and his angelic voice sneak in. "Can he kick it?" a mammoth gospel choir roars, and Kendall answers them. "Yes," he raps. "Yes I can." At fifteen, Kendall Monson has cornered the market on young hearts everywhere, Lucy's included, with his straight-to-video brand of moping melodrama. Last summer, Lucy and I waited in line at the mall for three hours for her limited edition copy, with commentary, of *Endless Kendall*. He's the star of Doritos commercials. He has his own fragrance line, a stale amalgamation of lilac and boy sweat that Lucy insisted Tom try out for an entire week once. "How about it, Dad?" she'd ask, turning Tom's neck toward me. "Doesn't he smell Kendall sexy?"

But two days ago — late Thursday — Kendall Monson staged a sudden, grisly finale. It interrupted *Idol*. It took over the Internet. On the news, it went Kendall, then Iraq, then Kendall again. "Kendall Monson is dead," a hundred thousand channels declared. He'd hung himself in the basement closet of his grandfather's bungalow in Modesto. The life went out of him in a pair of blue footy pajamas; he'd wet himself and was clutching a toy stuffed bear when it left. *Can he kick it? Yes. Yes he can.*

Sheila called me right after it happened. I could hear Lucy weeping in the background, the hollow boom of a newscaster's somber voice crashing in and out. On TV, a crowd was already gathering outside Kendall Monson's grandfather's house, little girls in Kendall nightshirts, their mothers looking tired, tiny zombies scribbling messages on the outside of burning luminaries. "We miss you, Kendall. Come back to us." This, after he'd been gone for just over three hours.

Tom was pleading with Sheila. "What did Kendall do?" I heard him say, fighting for the phone. "Oh geez," he cried. "What the crap happened to Kendall?"

"What should we do?" Sheila asked me. I was sitting in front of my set, hunched over a TV tray, working through the main course of a Swanson Hungry Man, digesting Kendall Monson and three pieces of undercooked microwave chicken.

"It's all over everything," I told Sheila. "What can we tell her that she doesn't know already?" I paused. "You need me there?"

"I think we'll stick it out," she said. "Roger," she told me, "I just might miss you a little."

I was watching the grandfather exit the house, a striped blue-and-white cardigan stretched over his hunched spine. He was wearing khaki pants with an elastic band across the waist. Brown loafers. There was a box of powdered doughnuts stuffed under his arm. He handed the box of doughnuts down the mourning line, head down, as if he were passing the collection plate at a church service. When the doughnut supply was exhausted, he turned and acknowledged the cameras — what must have been a helicopter — with a nod of his frail and wrinkled head. He got into his station wagon and tried backing it out of the driveway. An excited little girl hurled herself onto the rear window. She started pounding on the glass, screaming. "Are you watching this?" I asked Sheila.

"Do you think Lucy's OK?" Sheila asked. My daughter's sobs were unmistakable now. "She's not going to be one of these nightshirt TV girls, is she?"

"Come on," I said. "It's not like Kendall Monson was a real person."

There was a serious pause on the line then, and all I could hear was the sound of Sheila's pronounced inhales and exhales, the wind rolling in and then creeping out of her. She was reaching back, I could tell. Remembering a year of us for every breath. The silence was weighted, like the moment preceding an electric shock that lights on a fist of fingers closing around a doorknob in a carpeted room. The nanosecond when the small hair over your palm peaks upward. We still hadn't talked about Louie Berg.

"God," Sheila said on the phone, Tom squeaking around behind her. "That was such an awful winter. Roger," she said, "are you sure you're OK?"

There was another pause.

"Kendall Monson," my wife started up again. "Doesn't it bring back memories?"

I laughed. "Just last night," I said, "I was dreaming of Louie Berg."

But today, on the phone, I'm the one asking Sheila all the questions.

"Is Tom going to be OK?" I ask her and a toilet flushes. A hand dryer roars to life. "Wait," Sheila asks. "Where are you? Are you in some bathroom?"

"I'm nowhere," I tell her. "We're eating."

"Roger," Sheila asks, "are you hiding?"

In the lobby of the Lottaburger, a tray littered with wrappers and small ketchup cups sits at the center of our table. In my absence, my burger and Vanilla Coke have been extradited from the mainland of the tray; they currently occupy the lonesome islet of napkins on my side of the table. Lucy and Tom have finished everything off, and Tom is working on his drink now, chewing the ice. He shows me the cubes on his tongue as I sit. "Look at that," I say. "It's some kind of glacier." Lucy has her arms folded on the tabletop. All I can hear is the sound of my own chewing. A flake of lettuce, greased in mayonnaise, works its way down my chin and I go to wipe it away with my shirtsleeve.

"Ugh," Lucy says. "We should become vegetarians."

"Since when do you know what that is?" I ask her, and she rolls her eyes.

"Since school," she says.

"You know," I say. "People who only eat vegetables have really small poop."

"Whatev," Lucy says.

"You mean whatever," I say.

"No," Tom tells me. "She means whatev."

Lucy clears her throat. "Kendall Monson was a vegetarian."

"Well," I say to Lucy. "There you go." At the mention of Kendall's name, Tom drops his soda and reaches across the table at me, working his hand into a claw, pinching the skin between my thumb and index fingers. "Ouch," I say. He wants me to say uncle. "Tom," I tell him, "this sort of hurts." He squeezes harder and I release what's left of my burger onto my napkin.

"Say uncle," he says. His small eyes drop to slits.

"Tom," I say.

"Roger," he says. He grits his teeth. He draws out my name. "*Rooooger.*"

"Fine," I say.

"Fine, what?"

"Fine, uncle."

He lets go. He retracts his claw and wraps it back around his cup. "I'm full," he tells me. "Big poop coming," he says, and on the way home, he falls asleep.

I turn to Lucy in the passenger seat. "What was that all about?" I ask her, massaging my hand.

"There's a nerve there," she says, and I catch a trace of the old softness in her tone. "A pretty big one."

"Tell me about it," I say. Outside the car, it has started to snow. We pick up speed on the highway and, for a moment, we are a spaceship, the tiny white flakes rushing past our windows in a flowing stream, like stars. Some of them crash into our windshield, showing themselves briefly for whole planets of honeycombed ice before shattering on impact. Lucy and I are silent, looking out at the black hole of winter for a long time, before she asks the question.

"Dad," she says. "did you ever know anyone who committed suicide?"

Louie Berg sat across from me in the cafeteria once. He ate noisily from a bowl of ice cream and watched the big screen television against the wall behind me. *Jeopardy*, I think it was. We were having the pasta bar. He was kind of a big guy, Louie Berg; he liked his ice cream. He tucked his pant legs into the tops of the black snow boots he was always wearing. Big black boots, even in the spring. They had one of those soft-serve machines in the cafeteria, and Louie got up once during our meal to refill his bowl. I remember watching him pile it on, employing his doughy hand at the lever of that machine, spinning his bowl beneath it like he was shaping pottery, coming up with the perfect sculpture of chocolate and vanilla.

"There," he said when he sat back down, like he was presenting me the bowl. I'd never met him before — until he spoke. I'd only heard him incorrectly guess the *Jeopardy* questions to the television over my shoulder. "What is Seattle?" he said when an answer came up about the capital of Washington state. I could see Alex Trebek floating in the smudged lenses of his glasses. When the correct question surfaced — "What is Olympia?" a solemn contestant's voice echoed behind me — Louie Berg moaned and went to work on his dessert, his spoon clinking around his bowl, making a sound like he was fencing. "Whoops," Louie said about his error in trivia, looking up at me with the spoon in his mouth. "Brain fart," he mumbled, and then he laughed. There was a brown dab of chocolate on his cheek, just to the north of his chapped lips. It was all so random. Chance. A day earlier I'd asked Sheila to a movie, and just that morning, in Spanish, I'd written an entire composition with the aid of the only two words I could ever remember correctly. *Perro*, dog, and *correr*, to run. *The dog ran*, I wrote over and over again, with limited success.

"You got a little something," I said to Louie Berg, touching my face.

His eyes lit up. He reached for a napkin and dabbed it over his skin. "Oh," he said. There was a waver in his voice. Too much phlegm. "Thanks. You're a real lifesaver."

Two days later, he jumped. It sounded like someone shaking a rug out on the street. I was one of three smokers to see it, to watch Louie Berg land right there in front of our stoop. A few more feet and he would have hit traffic. "One less Pall Mall," I told Sheila, "and I wouldn't have seen a thing."

It was someone else, a professor from the science and technology building across the street, who got to Louie first, who cradled the mess of his head there on the sidewalk until the paramedics came.

The three of us standing on the stoop could only watch. The hollow sound of Louie's death, like a gunshot or a loud concert, had deafened us temporarily, thrown us off our centers of gravity. In the elevator afterward, on the way back up to my room, I found a pattern — small brown dots of Louie's blood — draped along the edge of my shirtsleeve. Slowly, with my door closed, I took off the shirt and folded it up in a drawer. Later, when Sheila was over, I showed it to her.

"It was a pretty big splatter," I said. "I'm not sure what to do with it."

And as long as the shirt was there in the room with me, I woke up at least once a night to study it. I'd open the drawer and stare down into the darkness, thinking that maybe Louie'd let me in on a secret that would reveal itself in the small stain of his blood. That maybe that day in the cafeteria he'd shown me a small preview of coming attractions. The way he was eating his ice cream, sliding it around the bowl — was he thinking of it then? Of dying? The way he said thank you. How had I not seen it coming? You go over and over a thing like that in your mind.

Right now, I'd bet a good chunk of money that Kendall Monson's grandfather is stopped at a light in downtown Modesto. He's frozen in the freezer section of his favorite supermarket, struck dumb in the lights of a local TV news interview. He can't help it, he's scrutinizing the last meal he and Kendall shared. They'd gone out, maybe. They'd ordered pizza, and Kendall's grandfather is stuck on the toppings Kendall chose. The cheese, the pineapple. How Kendall'd ordered a Coke with grenadine. The way he'd balled a napkin up in his fist. If there was ever a clue, he thinks, it lies there. In the smallest of choices. In everything taken together. "Would Kendall still be alive," he thinks, "if it weren't for the pineapple, for the cheese and the Shirley Temple?" If he hadn't swallowed those things in the first place. If, on the way to his stomach, they hadn't rubbed his heart in just the wrong way.

It's true, I do dream of Louie Berg. Whenever I get an alumni letter, or catch a glimpse of *Jeopardy* flipping through the channels, I can close my eyes and see him again. I'm lying out on the sidewalk in front of the smoking stoop at Abel Hall, a human X marking his final resting spot, and Louie's coming down hard, plummeting from that great height, belly fat rippling, screaming at the top of his lungs. "Thank you!" he shouts over and over again.

Thursday evening, it was Kendall Monson who invited Louie back in. "Calling all ghosts," the little idol must have said from that dark corner of his closet in California. From his noose. Tonight, when I dream of Louie Berg, he looks a little different. Older, maybe. There's a wash of gray in his hair. He's dropping down on me at an even greater speed and just before he grinds me into the pavement, takes me along with him to ice cream heaven or fat boy suicide hell, he makes a face, sees that I don't fully recognize him. He knits his brow, looks hurt. "What?" he says. "It's me. Louie." And when I don't respond, he pulls his knees into his chest, makes himself into a cannonball, and tells me to spread my arms out. "Wider," he says. "There you go, Roger. A little wider. Just like that."

Around two-thirty in the morning, I get out of bed for a glass of water, hoping to wash the taste of Louie Berg down proper. I pass Lucy in the living room, a hairbrush in her hand, hunched over the puzzle of Mount Rushmore. This morning, waiting for Tom and Lucy to arrive, I put together a good deal of Roosevelt's chin.

"Roosevelt," I told Lucy earlier, as she stood over my shoulder, taking off her coat. "Roosevelt was the adventurer." Tom was behind us somewhere in the foyer, skiing.

Now, Lucy is plucking random pieces from the puzzle box and trying them in the gaps in the picture. She turns the pieces, shakes her head, and then throws them back. I watch her do this, try over and over, before speaking.

"Did you cook something?" I finally say. In the kitchen, I find my answer: a small circular baking pan sitting on the stovetop. Lucy's forgery of a Jackson Pollock, made with real cheddar cheese. When I walk back into the living room, she's holding up a paper plate with half a dozen pizza rolls stuck to it.

"Want one?" she asks. "Tom was snoring."

I sit down on the couch to contemplate her offer, the little pockets of frozen pizza she has zapped to charcoal briquettes. "The oven can be tricky," I say. "It heats a lot faster than our old one."

Lucy looks at the plate, then at me, and then back at the plate again. "I've been thinking," she says, "about this puzzle." When I bite down on my roll, the crunching sound is epic. The rolling of a boulder, the snapping of a tree branch. Lucy works her hairbrush over the top of her head. "I mean, it's a new puzzle, right?" she asks. "Never opened?" She finds a knot, closes her eyes, opens them again. "I looked everywhere for the pieces." She points at the unfinished edges, the hills with the holes in them. "But maybe you didn't get them all. Maybe the box is defective."

I remember watching Louie's legs, his feet, twitch there inside his boots, when he didn't keep going, when the ground stopped him for good.

I stare at my daughter's face for a long time and wait for something there to break. To give.

"Maybe," she says, "you never had the pieces in the first place."

JAMES MADISON REDD

Visiting   *Fiction*

So the preacher down at Worley Hill, for some reason I don't care to
know, came and gave me a kind word at my parole hearing. In that jail,
I kept reasoning with myself, especially after my love Doris died, that
I was gonna redeem my good name. Folks around the county didn't
trust me no more after what I'd done, and I didn't blame them. So
I went to the preacher who'd give me that good word, turns out his
name was Eaves, and asked him what I could do to help my name. He
sent me out visiting.

Before Eaves came around, what I'd promised myself to do when I
got out of jail was have a fifth of bourbon, and then sleep with Doris
until sunup. But my stomach couldn't stand liquor anymore after all
that prison food, and Doris was up there singing with the angels. So
instead, there I was, not two weeks out of jail, and rather than living
up the good life, I was visiting the fifth strange house of the day. The
preacher had coached me up, though, said I was a great man. Better
than any other feller in the county cause I was dedicating my time to
the church, visiting sick folks and whatnot. Believe me, he didn't fail
to remind me about the debt I owed him for what he'd done; I still
think he'll never let me live it down. Preacher had it in for me and I
don't know why — maybe he was testing me; I don't know — because
he could have sent me to just about anybody. But all the folks I visited
that day turned out to be hell on wheels.

The first house I saw had a lady come up to me in nothing but a
house robe, tied up real loose. Said she hadn't had a man in some
time; she was about fifty something with her hair done up in a perm.
I left soon enough. The next three, there wasn't nobody answer the
door, even though I heard folks talking in some of them and saw their
pickup trucks out front. Then I drove up on the Isbell's house just
off Highway 365. They got an old house, and I mean old even for
round here. I thought at first that the preacher had give me the wrong
address. This house had the grass grown up so tall you couldn't see
the windows, way up past the porch so's you couldn't see it unless you
came right up to the door. I drove into what served as their driveway.
They had a busted up Chevy with a cave-in trunk pulled right up to the
porch. I figured they couldn't own more than one car, so they had to be
home. When I knocked on the door, I could hear them Isbells talking
and talking over each other, and I thought for a second I saw a window
blind scoot down. They kept talking, and I'd seen enough of that kind
of treatment for one day. So I didn't give up and just went around to

the back door and knocked louder until I heard Clara Isbell scream. Her scream was louder than I could ever knock, even if I made my hands bloody. Then Clara opened up her window blinds.

"I done called the cops, Randy Grisham," she said. "You ain't gonna come in here none and beat us like you did that old lady in Biggersville."

Her son, James, a fellow about thirty years old and still living with his momma, repeated, "Nope. No sir. We called the police. You're done for good, Randy."

And hell if I didn't scream and holler too, tell them that I wasn't come out there to beat nobody. "The preacher, Rev. Eaves, sent me out to come and visit you and make y'all feel welcome to the church."

"Well, Lord, Randy, if that's your story, then you'll be in mighty fine shape when the sheriff comes."

"Yep," James followed, "Sheriff gonna drag your sorry ass to jail in no time flat."

And you know me; soon as I heard they'd called Sheriff Dodgson, I was gone. But the sheriff had heard all their craziness before, and he came out skeptical but still looking for something to put me away — he don't like me cause he caught me screwing his virgin daughter on their great-grandmother's piano some twelve years ago. He told me later that he was inclined to do up charges, putting me in trouble with my parole officer. But Eaves stood by me and confirmed my story, only making me more in debt to the bastard. Still, that was all the visiting I had in me for one day.

About two weeks later, them Isbells came and saw me at my junkyard. I was out working on that same Ford that you were wanting to buy. I had the guts of it out scattered all over the place, and I had Adell and Tom Wheeler piecing together the engine parts. Adell, my daughter, was about sixteen then. When I'd left she hadn't even made it past the giggling teen stage, but now she was wearing short cut jeans and had her curly blond hair long as her shoulders. I told her that she ought to start messing around with Tom, the old Rev. Wheeler's boy; I had the boy working for me then doing paint jobs. He was smart and talented and had some money coming to him. He'd even wrote her a song with a high class title, like "Sweet Cherubim." That Tom wouldn't talk to her none, though, and after a while she didn't seem interested, no matter how much I tried.

Clara and James Isbell pulled in that day talking up a storm. Talking the way they always do: Clara going first and James taking up the rear end, saying just what his momma said only in different words. I found out that they were looking for an alternator for their Chevy.

"Since James been sick," Clara said, "we ain't been able to make no money, Mr. Randy. We can't even afford to buy him nothing for his pain."

"Hurting all over, Mr. Randy. No money." James was crouched a little with his legs about as far apart as they could be, and he tossed the old alternator back and forth between his hands.

"Look, y'all. I'm in as bad a shape as you are," I said. "Since I been in jail there ain't been no money to go around. Had to spend the last of my wife's tiny insurance policy to get my business back on its feet again." I tapped the new sign I'd bought that no longer had my name in the business title. "Ain't hardly had no customers since decent folk don't want to deal with me no more."

"Are you saying we ain't decent folk, Mr. Randy?" Clara shook her three-fingered hand violently. "Lord, the preacher wouldn't like to hear you call us that. Ain't he had a say in whether you stay out of prison or not?"

"No, sir. We decent. Yes, sir."

Adell chimed in defending me: "My daddy hadn't said nothing to hurt y'all none. Now I don't need him going to jail because I sure as hell ain't going to no foster home." She wiped her greasy hands on her long legs. "And I don't need him giving your finagling asses nothing neither, so as it's gonna be hard to make ends meet."

I thought then that if Tom Wheeler had any sense, he'd say something to her; she was more fiery than hellfire and would make any man a proud, Southern wife. Tom was sitting on his knees looking up at Adell and her greasy legs and nodding. But it was Clara and James who talked.

"Young ladies shouldn't curse and talk back to their elders, now." Clara looked Adell head to toe. "Unless you're not a young lady."

"Young ladies, yep," James said. "Not whores dressing like you."

Clara and James accusing Adell was about all I could take. They could tarnish my name up and down this county and the head honchos from everywhere in Mississippi could throw me in whatever pen they devised, but I wasn't going to have nobody slam my sweet Adell's good name. I grabbed that alternator from James and tossed it across the road. "You folks have worn out your visiting privileges at my house." And I gripped my wrench until it about broke all the fingers in my hand, my face blazing like I'd been out in the sun too long, and before I put any amount of thinking into it, I realized I was aiming to hit Clara in the nose.

"Lord help us, he's gonna do it again, James!"

"Lord God."

And I stopped just long enough for her and her son to take three strides toward the road and her house. Then I punched my new sign, denting in the word "Mechanic" and bloodying my fist. Maybe it was the heat or maybe the pain and loss of blood made me dizzy, but I felt so tired that I slid down to my knees and saw all the junk around me: the clocks, wind chimes, and cars, the oil rags, saw blades, and piles of wood. But Adell came and kissed my head and wrapped my hand, and Tom brought some ice, and eventually I could see all right again.

Well, I thought I'd never see those folks after that. But wouldn't you know when I was over at the preacher's house one Friday playing Spades with him and a layman, I'll be damned if he didn't tell me I was going to have to go over there again. He said the Isbells had come and told him what I'd done, and he had apologized for my actions. He said he had promised them that in recompense I'd go over there and patch up their leaky roof.

"Here's another chance to redeem your good name," he told me.

I thought about doing a good deed for the preacher by popping *him* one in the nose, but I knew he was right. There wasn't no way for me to clear my name unless I went out and done something to deserve it.

But the preacher hadn't said nothing about how big a hole it was. About a quarter of the roof was caved in, and they hadn't even bothered to move any of James' stuff out of the bedroom that it covered. James had been sleeping on the couch in the living room. I felt bad for them for the first time cause of that. I knew what it was like not being able to sleep in your own bed. Never mind my new found sympathy for their sleeping situation, it wasn't long and I was back to hoping they wouldn't say nothing to me. When I first set up my ladder and looked through that hole in the roof, I saw James in there, and that fool was wearing a woman's skirt. Redder than hell, it was, with white polka dots. I'd seen plenty of fairies before in the jail so I wasn't too surprised and just set to work.

Luckily, the preacher said I could use the church money to cover the materials, so I took to tearing off the old shingles from that section and ripped up the rotted wood that had fallen. I wasn't up there a few minutes when Clara came out and saw that I was pulling stuff off her house. Boy, she got fighting mad. She started nagging at me about her thinking I was coming out here to fix her house and then I come and instead tear off what was left of it. Believe me, I tried to tell her that what I was doing was getting it ready for fixing it back right, but she wouldn't have none of it. She called Sheriff Dodgson again, and this time I waited for him. That's right. I waited. I knew the preacher would back me up, and that common sense would back me up too. In fact, Eaves had already called the sheriff and told him what I was doing, just in case. And it was some kind of a relief for me when the sheriff did come out and say, "Son bitch ain't lying, but I sure wish he was, Mrs. Isbell." Clara was real embarrassed. She apologized, but I could see by her silence and unusually steady gaze that she held a grudge for having been trumped.

Well, I came back on Saturday morning, and I got most of it done. Every now and then Clara came out and nagged me over something, but I didn't pay her no mind. I was happy enough just being there and reminding her that her bitchery had been overruled. It wasn't the best time of year not to have no lemonade to cool your throat, as the days were still hot and you'd get dizzy with heat. And I did get curious why James didn't never walk out the house no more with her.

When I came back the third time, I figured I'd be done with my work quick. I came during a regular workday this time cause it looked like it might rain. I'd need to get on it soon cause the rain might wash away some of my doing, and then get all in their house. I was going to ask the preacher to talk me up at church on Sunday morning so people might think good of me.

When I got out of my truck, I could hear hollering coming from inside the house. It was one of those screams that a man don't scream unless he don't know he's doing it; I'd heard them noises before, down in the pen when a man had tried getting out and made it about a quarter mile in the cotton fields before the dogs shredded him. I went in to check it out, and there was James Isbell laid out on the couch. He had an ice pack between his legs and a bottle of whiskey in his hand. That stupid queer ass son bitch I figured had done cut his dick off. He pulled the bottle to his mouth and tried to get a drink from it, but I could tell it was empty. This was the first time I was inside their house, and it sure as hell wasn't a pleasant sight. Cigarettes an inch deep on the carpet and cat shit covering every piece of furniture. But I didn't think down on them much because of that; my own house don't look much better.

Clara was to the door in no time flat, telling me, "Your job of charity is out on the roof, not in the house."

I told her, "I'm not about to do no work on your house when what's inside is what needs the fixing." After I said that, I heard James speak for the first time without Clara saying something first.

"It ain't gonna be fixed. No way. No sir." He sat up on the couch gingerly and looked like he might try to get up and punch me, even with that ice pack on his balls.

"Now you happy?" Clara asked me. "You got him upset. Ain't it enough that he's suffering physical, like he already is?"

"Well, if he's suffering so much," I said, "why don't you get him a doctor or something?"

"Can't afford no doctor, first off," Clara said. "And even if we could, we wouldn't." Clara smoothed her skirt and sat in the chair across from the couch.

"No. Lord no," James began. "No sawbones going to come here. Saw it off." He clenched the ice so hard that melted water began to seep out the top of the bag onto the couch.

"That's right," Clara said. "I know you'd love it for my only boy to be without any way to carry on this family tradition, but I ain't going to have it, and he ain't neither."

"Lord help us, we ain't." James nodded until I worried his head was going to fall off.

I was up there to fix their roof, and to help them out, and there they were accusing me and not trusting me a damn bit. I wasn't letting up, though. Those crazy people were the only chance I could see to redeem myself and I wasn't about to let them get in the way of helping their own selves. "Well, hell," I told them, "at least you could do something about the pain, and as you can see, whiskey ain't the answer. Matter of fact, I might know a way to help, without no money at all." They sat and stared at me, quiet for the first time. I stuffed a wad of chaw in my lip, enjoyed that silence for a moment and said, "I'm gonna be damned if Lee Posey don't have the cure for that pain."

And I knew that crazy son bitch would. When I was down in county jail waiting to be transferred to Parchman, they brought Lee Posey in one Sunday evening. Cops used to bring him in the jail all the time for suspicion of dealing drugs. Which he was, but they couldn't never find it on him, or in his house; I still don't know where he made it. When he showed up that day to the jail, I was bawling my eyes out. I'd done whooped that old lady like she was a punching bag for what she'd said about my daughter and what she'd done in her English class. My fists were like string cheese and the cops didn't give a shit about giving me no treatment. Well, Lee took a look at my fist and pulled some kind of bag out of you know where and the son bitch opened it up and put a bit in his hand and got some water out the sink and soaked it in it. Then he told me to snort that shit; he told me it worked better through a needle, but said I'd get to feeling better soon either way. And I took it expecting not too much, but it wasn't ten seconds and I was sucked into the wall, couldn't move a muscle, feeling like I was out my own skin.

That's how I knew when I called Lee Posey from the Isbell's phone that he could help whatever pain James was in. And Lee came within thirty minutes, like he knew he was about to be called up and ready to go. He'd dressed the part, carrying a doctor bag and a stethoscope around his neck; he'd even shaved his beard, leaving just a mustache. Well, I'd told James that there wasn't no real doctor coming, but seeing Posey dressed that way just threw him into a fit. Lee calmed him down right quick, though. Showed him he didn't have no saw or knife or nothing and soothed James by telling him he was there to cure his pain, not make some more. It might have been hard for me to calm down James, but not for Lee. Lee was a mighty persuasive feller, and he knew something about near everything. He'd been a medic in Nam, and he had some crazy stories about drugs and killing that you'd never get out of your head once he'd told you. I couldn't hear what he told James at that point cause he was whispering in his ear, but the young man had gotten quiet. James closed his eyes, and Lee reached in his doctor's bag and pulled out the biggest needle I ever saw. He sucked up some dark, thick liquid into it and then turned it up and thumped it a couple of times. He fitted on a tourniquet high on the leg and then found a vein and jammed the needle in there, pushing the plunger down while James screamed, calling him a "goddamn lying son bitch." He kept cursing till Lee pulled out the needle and stood back, and James got quieter and quieter and smiled and closed his eyes.

Lee worked James's balls, feeling for anything strange; they were huge, looking like he only had one ball that was the size of a fist. I'd never seen a man touch another man's particulars, but I reckoned James didn't mind since he was a queer anyway. Then Lee set to work on cleaning up the kitchen; said he was going to use it as an operating room. I was scared as hell and so was Clara. While he was prepping the room, he told Clara that James had an advanced hernia. And he made her all confused by dropping these medical terms and saying what it was that James was suffering from and how he was going to cure it. He told her that James wouldn't suffer during the surgery; he'd jammed him full of morphine that would knock him out for a long time. Finally, he said, "He won't lose his testicles, and it's not going to cost you any money. I'm operating for the curiosity of it." Clara seemed content after that and shut up and went to the living room.

Lee Posey was ready; he had the sharpest knife you ever saw and needles and thread strong as oak. He told me to clean up. I told him there wasn't no way to clean all the mess in that house, and he told me, "Well, now it's your calling to fix it, if you want this deed to be carried through." It took a bit to scrub the molasses off the kitchen table so James could lay on it, and it took even longer to wash out all the motor oil I had built up in my hair. I saw some things then that I don't even know how to talk about; my God, I still wonder at the ways that Posey manipulated that man. He was like a mechanic, working on James the same way I would mold a piece of scrap metal. You'd of thought there'd been more at stake, but he didn't never sweat none that I saw. All you need to know I done during that surgery was fill that feller up with morphine every now and then, and I threw up when Posey split open James' ball sack.

When we finished, there was blood all over my clothes, and I walked out into the living room where Clara waited. She saw that blood and started crying. I'd seen her throw fits before; she'd gnash her teeth and wail and cry and say she worried she would go on to the by and by, but always those rants were a plea for charity. I'd never seen her actually show compassion. So I made the decision to put aside whatever ill will I had against this family and hold her three-fingered hand.

When I touched her, though, she jumped back. I was a bloody mess. So I asked her for a change of clothes, and she led me into James's bedroom. The rain had come while Posey operated, and the water flowed through the hole onto the soaked mattress. She opened up James's closet, scooting away some dresses at the front to reach into the back for a stained T-shirt. When she handed it to me, she said, "Thank you for your help with my boy."

"Hardly anything to ask," I said and pulled the shirt over my head. "Just make sure you let the word get spread that I ain't as bad as everybody thinks I am."

"Well, you seen these dresses in his closet." She closed the closet door. "Don't let the word get spread that my son done what he's done."

I hadn't taken any recognition of them as hanging in *his* closet until then, but she continued on anyway. It was her habit to talk until she'd said too much.

"You've noticed my boy repeats everything I say and follows me everywhere I go," she said, and asked me for help with moving the bed. We managed to scoot it across the room away from the rain. "Well, he thought that I didn't have nothing wrong with me and so if he acted just like me and looked just like me he wouldn't suffer no more. Don't think less of him; he don't know no better." She picked up a huge bucket and put it on top of a dresser to protect it from any more water. "He worked hard and I reckon that's how he got what he got. Picking up cans all up and down these roads everyday, and then making some little money lugging big loads of topsoil back and forth across Mr. Massey's fields," she said. "Now he can't work and we can't manage."

We left the room to the storm and walked back into the living room where Lee Posey sat already cleaned up. Knowing him, he had a change of clothes with him when he came.

Posey must have heard our conversation, because he said, "He'll be able to work again soon. He won't be able to do any heavy lifting, but I bet you can find him a janitor job or something somewhere soon."

She smiled for once. "God has sent you both from above."

Posey handed Clara a needle and some morphine and gave her his phone number. "When you need anything, call me." He showed her how to use the needle and then began to leave. I told Clara I'd finish with the roof when it stopped raining and then I walked outside with Posey. He paused on the porch watching the rain fall. I studied his features; he still had that hard gaze about him, the kind that wouldn't be diverted unless he chose for it to be.

"I had known when I called that you wouldn't charge much to help," I said, "but you didn't charge anything at all. And you *operated* on that son bitch."

He pulled the hood of his jacket over his head. "They'll call me again soon, like any good customer." Then he tested the rain with an open palm and left.

I tell you what, after I saw how happy I'd made Clara, I felt like I was on my way to redemption. I didn't even care whether they were trying to finagle a free penny from me or not. I'd helped some folks out of the goodness of my heart, and I considered myself as great a man as the preacher had said I was, whether he believed what he said or not.

It was then that I got careless.

I was so proud of what I'd done that I couldn't hardly wait to get back on that roof to work and get a fresh sense of pride. I spent the rest of the week finishing up that Ford that I was going to sell to you, waiting for the rain to let up. Then, one hot, sunny day, I set out to finish what needed finishing. The rain had done some damage to the roof and I set to tending on that. I worked through lunch because I wanted to get done before Sunday. Well, I tell you this much, I don't remember most of that day, except the sweat that kept dropping from me, making me almost slip off the roof a couple of times and I couldn't hardly see straight. I sweated so much that my cigarettes got drenched. Eventually I kind of got used to all the sweat and it slowed down to where it wasn't so bad. I thought I must have eat something real bad that morning 'cause I threw up at some point. I could have swore not long after that I saw James come out with a hand on his nuts and the other hand waving at me. And it was about that time when I was near to maneuver one of the last shingles into place.

I remember waking up briefly, being splashed by a garden hose, and then I was in the back of James and Clara's car wondering how they got it fixed and I realized we weren't moving. Not too long after, the ER folks were pulling me out of another vehicle at the hospital, and Tom and Adell were there and I wanted him to hold her hand, and then Clara and James were standing over me in a freezing white room. I wasn't sweating anymore, and I had a needle in my arm.

"Hey there, tough fella," Clara said. "Looks like you made it all right."

"Yessir," James said. "Tough as nails. It's all right."

I felt real dizzy, and their talking over each other didn't help the worst headache I'd ever had in my life.

"We're glad we could repay the favor and help you out, Mr. Randy," Clara said and adjusted her feather-trimmed straw hat. "But we lost something on the way, and we need your help."

"Lost it. Don't work no more. Need it."

"I thank you kindly for what you did for me," I said. I was very tired and wanted to do nothing but sleep and be rid of those two. "I hope you didn't lose nothing too important in your helping," I said half out of a dream.

"We've lost our car in your service," Clara said, "and we know that a generous man like you who has hundreds of cars his own wouldn't mind lending us one."

"Give it."

I was done with fixing their house, and in that daze I was in, I felt it not out of the question to get them out of my life by throwing a car their way. I knew it had been three years since you'd pledged to buy that car, and I might not make any money out of it since you'd never showed up once I got out of prison. Don't get me wrong, I knew what kind of duped I was being by them two. I was letting myself forget what I'd learned the hard way from those years in prison: man will bluff, trick, scheme, devise, and swindle to get what he wants if he thinks he can get it. And using another man when he's down and out in order to get yourself up and in with the world ain't too far beyond human nature. But I knowed that that's what I done to them to get back my name, so I guess I couldn't point a finger at them without pointing my thumb back at me.

Any further objections I had they managed to talk me out of pretty easy by sticking around, pledging to watch over my sick bed for as long as necessary. So I gave them the keys and told them I was gonna let them borrow it. "I'll come over when I want it back," I told them. "Till then, y'all don't have to worry none about bringing it my way."

You know what, though? It ended up out all right for me that they took that car. You wouldn't believe it, but them Isbells, they started showing off their nice car to all the folks in Vandler County and telling them who it was that gave it to them. They'd show up near dinner time and show them folks an act of charity, and then ask them for another one: a hot meal. I reckon Clara and James Isbell were the best advertisement for my name I ever had. Turns out their two big mouths can sell cars better than my one.

POETRY'S AFTERLIFE: VERSE IN THE DIGITAL AGE
By Kevin Stein
276 pp. University of Michigan Press
Paper. $26.95

O Taste and See: A Review of Kevin Stein's *Poetry's Afterlife*

Once, on a rare visit to the Northeast where I live, my father spent a whole day walking from just above Midtown Manhattan to Wall Street without stopping anywhere to eat. The fact was he could choose neither a food nor a restaurant. He wanted something recognizable. He wanted his money's worth. He wanted something he was sure to like. Instead of taking a chance in China Town or Little Italy or even a hot dog stand at the southern edge of Central Park, he went hungry, waiting until we returned to my house that evening. My dad is a life-long southerner, who rarely leaves his small-town zip code, much less the region. He is a dentist, who has been practicing for the last forty years in the same office in which his father practiced. He is a self-described "character." He likes things simple: a single diagnosis, a clear method of treatment, a straightforward business plan. This clear singularity soothes and ensures success; having more than two choices overwhelms and frustrates him. "Routine, just routine" is his standard and preferred response when asked how he is. To him, *routine* is synonymous with *status quo* — "the state of affairs previously existing," since change is at the least troubling; at worst, catastrophic.

My father's response to change and the unknown resembles much of what I hear from the more traditional literary voices about contemporary poetry. It doesn't look (or sound) like the same landscape that was once merely carved into aesthetic camps — William Carlos Williams versus T.S. Eliot, or the Beats versus the Slicks. It is hard to gauge its value. What constitutes worth when the *filmic poem* is spoken, sound-tracked, and imagistic? Where what we see seems as important as what we hear? What does it mean for the patient skills of craft and knowledge that poetry writers and readers must develop when poems are more immediately and freely accessed on-line than from within the pages of a book or literary journal that must be searched out, borrowed, or bought? How do we know a poem is good when language is not the only thing to be considered? Or when there's no longer a single authorial voice? Or when the "expert" poet's work and the novice's are only separated by a click? How do we "stay on top of" or "get ahead" in the myriad poetries that exist in and outside of the academy?

Kevin Stein's *Poetry's Afterlife* is necessary for the way it addresses these questions. It illuminates how poetry is composed, delivered, and received in this digital age alongside its inclusions of more recognizable literary criticism on the poetry of James Wright, historical analysis of the role played by newspapers in poetry's American life, and pedagogical essays on "Voice" and "Why Kids Hate Poetry." It is a book for poets, anyone teaching poetry, anyone who is trying to assess poets and poetry, and anyone who just plain loves poetry apart from what is said about it — loving it for what it is or has been. Stein helps us to re-frame our perception of poetry, subtly nudging us toward understanding how poetry is often categorized and analyzed in the terms of capitalism — or more specifically, monopolies. This book helps us to consider that perhaps for too long we have been expecting the artistic equivalent of the golden arches along turnpike rest stops, and that our poetic choices have been akin to Coke or Pepsi, paper or plastic (to borrow from the opening chapter title). The great strength of this book is in Stein's ability to elucidate the various poetic camps and embrace the multiplicity. While many "believe this blizzard of aesthetic dialogue freezes not perpetuates American poetry's continuing evolution," Stein argues that it is this very argumentation between and among the camps that "promotes rather than extinguishes poetry's vibrant future" (17). Poetry has changed up its routine.

In the book's key chapter, "Poems and Pixels: The Work of Art in an Age of Digital Reproduction," Stein adapts and channels Walter Benjamin's earlier essay, "The Work of Art in an Age of Mechanical Reproduction." This chapter addresses the polar tug and crux of the artistic, and specifically, poetic arguments today: How do we evaluate the elite reception of art versus those experiences received via technology? Stein applies Benjamin's "hierarchy of aesthetic experience" to the various ways we receive art these days, acknowledging that the "reality of this hierarchy . . . ought not to devalue utterly those occasions which reside below the summit. How, then, explain one's rush of joy listening to a compact disc version of Mozart's twenty-eighth or the pleasurable edification of hearing Yusef Komunyakaa's reading a poem on one's iPod?" (89). These digital experiences of art, he suggests, will not replace the elite, intimate experiences of being in the physical presence of art; rather, they are part of the multiple receptions and, as such, are democratizing. While clicking on Google images to call up the Mona Lisa with the competing banner ads and pop-ups is not equal to standing in the Louvre, contemplating the strange delicateness of the image, the other art works surrounding it, the grand scale of the gallery itself; it is "efficient," immediate and egalitarian — and should not be dismissed even as it is a secondary or even, tertiary artistic encounter (89).

While some may see this book as being too all-embracing of current poetries — from *Filmic* or *Cin(E)-Poetry* to alterable text electronic poetry to collaborative authorship and computer screen/gallery sites in place of the fixed, the singularly authored, the page, the book — what educates and even soothes is Stein's connection to and clarification of poetic tradition in these new contexts, and his great commitment to American pluralism. While he does not overlook how "infuriating [it is] to rake through the democratic haystack to find the authentic needle one's been searching for, [where] the bloviators and the bloggers and the simply uninformed stand shoulder to shoulder with the expert and the well-skilled," he nonetheless asserts that, "America is a pluralistic society . . . [whose] variety of voices must be heard if [she] is to speak for herself *as* herself" (97). This break-up of the poetic rebellion routine, where one set of aesthetics simply upsets and rousts the previous (the poetic *status quo*), refreshes. Even as this technological world changes and dizzies poetry, it may also enable it toward "unceasing growth" (137). Instead of eliminating the need to understand the tradition and craft of poetry, these new poetries may require readers and writers to employ and increase their skills across these various aural, visual, and linguistic landscapes. These choices need not keep us stunned nor wandering hungrily; rather, they beckon us to see, hear, taste.

Lea Graham's first book of poetry, *Hough & Helix & Where & Here & You, You, You* was released August 2011 through No Tell Books. She is assistant professor of English at Marist College in Poughkeepsie, New York, and a native of Northwest Arkansas.

STEEL TOE PRESS
Chad Heltzel

MONEY FOR SUNSETS
By Elizabeth J. Colen
90 pp. Steel Toe Press
Paper. $12.00

At the end of the first strophe of "80 East," from Elizabeth Colen's excellent debut collection *Money for Sunsets*, the speaker, having driven across a section of the American Northwest with her partner, notes, "You said you'd take the blame if we became wreckage on the plains." The poem continues, detailing the cheap motels along the way, their stained sheets, and the "unplastered gashes in bathroom walls the night wants in." By the time the speaker ends the poem, stating, "When I come out of that office with diamond-shaped keychain you'll look at me as though it's been years," we realize the emotional journey the poem has captured in four verse paragraphs. Moving from glimpses of human wreckage to the damaged rooms in which the women stay to the passage of time in a gaze, the poem suggests a lifetime of shared love and pain in the brevity of a car trip. In fact, the wide emotional range the poems cover is their greatest strength. The poems guide readers through surprising twists, moving from playful to somber, apocalyptic to cautiously hopeful.

Throughout, the poems possess a cinematic quality. In "11 Bang-Bang," Colen opens with a succession of evocative visual images: "Box of hair on a beach. Scattered and new, ashes. A fine-feathered boy made of glass. Pin pricks, a hole in the wall." Each fragment works like an extreme close-up, never fully explaining the association between one image and the next. Notably, Colen uses the prose poem throughout the collection as an effective vehicle for the poems' cinematic effects. Not writing in lines, she avoids creating pauses in the syntax of enjambed sentences or dissociating thoughts over a line break. Instead, she moves from one moment to the next, as if tracking or cutting between images or ideas. The richness of the images also fills them with strong emotional overtones that create heavy tension, which here build to revelation of a death: "What the boy was wearing when he died could fit inside your palm, or, if you like, could hang off the two fingers left of your right hand. They wouldn't let us see his face. Scattered and torn, a boy made of glass, shattered." Even as strong as those images are, a sense of fragility hovers over the emotional center of the poem. The tension created by the interplay between the carefully collected remains and the eventually revealed broken boy set up explorations of violence, identity, and the intersection between the two that are also prevalent throughout the collection.

In "American Beach," "a deep green" ocean where "gulls flock like plastic bags" — both suggesting pollution — imagistically contrasts with a beach shack, its "paint sanded off by sand" and with sand castles being slowly eroded by the tide — indicating nature reclaiming the land. Later in the poem, after a condom has been thrown into a fire, the speaker notes, "What saved us melted. We felt so adult. It only hurt when we stopped." The speaker's loss of innocence is tied to her maturation, and this idea is parallel to the land's losses and recoveries. The natural tension correlates to the personal, emotional tension. Importantly, however, this process is not painless, and what is gained always implies damage.

Even in poems that seem very different tonally, Colen's signature movements are still clear. In its opening lines, "Grand Canyon" manifests a parent's homophobia through dark humor: "I say wife and my father hears knife. I think it's got something to do with religion." Although the poem starts amusingly, the speaker continues, asking the father to recall a series of details from a hiking trip. By the end, the statement, "Remember your thirst like it was something that mattered," takes on a serious double meaning, an urgent plea for understanding and acceptance.

The final poem, "Aposematic," perfectly encapsulates the ideas in the central themes in the collection. The speaker moves from describing the disposal of glue-trapped rats and the violent gestation practices of the tarantula hawk wasp to personal revelations of how the men her mother brought home affected the household. Though the poem is centrally concerned with female sexuality, the final lines seem applicable to much more: "I am going to keep on believing in the devil, until the earth is proven otherwise uninhabitable. The great unimaginable caverns below us are really doorways into our souls. So what's this about the eyes as the windows, cracked, shut, bleeding, smeared with weather and worn. Great untapped mercies live within us." Indeed, Money for Sunsets is a collection that works to find a place to free, however tentatively or painfully, those untapped mercies dwelling within our depths.

Chad Heltzel's PhD is from the University of Illinois at Chicago. He is a coeditor of *Little Red Leaves*, and his poems and reviews have appeared in *Cream City Review*, *Faultline*, and the *Sarmatian Review*, among other journals.

CONTRIBUTORS

LESLEE BECKER has published a story collection, *The Sincere Cafe*, and individual stories in *The Atlantic, Ploughshares, The Kenyon Review, Epoch, Iowa Review*, and elsewhere. She is the recipient of a Wallace Stegner Fellowship, the Pirate's Alley Faulkner Society Award, and the James Michener/Copernicus Society Award. She teaches in the MFA program at Colorado State University.

BRUCE BENNETT is the author of nine books of poetry and more than twenty chapbooks. His most recent books are *Something Like Karma* (Clandestine Press, 2009) and *Subway Figure* (Orchises, 2009), and his most recent chapbook is a sonnet sequence, *A Girl Like You* (Finishing Line Press, 2011). He is professor and chair of English and directs the creative writing program at Wells College in Aurora, New York.

LINDA BIERDS's eighth book of poetry, *Flight: New and Selected Poems*, was published in 2008 by Putnam's. Her awards include four Pushcart Prizes, *Virginia Quarterly Review*'s Emily Clark Balch Poetry Prize, and fellowships from the Ingram Merrill, the Guggenheim, and the MacArthur foundations, and twice from the NEA. She is a professor of English at the University of Washington.

MARY BUCHINGER's poems have appeared in *Booth Magazine, The Cortland Review, New Madrid, Nimrod International Journal of Prose and Poetry, RUNES: A Literary Review, Slice, The Massachusetts Review, Versal* (the Netherlands), and other journals; her collection *Roomful of Sparrows* (2008) was a semifinalist in the New Women's Voices Series. She teaches writing and communication at the Massachusetts College of Pharmacy and Health Sciences in Boston.

JOSH CASEY's fiction has previously appeared in *The Rambler, The Mochilla Review, Relief,* and online at MNArtists.org. He lives in Omaha, Nebraska, with his wife, Hannah. He is currently at work on a collection of short stories.

SAVANNAH CLEMENT is an actor and budding photographer. After high school she chose to bypass college and instead became a "student of life" (she'll probably never graduate). She is a great admirer of portrait studies but mainly finds herself shooting objects, structures, and the great outdoors. She lives in Hell's Kitchen, New York, with her puppy, Luna. For a closer look, find her on Flickr under Savvy Clement, or go to www.SavvyClement.com.

JOSH DENSLOW lives in Dripping Springs, Texas. His stories have appeared or are forthcoming in *Black Clock*, *A cappella Zoo*, *Storyglossia*, *Upstreet*, and *Twelve Stories*. He has written and directed five short films that have played at a few festivals. His short story collection *Frequently Mistaken* and his novel *TOUCH* are both looking for homes.

RAIMA EVAN is an assistant dean at Bryn Mawr College. Her fiction has been published in *Calyx*, *Philadelphia Stories*, and *Women & Performance*. Her one-act play, *Goodnight Firefly Ravine*, was produced at Actors Theatre of Louisville and published in *Dramatics Magazine*. "The Magician's Assistant" is dedicated to her family and especially to her parents, who told her stories about growing up on the Lower East Side.

PETRA FORD lives in Chicago with her son, photographing everything that passes in front of her camera lens. Days are typically spent shooting lifestyle, fashion, and beauty photography, but her true passion lies in finding and capturing life's unposed, unseen moments. Ford believes that the world is full of expression, irony, and beauty in the ordinary, and she adores interesting juxtapositions and the relationships between different people and between a person and his or her environment. Her work has been published in the spring 2008, fall 2008, and fall 2009 issues of *Fifth Wednesday Journal*, *INK Magazine*, and *Chicago Special Parent* and has been shown at Calmer House Gallery, MaNa Gallery, and Wings Gallery.

Originally from rural Alaska, **MOLLY LOU FREEMAN** took degrees with honors in poetry from Brown University (BA) and from the University of Iowa Writers' Workshop (MFA), where she won an Academy of American Poets Award and was nominated for a Pushcart Prize. Her poems have been published in *The Alaska Quarterly Review*, *The Bellingham Review*, *The Colorado Review*, *The Michigan Quarterly Review*, *The New Orleans Review*, and the University of

Alaska Press anthology *Crosscurrents North*. Her chapbook, *In Wind: A Paper*, was published by the University of Iowa Center for the Book. Founder and editor of the review of American and French poetics and design *carnet de route*, she has twice been awarded grants from the French national literary endowment. She teaches at the International School of Paris, France.

RACHEL FUREY received her MFA from Southern Illinois University and is currently a PhD student at Texas Tech. She is a winner of *Sycamore Review*'s Wabash Prize for Fiction and *Crab Orchard Review*'s Charles Johnson Student Fiction Award. Her work has also appeared in *Women's Basketball Magazine*, *Freight Stories*, *Terrain*, *Waccamaw Journal*, *Hunger Mountain*, *The Prose Poem Project*, *Sweet*, and elsewhere.

RICHARD HACKLER lives in Marquette, Michigan, and is an MFA candidate at Northern Michigan University.

CHAD HELTZEL received his PhD from the University of Illinois at Chicago. His poems and reviews have previously appeared in *Cream City Review*, *Faultline*, *Hamilton Stone Review*, *Sarmatian Review*, and *Konundrum Engine Literary Review*. Chad is a coeditor of the online journal *Little Red Leaves*. He lives in Chicago.

BOB HICOK's most recent book is *Words for Empty and Words for Full* (Pitt, 2010).

KATE KOSTELNIK's fiction, which earned a 2007 New Jersey State Arts Council Fellowship, has appeared in *42 Opus*, *Invisible Insurrection*, *Hayden's Ferry*, and *Superstition Review*. Her scholarship, "Revisions from Within: The Potential of PhDs in Creative Writing," was published in the journal *Creative Writing Teaching: Theory and Practice*. She's working on a novel, a story collection, and a chapter for *A Guide to Creative Writing Pedagogies* that explores writing center theory in creative writing classrooms.

KAREN AN-HWEI LEE is the author of *Ardor* (Tupelo Press, 2008) and *In Medias Res* (Sarabande Books, 2004) and winner of the Kathryn A. Morton Prize and the Norma Farber First Book Award. Her chapbook, *God's One Hundred Promises*, received the Swan Scythe Press Prize. The recipient of a National Endowment for the Arts grant, she lives and teaches in southern California, where she is a novice harpist.

MICHAEL LEVAN received his MFA in poetry from Western Michigan University and is currently a PhD candidate in English at the University of Tennessee, where he serves as nonfiction editor of *Grist*. His work can be found in recent or forthcoming issues of *New South*, *Third Coast*, *Harpur Palate*, *The Pinch*, and *Cimarron Review*. He lives in Knoxville with his wife, Molly, and son, Atticus, with whom he hopes to share his love for all things Cleveland, especially its sports teams, no matter how far from first place they may be.

JANE MEAD is the recipient of awards and fellowships from the Lannan, Whiting, and Guggenheim foundations and the author of three collections of poetry. She is on the faculty of the Drew University low-residency MFA program and farms in Northern California.

HARRIET J. MELROSE's poems have been published in *TriQuarterly*, including the last print edition guest-edited by Edward Hirsch. Her work also has appeared in *The Gettysburg Review*, *Boulevard*, and in many smaller university and regional literary magazines and anthologies. She won an Illinois Arts Council Literary Award for a poem published in *TriQuarterly* 110/111. Her poetry book manuscript, *What the Poet Knows*, was a finalist in the 2009 New Issues Poetry Prize first book competition.

WENDY OLESON has an MFA from Oregon State. Her fiction appears or is forthcoming in *Copper Nickel*, *SmokeLong Quarterly*, *Hobart* (online), and *McSweeney's Internet Tendency*. Her poetry appears in *the delinquent* and is forthcoming in *Rattle*. In 2010 Wendy was a finalist for *Hunger Mountain*'s Katherine Paterson Prize. She's currently at work on novels for children — both YA and MG readers — and a novel and story collection for adults.

GAYATHRI PRABHU is the author of the novels *Maya* and *Birdswim Fishfly*. Born and raised in India, she holds three master's degrees and a PhD from universities in India, the United Kingdom, and the United States of America. She is currently in search of her ancestral roots along the Arabian Sea in southern India while working on her next novel.

SRIRAM RAMGOPAL has been a photographer for over a decade. His first experiences with photography were with a Polaroid camera he claimed from his parents when he was twelve. Ramgopal is a medical graduate from the Boston area. He currently works as a research fellow studying pediatric epilepsy. He is the cofounder of Sangam India, a not-for-profit group focused on urban slum development. Some of Ramgopal's photography can be seen at www.insightfulart.com.

JAMES MADISON REDD is a preacher's son hailing from Booneville, Mississippi. His work was nominated for inclusion in *Best New American Voices 2009*, and he is a winner of the Mari Sandoz/ *Prairie Schooner* Award for Short Story. Read the winter 2011 issue of *Parting Gifts* to enjoy more of his work. Currently, he is continuing his doctoral studies and writing a novel called *Revival!*

ROGER REEVES's poems have appeared or are forthcoming in *Poetry, Ploughshares, American Poetry Review, Boston Review, Gulf Coast,* and *Tin House,* among others. Kim Addonizio selected "Kletic of Walt Whitman" for the *Best New Poets 2009* anthology. He was awarded a Ruth Lilly Fellowship by the Poetry Foundation in 2008, a Bread Loaf Work-Study Scholarship, an Alberta H. Walker Scholarship from the Provincetown Fine Arts Work Center, and two Cave Canem Fellowships. Recently, he earned his MFA from the James A. Michener Center for Creative Writing at the University of Texas. In the fall, he will be an assistant professor of poetry at the University of Illinois at Chicago.

ED ROBERSON is the author of eight books of poetry, including *Voices Cast Out to Talk Us In*, a winner of the *Iowa Poetry Prize*, and a recent collection, *The New Wing of the Labyrinth* (Singing Horse Press, 2010). His latest book, *To See the Earth Before the End of the World*, was released by Wesleyan University Press in fall 2010. He is Distinguished Artist in Residence at Northwestern University. Learn more about Ed Roberson at his website, www.edroberson.net.

MOLLY JO ROSE lives in the South with her husband and son. The former of the two, Michael Levan, is published inside these pages, which, to her mind, is a lovely thing.

JASON ROUSH is the author of three books of poems: *After Hours, Breezeway,* and *Crosstown*, all published by Orchard House Press. His poems and reviews have appeared in *Bay Windows, Brooklyn Review, Cimarron Review,* and *The Gay and Lesbian Review Worldwide*. He teaches at Emerson College and the New England Institute of Art, and he is currently working on his fourth collection of poetry, titled *Dispossession.*

ROB SHORE has worked as a writer, producer, and photographer. His writing and photography have been featured in *Smithsonian Magazine*, *Fifth Wednesday Journal*, *Juked*, *Porchlight*, *Anderbo*, *Worldview Magazine*, and *The Best American Poetry Blog*. His essay "Time Travel" is forthcoming in the book *Being There: Learning to Live Cross-Culturally* (Harvard University Press). He also wrote and directed the documentary film *And Many More*. Rob currently lives in Washington, D.C., where he oversees the production of new media at the FrameWorks Institute.

STACY SIMMERING is from Bell City, Missouri, and has been living in the UK for the past three years. She studied at the Photography Institute of London. She writes that her four kids inspire her every day to pick up her camera and photograph those moments that pass us by so quickly. This is her first publication.

CHAD SIMPSON is the author of *Phantoms*, a fiction chapbook published by *Origami Zoo Press*. His stories have appeared in *McSweeney's Quarterly*, *American Short Fiction*, *Crab Orchard Review*, and *The Sun*, among others. He lives in Monmouth, Illinois, and teaches fiction writing and literature classes at Knox College.

KEVIN SPENST's work can be found in *Can't Lit: Fearless Fiction from Broken Pencil*, *The Martian Press Review*, *Pages of Canada*, *Only Magazine*, *The Maynard*, *The Enpipe Line*, and *Ditch Poetry*, among many others. His manuscript *The Gang's All Down by the Abecedarium* was shortlisted for the Robert Kroetsch Award for Innovative Poetry. Over the past year Kevin's website, kevinspenst. com, has conducted interviews with poets such as Rob McLennan, Pearl Pirie, Aaron Betz, and Christine Lecler.

MARY SZYBIST's second collection, *Incarnadine*, is forthcoming from Graywolf Press in 2013. In the fall of 2011, she will be a resident at the Rockefeller Foundation's Bellagio Center. She lives in Portland, Oregon, where she teaches at Lewis & Clark College.

SHARON OARD WARNER has published a short story collection, *Learning to Dance and Other Stories*, and the novel *Deep in the Heart*. She has also edited an anthology, *The Way We Write Now: Short Stories from the AIDS Crisis*. Currently she is completing a new novel, *Sophie's House of Cards*. Warner teaches creative writing at the University of New Mexico and serves as founding director of the Taos Summer Writers' Conference.

BOOK REVIEWS
AT FWJ

In keeping with our mission of bringing a sharp readership together with the best storytellers and poets working today, *Fifth Wednesday Journal* is pleased to publish a book review section in every issue.

Literary books in all styles will be considered; however, an emphasis will be placed on the types of writing we publish in the journal, including short fiction, poetry, essays, and nonfiction works. Books devoted to black-and-white photography, either by one artist or several, also will be considered.

Publishers interested in having manuscripts reviewed by *Fifth Wednesday Journal* should send inquiries, galleys, and books to:

Daniel Libman
Book Reviews Editor
P.O. Box 67
Oregon, IL 61061

FIFTH WEDNESDAY
JOURNAL

FIFTH WEDNESDAY
JOURNAL
Defining literature. In real context.
www.fifthwednesdayjournal.org

DONATION FORM

Donations may also be made online with a credit card at www.fifthwednesdayjournal.org/donate.

Donate to *Fifth Wednesday Journal* in three easy steps. Every dollar makes a difference!

▶ CHOOSE YOUR DONATION LEVEL.   AMOUNT

✱ Up to $49 .... $_____

✱ $50-$499 – Special Friend .... $_____
Listing on the Patrons page in the magazine in the issue following your donation.

✱ $500-$999 – Special Reader .... $_____
Listing on the Patrons page in the magazine for two years with a complimentary lifetime subscription.

✱ $1,000 or more – Editors' Council .... $_____
Listing on the Patrons page in the magazine for three years with a complimentary lifetime subscription.

▶ DESIGNATE THE PURPOSE OF YOUR GIFT.   AMOUNT
(Choose one designation, or divide your gift among two or more funds.)

✱ Writers' Fund .... $_____

✱ Special Events Fund .... $_____

✱ Web Fund .... $_____

✱ General Operating Expenses *(default if none is indicated)* .... $_____

▶ TELL US WHOM TO THANK! *(Your donations will be tax deductible to the fullest extent allowed by law. We will send you a receipt.)*
Your Name: _____
Your Address: _____

Whose name should we list on the Patrons page? *(For amounts of $50 or more.)*

✱ Please use my name as shown: _____
✱ List my donation in honor of: _____
✱ Keep my donation anonymous.

Please mail this completed form with your check to:
Fifth Wednesday Books / P.O. Box 4033 / Lisle, IL 60532-9033

Questions? Please e-mail editors@fifthwednesdayjournal.org   **Thank you!**

For the latest FWJ news, join our mailing list. Email: _____

FIFTH WEDNESDAY JOURNAL

Defining literature. In real context.
www.fifthwednesdayjournal.org

ORDER FORM

Orders may also be placed online with PayPal or credit card at www.fifthwednesdayjournal.org/order.

► SUBSCRIPTIONS	INSIDE THE U.S.	OUTSIDE THE U.S.	TOTAL
3 years (6 issues + T-shirt) (T-shirt size S M L XL circle one)	✹ $54	✹ $80 USD	$____
2 years (4 issues)	✹ $37	✹ $57 USD	$____
1 year (2 issues)	✹ $20	✹ $32 USD	$____

► **SINGLE ISSUES**
Quantities of 1–4 only*

Fall 2011	____ QUANTITY x $11	____ QUANTITY x $18 USD	$____
Spring 2011	____ QUANTITY x $10	____ QUANTITY x $17 USD	$____
Fall 2010	____ QUANTITY x $10	____ QUANTITY x $17 USD	$____
Spring 2010	____ QUANTITY x $10	____ QUANTITY x $17 USD	$____
Spring 2009	____ QUANTITY x $10	____ QUANTITY x $17 USD	$____
Fall 2007	____ QUANTITY x $10	____ QUANTITY x $17 USD	$____

Spring 2008, Fall 2008, and Fall 2009 issues available by special order only. Contact us for details.

► **T-SHIRTS**

XL	____ QUANTITY x $14	____ QUANTITY x $20 USD	$____
L	____ QUANTITY x $14	____ QUANTITY x $20 USD	$____
M	____ QUANTITY x $14	____ QUANTITY x $20 USD	$____
S	____ QUANTITY x $14	____ QUANTITY x $20 USD	$____

TOTAL AMOUNT INCLUDED WITH ORDER $ ____

SHIPPING INFO
Name: _____
Street Address: _____
City, State, ZIP: _____

Please mail order with payment to:

Fifth Wednesday Books / P.O. Box 4033 / Lisle, IL 60532-9033

*For pricing of 5 or more copies, please e-mail editors@fifthwednesdayjournal.org.

For the latest FWJ news, join our mailing list. Email: _____